# GREAT BASTARDS OF HISTORY

First published in the USA in 2010 by

Fair Winds Press, a member of

Quayside Publishing Group

100 Cummings Center

Suite 406-L

Beverly, MA 01915-6101

www.fairwindspress.com

12 11 10 09 08        1 2 3 4 5

ISBN-13: 978-1-59233-401-8
ISBN-10: 1-59233-401-6

**Library of Congress Cataloging-in-Publication Data**

Fiorillo, Juré.

  Great bastards of history : true and riveting accounts of the most famous illegitimate children who went on to achieve greatness / Juré Fiorillo.

     p. cm.

  Includes bibliographical references and index.

  ISBN-13: 978-1-59233-401-8

  ISBN-10: 1-59233-401-6

  1. Biography. 2. Illegitimate children--Biography. 3. Successful people--Biography. I. Title.

  CT105.F45 2010

  920.02—dc22

                                                                                2009018754

Cover and book design: Peter Long

Book layout: Sheila Hart

Photo research: Anne Burns Images

Cover image: Portrait by Federico Fiori, 1605, Palazzo Piti, Florence, Italy/Bridgeman Art Library International; modified by Peter Long.

Contributing writers: Juré Fiorillo (Introduction, Alexander Hamilton, James Smithson, Alexandre Dumas fils, Billie Holiday, Eva Perón, Fidel Castro); Alan Axelrod (Elizabeth I, James Scott, 1st Duke of Monmouth); Edwin Kiester Jr. (William the Conqueror, Bernardo O'Higgins, Henry Stanley, Jack London, Lawrence of Arabia); Ed Wright (Leonardo da Vinci, Francisco Pizarro)

Printed and bound in Singapore

# GREAT BASTARDS

# OF HISTORY

## TRUE AND RIVETING ACCOUNTS OF THE MOST FAMOUS ILLEGITIMATE CHILDREN WHO WENT ON TO ACHIEVE GREATNESS

## JURÉ FIORILLO

FAIR WINDS
PRESS
BEVERLY, MASSACHUSETTS

# CONTENTS

# INTRODUCTION

*"WHY BASTARD? WHEREFORE BASE?*
*WHEN MY DIMENSIONS ARE AS WELL COMPACT,*
*MY MIND AS GENEROUS, AND MY SHAPE AS TRUE,*
*AS HONEST MADAM'S ISSUE?"*
*—KING LEAR*

CHANCE CHILD, WHORE'S SON, BAR SINISTER, LOVE CHILD, CATCH-COLT, bachelor's baby, and bastard are but a few of the appellations given to children born out of wedlock. Throughout history, illegitimacy has carried a stigma and posed a heavy burden for those branded as bastards. Those who were unfortunate enough to carry the label *illegitimate* have faced extreme hardship and many obstacles in life.

This book takes a look at the lives of individuals who rose above the circumstances of their birth and made a lasting impression on history. They experienced severe adversity in the form of poverty, neglect, ridicule, and scorn as a result of being illegitimate. For example, although founding father Alexander Hamilton achieved great success in his life, he was never able to escape the stigma of being born out of wedlock. Despite Hamilton's many achievements, John Quincy Adams frequently referred to him as the "bastard son of a Scottish peddler."

To the world's great benefit, Leonardo da Vinci's illegitimacy barred him from entering certain professions. Unlike his father, da Vinci could not pursue a career in finance. Eva Perón could not marry Colonel Juan Perón because an Argentine law prohibited military officers from marrying women born out of wedlock. She had to alter her birth certificate to become Argentina's First Lady.

In ancient Rome and Greece, illegitimate births were common and viewed as normal occurrences in life. The circumstances of a child's birth were noted for legal, rather than social or moral, reasons. Children born out of wedlock had fewer rights to parental inheritance, and thus were designated "illegitimate" to differentiate from "legitimate" heirs.

The pragmatic attitude toward illegitimacy held by the Greeks and Romans changed with the advent of the Middle Ages and the spread of Christianity. In the Christian stronghold of Europe, illegitimacy was viewed as a scourge—a tear in the moral fabric of a God-fearing society. An illegitimate child was the living embodiment of immorality, of sex outside of the sanctity of holy matrimony. This opinion held firm, even as the Renaissance dawned.

On a more pragmatic level, illegitimacy was shunned and disparaged because it strained the state's finances. Because the majority of unwed mothers were poor, society was often saddled with the responsibility of supporting the unfortunate offspring. Long before he set off for Africa in search of the missing doctor David Livingstone, explorer Henry Morton Stanley was confined to the crowded quarters of St. Asaph Union Workhouse, a dumping ground for unwanted children, as well as the detritus of Welsh society. In some European countries, criminal charges could be brought against parents who abandoned, or were unable to support, their illegitimate children.

In France, discrimination against illegitimate children was especially harsh after the passage of the Napoleonic Code in 1804. According to the code, illegitimate offspring were considered parentless. Parental acknowledgment was strictly voluntary. Bizarrely, maternity was not assumed or acknowledged; a woman had the right to renounce her child. A child wishing acknowledgment from his or her mother had to prove maternity in a court of law. Such recourse was forbidden for proving paternity. Wayward fathers were not required, or expected, to claim their illegitimate children. However, they could claim parentage at any time. French playwright Alexandre Dumas Fils was several years old when his father, the legendary novelist for whom he was named, legally acknowledged him as his son.

In England, an illegitimate child was deemed *filius nullis*—child of no one. Not only were non-marital children considered parentless by law, but they were also denied the right to inherit property and royal titles. When serial husband King Henry VIII had his second marriage annulled, he effectively made a bastard of his three-year-old-daughter, Elizabeth. By law, Elizabeth's status barred her from inheriting the throne; she was only able to wear the crown because Henry stipulated so in his will.

Attitudes toward illegitimacy have changed tremendously over the past two centuries. Many of the restrictions placed on the rights of illegitimate children have been lifted or relaxed. In 1968, the United States Supreme Court extended the 14th Amendment to apply to illegitimate children, securing their rights to parental inheritance. The United Kingdom discarded the notion of filius nullius, supplanting it with the Children Act, which recognizes non-marital paternity and parental responsibility. In 2005, France removed the distinction between illegitimate and legitimate children set forth in the Napoleonic Code. Today, illegitimacy is less stigmatic, especially in Western cultures. Natural children have a much lighter burden to bear than their historical counterparts. They also have an enforceable legal right to parental support in most countries. This is indicative of the changing attitudes toward non-marital offspring.

The individuals covered in this book surmounted enormous obstacles and broke through seemingly impenetrable barriers in their pursuit of their goals. With their legacies firmly established, these individuals are among history's most unforgettable—and greatest—bastards.

# CHAPTER 1

# WILLIAM THE CONQUEROR

## A LUCKY BASTARD
## 1028?-1087

HE WAS FRENCH, SPOKE BARELY A WORD OF ENGLISH, HAD ONLY
A DUBIOUS CLAIM TO THE THRONE, AND WAS A BASTARD BESIDES.
YET THE WARRIOR DUKE OF NORMANDY MADE HIMSELF ONE OF
ENGLAND'S MOST SIGNIFICANT KINGS IN A YEAR EVERY ENGLISH
SCHOOLCHILD IS TAUGHT TO REMEMBER-1066.

HE NEEDED A WIND FROM THE SOUTH. IN THE SUMMER OF 1066, WILLIAM,
Duke of Normandy, the illegitimate son of a rogue duke and a leather-tanner's daughter, had
assembled an invasion fleet at the English Channel port of Saint-Valéry, poised to launch an
attack on England to press his claim to the English throne. A southerly wind would allow the
flotilla to unload his ten thousand warriors and three thousand horses on the beaches of Sussex
and push on toward London. But for almost a month, a stiff and steady wind had been blow-
ing from the north, keeping the would-be invaders in port. Now it was September. Opportunity
might be slipping away unless the fickle Channel weather changed.

Across the Channel, a rival claimant, Harold Godwinson, Earl of Wessex, had already proclaimed himself king. Harold, a member of a family that controlled vast areas of England, was a
large, burly man and a born leader. He had mobilized and trained a powerful army and had chosen strong positions in anticipation of a possible attack. He had been a longtime chief advisor to
the English king, as had his father before him. William the Bastard would clearly have a difficult
struggle after he landed—if the wind shifted and allowed him to land at all.

**"The king is dead!" The famous Bayeux Tapestry depicts Duke William of Normandy, left,
notified of the death of King Edward "the Confessor," opening his path to the English throne.
The Tapestry is 230 feet (70 m) long and depicts the events leading up to and during the
Norman invasion of England.**

Both armies were becoming restless and eating through their supplies. Forage for William's three thousand horses was becoming a problem, not to mention that the cavalry was producing a mountain of manure.

Neither leader had a clear title to the English crown. Now a third candidate with an even more dubious claim appeared. Harald Hardråde of Norway had landed a large army near York in northern England. He had allied himself with Harold Godwinson's younger brother Tostig, who had his own aspirations plus his own army. Hardråde argued that much of the population of northern England were Norsemen, and their allegiance was to him, not to the Anglo-Saxons of Wessex. The Norse had a right to the kingship.

To emphasize his rights and power, he torched the English-garrisoned town of Scarborough, near York. Harold Godwinson, ever ready for battle, turned his waiting force around, took two-thirds of his infantry, and in a series of day-and-night forced marches still regarded as a military miracle, confronted Hardråde and Tostig at Stamford Bridge outside York. Harold's surprise appearance completely overwhelmed the Norwegian force. Hardråde and Tostig were killed in the battle, and the remaining invaders fled to their ships as fast as their legs would carry them. Then he turned his army about to deal with those pesky people from Normandy.

In his absence a significant change had occurred in the south. The northerly Channel gusts that had immobilized William for a month gave way to a more

## 1066:

**January 1** Harold remains at Edward's bedside. Declares afterward that Edward "entrusted the realm" to him.

**January 5** Edward dies. Harold claims throne and is supported by the council of nobles and elders, the witan.

**January 10** William is notified of Edward's death and Harold's accession to throne.

**January** William decides to press for throne and invade England. Begins training and assembling an army and fleet for summer cross-Channel invasion. Force eventually numbers 600 ships and 7,000 men.

**Spring** Harold begins buildup to combat imminent attack.

**August–September** Stiff south-blowing winds pin William's invasion fleet in port for six weeks.

## 1087:

**September 9** Dies in Rouen of internal injuries after fall from horse.

**September** Another relative, Harald Hardråde of Norway, claims the throne in name of Norsemen in England. Hardråde is supported by Harold's brother Tostig. Hardråde lands an army in northern England. Harold marches his army north to repel invaders and defeats them at Stanford Bridge.

**September 27** Winds subside, and William begins landing force on southwest coast of England, in Sussex.

**October 1:** Harold turns army south to combat William.

**October 14** English and Norman armies meet in the epic Battle of Hastings. Harold is killed by an arrow in the eye, along with two younger brothers. Leaderless English defense collapses, and William is victor.

**Christmas Day** William is crowned William I of England in Westminster Abbey. William begins to consolidate power and institute reforms that cement all power in royal hands.

welcoming southerly wind as summer slipped into fall. William did not waste a minute. On September 26, 1066, he ordered the invasion fleet into the Channel. His army stormed ashore unopposed and began expanding their foothold toward the town of Hastings, on the road to London. Two days later, Harold's weary forces appeared, igniting what has been called one of the pivotal battles of history. William emerged triumphant, thanks to the wind shift and Harold's distraction upcountry. Because of his questionable birth, the Duke of Normandy had been disparaged and jeered as "William the Bastard." After the breaks began coming William's way in 1066, the American historian John Dillingham declared the sobriquet should be amended to "William, the Lucky Bastard."

## A FAIRY-TALE ROMANCE, SORT OF

One day in 1025 or 1026, according to legend, Duke Robert I of Normandy looked over his castle wall at Falaise and spied a beauteous young woman at the pond below. Next day he saw her laughing and dancing with other villagers and was completely captivated. Herleve was the daughter of the local tanner. Soon, "he had his way with her, as dukes will," one historian wrote, and she gave birth to a son legendarily on a bed of bulrushes after dreaming that her intestines had been spread all over Normandy and England. (William's later opponents were to taunt him about the allegedly abhorrent and supposedly persistent smells of a tannery, sometimes greeting his public appearances with a path strewn

# La terrible et merueil= leuse vie de Robert le

diable Nouuellement Imprimee a Paris.    b.

¶ Imprime a Paris par Claude Bichart: Demourant en la Rue
de la Juifrie: a lenseigne de Lescu de France.

with smelly hides. William did not take such insults lightly. When villagers in Alençon thus greeted him, he ordered their hands and feet cut off.)

William was brought up in the ducal palace as the duke's heir despite his illegitimacy, to the dismay of court purists. He was a bright and strong-willed boy, and Robert encouraged his possible leadership qualities. Then in 1035 Robert abruptly volunteered for the Crusades and went off to the Holy Land. Word eventually filtered back that the duke had died in Nicaea, en route home. Determined to maintain the ducal lineage, the Norman court proclaimed the boy the new Duke of Normandy.

The next few years were hardly serene for the young duke. After Robert's death, Normandy fell into chaos. Nobles across the Norman lands organized personal armies and built their own fortified castles. There were a series of peasant uprisings and internal rebellions, some of them promulgated by the duke's own jealous relatives objecting or claiming to object to a mere child being elevated to the dukedom, and a bastard at that. Plots were directed at young William's life. One night he was awakened and told he must flee, his life was in danger. He was placed half dressed on a horse and escaped. Many of his most loyal supporters were killed, including his guardian, his tutor, and his steward. When the plot was thwarted and the uprising put down, he was brought back and restored to his role as duke-in-training, and he took to it with a vengeance. His father would have wanted it that way; although some describe Robert as easygoing and amiable, he was also known as "Robert the Devil."

Bastardy was not the stain it was to become in terms of moral attitude or inheritance, and anyway bastardy ran in the family. His rivals saw riches to be gained and ducal prerogatives to be claimed. Nonetheless, being an illegitimate heir was a drawback to being accepted.

William quickly demonstrated that he would not be a mere figurehead manipulated by others. At age twelve, he was giving commands to the army. Knighted at fifteen, he began a campaign to neutralize internal opposition and expand

**William's father, Robert the Duke of Normandy, pictured here, died when his son was only nine. His father never married his mother, the daughter of a local tanner.** Title page from 'La Terrible et Merveilleuse Vie de Robert le Diable,' published by Claude Bihart in 1563 (engraving) (b/w photo), French School, (16th century) / Bibliotheque Nationale, Paris, France / Lauros /Giraudon / The Bridgeman Art Library

Normandy's borders. At eighteen, he commanded his first major battle at Val-ès-Dunes; his internal enemies had joined forces in the western part of the dukedom, with some support from neighboring Brittany and Flanders. Backed by King Henry I of France, William met them at the River Orne and overwhelmed them. The opposition continued; his uncle, William, Count of Arques, had always objected to his brother's illegitimate son as duke. He lined up Anjou, which had become the Normans' chief commercial rival, Flanders, and even Henry of France, William's one-time benefactor, who had turned against him. All these enemies then teamed up against William, but in 1054 he defeated their combined armies with a great victory at Mortemer. He was not yet thirty years old.

## AFTER DUKE ROBERT'S DEATH, THERE WERE A SERIES OF PEASANT UPRISINGS AND INTERNAL REBELLIONS, SOME OF THEM PROMULGATED BY THE DUKE'S OWN JEALOUS RELATIVES OBJECTING OR CLAIMING TO OBJECT TO A MERE CHILD BEING ELEVATED TO THE DUKEDOM, AND A BASTARD AT THAT.

While solidifying his rule in Normandy, William also began to look abroad. He took on the Muslims in Spain, recapturing Tarragona, and even invaded Sicily and the southern part of Italy. By the year 1060, however, he was turning more attention toward England, less than fifty miles from Normandy across the English Channel. Because of the proximity, England and Normandy had close trade ties—London was actually closer than Paris—and there were dynastic ties as well. King Edward of England, known as "Edward the Confessor," was more than sixty years old. England was a rich and prosperous country, and Edward had no legitimate heirs. He had never openly nominated a successor.

Edward has been compared to a rich old miser, playing off one child against another with tantalizing but vague hints about riches he might, just might, bequeath them in his will if they measured up. One after another, he teased the young wannabe kings with dreams of a glorious if distant future. William and Harold were two of the most likely candidates. But were any outright promises actually made? That question has been argued for nine hundred years. Thousands of lives were lost in 1066 in an effort to resolve it.

EDWARD REX BI

## A VISIT TO RELATIVES

In 1062, William considered Normandy secure and prospering and the overseas adventures under control. His erstwhile enemies had either pledged fealty to him or were sulking in their castles. He heard fewer taunts of "William the Bastard." It seemed an appropriate time to pay a family courtesy call on Edward the Confessor. They were relatives, after a fashion—Edward's wife, Edith of Normandy, was William's great-aunt by marriage. Amid the feasting and family celebrating, the old king was greatly impressed with the young man's leadership qualities and grasp of monarchial duties. Edward was a dictatorial martinet very conscious of royal prerogatives. He had peremptorily sent off his first wife of twenty years to a nunnery when she failed to produce an heir, and he "indicated" that he might look favorably on William as a successor and potential king

King Edward, right, bids Godspeed to Harold, a claimant to the throne, before his upcoming visit to Normandy in 1064 in a scene from the Bayeux Tapestry. Getty Images

of a combined England and Normandy. At least that was how William and his entourage told the story afterward.

Then in 1064 Harold arrived in Normandy. According to one version, he had been commissioned by Edward to size up William's kingly potential and to sound him out on a possible political alliance or a kind of co-king-ship under one flag. A second version explains Harold came on his own initiative, hoping to negotiate the release of his brother and nephew held as hostages in Normandy. A simpler version says he was just out fishing when he ran into a storm—even though he had shown no interest in fishing before. In any event, the quirky Channel winds drove Harold's boat ashore at Ponthieu, very much in William's sphere of influence. Harold was arrested as a pirate, which frequently happened to shipwrecked sailors. William had just emphatically subdued a rebellious Count Guy of Ponthieu in battle. So when William learned of Harold's imprisonment, he urged Count Guy in no uncer-tain words to release him. That would surely win him brownie points at the London court. The count immediately freed Harold and personally escorted him to William's palace at Rouen.

The two young leaders apparently hit it off famously. Both were sophisti-cated, ambitious, and skilled in political and court maneuvering. Their talents complemented one another: William was more decisive and forthright, Harold more the patient negotiator. Not surprisingly—it is also agreed—the topic of succession to the English throne came up; Edward had now worn the crown nearly twenty-four years.

Harold apparently implied that he was not interested in being king, but wanted to see that Edward's successor would respect the Godwin family's vast holdings and privileges. It seemed the commoner and William the Bastard might be an ideal one-two punch. William asked Harold to support him for the throne and to swear that he would do so. Harold was to place his hands on the table and take an oath pledging his support. Harold was either William's guest or his hostage, depending on one's viewpoint, but he may have considered the oath a harmless gesture that he could not politely refuse. Unknown to Harold, William had craftily placed under the table some holy saints' relics, making the simple ceremony a sacred event—which was to reverberate later. Harold then returned to England, where the two would meet in the future.

As in most Christianized countries in medieval times, the anniversary of Christ's birth was both a solemn and a celebratory occasion. The royal court in England in 1065 scheduled a Christmas festival of religious ceremony interspersed with feasting, singing, and dramatics before the king's throne. Yuletide 1065 was to be an especially joyous celebration, too; on December 28, Edward was to consecrate Westminster Abbey, the magnificent new church he had built on the banks of the Thames. On Christmas Eve, the king felt ill and retired, but next day, feebly wearing his crown and dressed in his royal robes, he valiantly attended Christmas Mass. There he suddenly slumped in his chair, felled by the first of a series of strokes. He lingered into January. Harold remained at his bedside, and Edward, according to the contemporary *Anglo-Saxon Chronicle* and some witnesses, "entrusted the realm," "granted the kingdom," and "commended all the kingdom to [Harold's] protection." Two days later, the royal funeral was held in the new Westminster Abbey. The following day, wasting no time, Harold Godwinson had himself crowned king.

## "LONG LIVE KING HAROLD"

The customary assembly of high-ranking nobles and earls, court officials, bishops, and church leaders, called a witan, had gathered for the funeral and promptly endorsed the choice. Their decision was pretty much a foregone conclusion. Edward's reported deathbed statements cemented it. Some of the witan approved Harold only reluctantly. He was a commoner, after all, and simply being the late king's brother-in-law didn't seem a strong qualification. The only candidate with royal blood was Edgar, the great-grandson of King Ethelred II, who had died fifty years before. But Edgar was only fifteen years old. His father had died when he was nine, and he had not even been named an earl because he showed so little promise. William of Normandy and Harald Hardråde were ruled out. The witan did not want a foreigner as king.

And what of Harold's oath to support William's candidacy? In the words of one historian, Harold "cocked a snook" at William—a derisive gesture roughly translated as "Go to hell." (Harold's defenders argue that the oath was meaningless, having been obtained under duress when Harold was a prisoner or hostage. Indeed, some historians theorize that Harold actually supported William's cause, but couldn't sway the rest of the witan.) Harold did not bother to notify William of the king's death. A two-sentence message from a Norman returning from a London visit brought the bulletin on January 10 as William was preparing for a hunt. "King Edward is dead. Harold is raised to the kingdom," he was bluntly told. William put down his bow, canceled the hunt, and returned to his palace. He sat there alone, his cloak drawn across his face, and spoke to no one. The news was not only a devastating disappointment, but it was also an unforgivable embarrassment. He had always assumed the supposed promise would be fulfilled, and he would become king of England on Edward's death; he had so informed many people, including the leaders of neighboring realms and even the pope. He recovered within a few days and now began to spread different news. He was planning to invade England, he let them know. He would overwhelm the Saxons and Norsemen and claim the throne for Normandy.

**HAROLD DID NOT BOTHER TO NOTIFY WILLIAM OF THE KING'S DEATH. A TWO-SENTENCE MESSAGE FROM A NORMAN RETURNING FROM A LONDON VISIT BROUGHT THE BULLETIN ON JANUARY 10 AS WILLIAM WAS PREPARING FOR A HUNT. "KING EDWARD IS DEAD. HAROLD IS RAISED TO THE KINGDOM."**

He instantly began preparing. Normandy, with its long coastline, had a seafaring tradition and a shipbuilding industry. The builders had mostly produced small fishing vessels. William directed them to convert to larger transports capable of carrying large numbers of fighting men and horses.

All along the Normandy coast that spring could be heard the rap-rap of hammers and the rasp of saws as the dukedom mobilized a fleet for the coming assault. Weather permitting, it would be launched in late summer or early fall. Some estimates said more than 1,500 vessels would take part. The lowest number was 696. Meanwhile, the duke began rounding up allies among his neighbors and reminding others not to attempt any mischief during his absence. He recruited warriors and knights from Brittany, Anjou, and France itself. He asked for the pope's blessing, and got it, on grounds that Harold had violated a holy oath sworn on the blessed relics of saints. The matter of William's legitimacy or right to the throne apparently presented no papal obstacle. The pope even presented the Norman pretender with a papal banner to be carried at the head of his troops.

None of this was kept secret, of course. In fact, William wanted it known. Soon frantic preparations began on the Channel's opposite shore. English shipbuilders started work on a matching navy; trenches were dug, fortifications and castles built. The most likely landing place for an invasion force would be along a twenty-five-mile stretch of Sussex beach with a few small harbors for landing vessels, west of the White Cliffs of Dover. Because no one knew where the blow might fall, these areas all had to be strengthened.

## A BAD SIGN?

In the spring of 1066, a burst of brilliant light illuminated the night sky above the English and French coasts. A star flashed across the sky, a long trail of fire behind it. Modern astronomers were to identify it as Halley's Comet, making its spectacular every-seventy-five-years appearance. Medieval stargazers had no experience with such a phenomenon, and it threw a panic into both sides. Frightened English soothsayers interpreted the fiery visitor as a heavenly warning of God's wrath at the preparations for battle. It was said to presage the fall of the monarchy, perhaps even notifying the ambitious bastard that he was becoming too uppity. Or it could be a prelude to some great disaster yet to come. William, however, reassured his followers that it was surely a sign of God's approval. God was blessing the endeavor, just as the pope had done. The comet streaked across the sky for seven consecutive nights and then went back into hiding. Calm returned, the hammers and saws and the military drills resumed, and near the end of August William pronounced himself ready. Both sides settled down to watch the weather.

In mid-September a violent fall storm blasted into the Channel from the Arctic, and a worried William saw savage winds and turbulent waters disrupt all his plans. Day after day, the wind blew and waves and whitecaps lashed the waters. It appeared his invasion might have to be postponed or canceled. Then on September 27, he awoke to a sunny sky and a warm wind wafting from the south. He quickly ordered the ships loaded with warriors and supplies and marched the men down to the shore, ready to strike. By October 1, they had crossed the Channel and landed at Pevensey on the Sussex coast. The news quickly reached Harold, 250 miles to the north, where he and his army were resting after the victory at Stamford Bridge. They had force-marched 250 miles

in only four days and had fought a major battle; now they were tired and their ranks depleted. Harold exhorted them to pick themselves up, reverse course, and backtrack those 250 miles to fight another important battle in patriotic defense of their homeland. By the morning of October 14, the two armies faced each other across hilly, open country four miles from the town of Hastings.

The battle began about 10 a.m. The English infantry had set up its trademark defensive formation: a so-called shield wall, men standing shoulder to shoulder, their great shields carried in front, overlapping and interlocked, a seemingly impenetrable barrier. Each man carried a two-edged sword; some carried spears, lances, or double-edged battleaxes. They were massed eight deep on Caldbec Hill, forming a line across a ridge bisected by the main road to London. The hill sloped gradually down to a meadow, where the Normans were positioning themselves for attack.

The two armies were roughly even in strength, between eight and nine thousand men. The bulk of Harold's army was infantry, built around the housecarls, a core of professional soldiers who formed an elite guard. The battle site was well chosen from the English point of view. The slope gave the defenders a commanding view of the field, which would force the attackers to fight uphill and slow down any advance.

William's army was quite different. Drawn up in line of battle, the Norman troops composed the center, with troops from Brittany, Maine, and Anjou comprising the left wing and French and Flemish units on the right. The cavalry, three thousand strong, comprised the elite unit, augmented by a thousand skilled archers, some armed for the first time with that powerful weapon, the crossbow. The balance of the troops was infantry. William's battle plan, repeatedly successful in his French campaigns, was to open with spear throwing and a rain of arrows, meant to cause confusion and fright, capitalize on that reaction by sending in the infantry, and then clean up the scattered defenders with a sweep by hard-riding cavalry, turning the battle into a rout. The shield wall,

◄ **William the Conqueror, helmet gleaming, leads triumphant Normans against English defenders in the epic Battle of Hastings on October 14, 1066. He was crowned king of England on Christmas Day of that year.** The Battle of Hastings in 1066 (oil on canvas), Debon, Francois Hippolyte (1807-72) / Musee des Beaux-Arts, Caen, France / Giraudon / The Bridgeman Art Library International

however, stood firm, casualties quickly being replaced from the ranks behind. A rumor spread through the Norman army that William had been killed. He took off his helmet and held it high to show he was very much alive, although his favorite horse had been shot from under him. Some units broke apart and fled. William and the remaining units fell back to regroup for a second try.

The second attack in early afternoon was a virtual carbon copy of the first. The French and Flemish had conducted the bulk of the initial fighting; this time it fell to the Bretons and Angevins. Still the shield wall stood firm, being steadily reinforced. Again an infantry charge sowed confusion, and the cavalry injected more confusion so that the battle line broke apart into small groups and hand-to-hand fighting. Then once more the attackers fell back to reorganize.

The sun was sinking as the third attack began. The ups and downs of life as a bastard had made William resourceful and able to revamp his plans on the fly, as he had in making his midnight escape to avoid capture as a boy. William decided on a change of tactics. Instead of a barrage of arrows fired directly at the frustrating shield wall, he ordered the archers and spear throwers to aim over the shields. The trajectory would carry the blizzard of arrows down on the heads of the clustered rear ranks. The tactic was an immense success. Unaccustomed to an attack from over-head and having lost the best-trained front-rank housecarls, the English rank and file known as fyrds turned this way and that in fright and bewilderment.

Trying to rally the troops, Harold plunged into the thick of the fray. He fell mortally wounded. Legendarily, a descending arrow struck him in the eye and lodged there. The Bayeux Tapestry depicted a fallen leader whose frantic aides tried to wrest the arrow free, to no avail. Harold, blinded, apparently succumbed within minutes.

This version of Harold's demoralizing death is based solely on the tapestry and is widely disputed. Archery experts declare that a falling arrow would not retain enough force in such a descent as to penetrate the well-protected eye. More likely, goes this explanation, he was killed by a sword stroke in the bitter hand-to-hand melee. But if details are questionable, the outcome is not. Harold's two younger brothers had been killed earlier. The English were now left without an authoritative commander. The defense lost all cohesion, dissolving into a torrent of badly rattled men trying to escape, Normans at their heels. The long day's fighting by an already worn-down band had cost the lives of an

estimated five thousand English. The Normans may have lost three thousand. After the bodies were cleared, William pitched his tent and spent the night on the battlefield, the victor's traditional symbol of triumph.

The following day, William withdrew to the town of Hastings to await the defeated leaders, earls, and bishops who would be sure to express submission and swear fealty. He vainly waited two weeks and then decided to move on London. Despite an epidemic of dysentery that flattened the troops and William himself, the English leadership began to appear, one by one, to kneel at his feet. The witan had gathered post-Hastings and chose fifteen-year-old Edgar to succeed the fallen Harold, but now Edgar came forward, too. On Christmas Day, 1066, William the Lucky Bastard was crowned king of England. No one now questioned his legitimacy or right to the throne. "William the Conqueror" had established that by force of arms. He ruled until 1087, transforming the country and establishing a reputation as one of the most significant monarchs in English history.

**The map depicts the marches of both William the Conqueror and King Harold, intersecting at Hastings in Southeast England, where William defeated Harold for the English crown in 1066.** Courtesy of the University of Texas Libraries, The University of Texas at Austin

# CHAPTER 2

# LEONARDO DA VINCI

## BASTARD OF THE RENAISSANCE
## 1452-1519

PATERNAL INDIFFERENCE AND DISINHERITANCE
ALLOWED LEONARDO DA VINCI TO AVOID THE CONVENTIONAL
FAMILY PROFESSION, YET HIS UNIQUE CAREER WAS DRIVEN BY THE
QUEST FOR PARENTAL AFFECTION THAT ELUDED HIM.

ALTHOUGH HOOKED INTO A BUSY LIFE AS A NOTARY IN THE CITIES OF
Tuscany, twenty-five-year-old Ser Piero da Vinci still found time to return to his hometown of
Vinci, a hilltop town of fewer than a hundred dwellings that was about a day's ride from Florence.
One of the delights of the place was the beautiful but insufficiently well-born Caterina. On his
visit in late summer 1451, he was most likely already betrothed to the daughter of a member of
his guild, but in the golden light of late summer, it was the beauty of Caterina that occupied his
mind as he ambled about the family's estates.

It was a passion that was reciprocated, and on one of their trysts that took place perhaps in
the seclusion of an olive grove or in one of the dilapidated outhouses that dotted the countryside,
their minds were probably on things other than the fact that nine months later one of the clever-
est bastards who ever lived would be born.

On the subject of his birth, Leonardo da Vinci once observed that "The man who has intercourse aggressively and uneasily will produce children who are irritable and untrustworthy; but
if the intercourse is done with great love and desire on both sides then the child will be of great
intellect, and witty, lively and loveable."

**The only known and definitely verifiable authentic likeness of Leonardo, this self-portrait
was drawn in 1512 when he was 50 years old.**

**1452:**
April 15 Leonardo is born to Ser Piero, a notary, and Caterina, a peasant girl; his parents never marry.

**1465:**
Albieri, whom Leonardo has become fond of, dies in labor as does the baby.

**1472:**
Leonardo becomes a member of the Florence painters' guild.

**1476:**
Charged with sodomy on April 9; the case is dismissed.

June 16 Birth of Antonio to Ser Piero and Margherita deprives Leonardo of his inheritance.

**1482:**
Moves from Florence to Milan, entering the patronage of Ludovico Sforza. By this time, Leonardo is writing in his notebooks regularly.

**1489:**
Studies anatomy.

**1453:**
Leonardo's father, Ser Piero, marries Albieri di Giovanni Amadori. His mother marries Antonio di Piero Buti del Vacca aka Accattabriga.

**1467:**
Around this time (the exact date is unknown) Leonardo becomes an apprentice to Andrea del Verrocchio, in Florence.

**1475:**
Ser Piero marries Margherita, daughter of Francesco di Gacopo di Guglielmo.

**1481:**
Receives a commission to paint the *Adoration of the Magi*.

**1483:**
Receives a commission to paint the *Virgin of the Rocks*.

Yet the love and mutual desire evident in his making would not necessarily be transferred to him in the guise of parental love.

## A SINGULAR BASTARD

Leonardo's father belonged to a long line of notaries, a profession that included functions now performed by professionals such as accountants, lawyers, and financial advisers. The da Vinci family oscillated between professional positions in towns such as Pisa and Florence, and their landholdings in the town of Vinci, where they cultivated grains, grapes, and olives. Their lifestyle was an enviable combination of urban professional and country gentleman.

While Leonardo's grandfather Antonio preferred the rustic quiet of Vinci to the bustle of Florence, his father, Ser Piero, enjoyed the busy life of the renaissance business world. At the age of twenty-one, Ser Piero graduated from his apprenticeship to full membership of the guild of notaries, the most prestigious of the seven guilds in Florentine society at the time. At the same time as he was beginning to climb the ranks of his profession, he was also sowing his wild oats, most notably with Caterina.

It is likely that when Ser Piero was cavorting with Caterina, he was already betrothed to another, Albieri di Giovanni Amadori, the daughter of a wealthy Florentine notary. Although some historians assert the engagement happened after Caterina's pregnancy was revealed as a measure to rescue Ser Piero from

**1493:**
A woman named Caterina, possibly Leonardo's mother, becomes a member of his household in Milan.

**1498:**
Makes his first attempts at planning a flying machine around this time.

**1504:**
On July 9, Ser Piero dies. Leonardo is the only one of his twelve children to receive no inheritance.

**1507:**
Is appointed Louis XII's painter and engineer. He travels to Florence in a lawsuit against his brothers of his inheritance from his uncle Francesco.

**1519:**
In May, Leonardo dies at Cloux in France.

**1490:**
Begins work in earnest on the bronze horse for his patron Ludovico Sforza. Leonardo begins a book on landscape and hydraulic works; it is never finished.

**1495:**
Begins his *Last Supper* painting in the convent of Santa Maria delle Grazie.

**1502:**
Becomes Cesare Borgia's military engineer.

**1505:**
Makes a second attempt to build a flying machine and begins sketches for the *Mona Lisa*, which he completes sometime later.

**1516:**
Permanently leaves Italy for France, where he will serve Francis I in his court in Amboise.

---

the consequences of his youthful excesses, it's more likely that the betrothal was the product of long-term planning, not for love, but for dynastic and business reasons. At the time of Leonardo's conception, Albieri was around fourteen years old, a marriageable age in Renaissance Italy.

When Caterina discovered her pregnancy, the da Vinci family didn't shun her. Leonardo was born on a spring evening in 1452, most likely on a property belonging to the da Vincis. The lack of records pertaining to Caterina's heritage suggests she was most likely from outside the district.

If one or both of the young parents hoped for the resolution of their predicament in favor of passion over society, this was soon dashed. About eight months after his son's birth, Ser Piero married Albieri. By way of compensation, the da Vinci family also found Caterina a husband, a man by the moniker of Accattabriga, which literally meant "troublemaker" but was a popular nickname also meaning "tough guy," particularly among soldiers and mercenaries of the time. Antonio di Piero Buti del Vacca may have been a soldier, but by the time he married Caterina, one year after Leonardo was born, he was a lime burner, a dirty and dangerous job involving the heating of chalk or seashells for the purposes of making mortar. He was two years younger than his wife, and it is likely his betrothal came with some financial inducement provided by the da Vincis to compensate for the shame Ser Piero had brought on Caterina.

Until Leonardo was eight months old, he was the only child of two unmarried parents. Then in the space of four months, he acquired two stepparents. His relations with both sets seem to have been good. When he was two years old, he received his first half-sibling when his mother gave birth to a girl, Piera. By the time he was eleven years old, he had five half-siblings on his mother's side. It took twelve years for Albieri to become pregnant, but tragically, both she and her firstborn died in childbirth.

**UNTIL HE WAS EIGHT MONTHS OLD, LEONARDO WAS THE ONLY CHILD OF TWO UNMARRIED PARENTS. THEN IN THE SPACE OF FOUR MONTHS HE ACQUIRED TWO STEPPARENTS.**

## MIDDLE CLASS LIMITS

By the time of Leonardo's birth, Ser Piero lived mainly away from Vinci. His career took him first to Pistoia, then to Pisa, then finally to Florence, where he hung out his shingle and began to climb the ladder of Florentine society, not the least by further marriages within the guild of notaries. His contact with Leonardo was erratic. Although Leonardo saw his mother and stepfather more regularly, he didn't live with them either.

With brothers and sisters arriving almost on an annual basis, and less money to go around, Caterina was probably too busy to pay too much attention to her firstborn. Instead, Leonardo went to live with his paternal grandfather and uncle Francesco, two of the more rusticated members of the clan, who avoided the clamor of the city, preferring the life of country gentlemen in Vinci, and gave the young genius a home. Leonardo is recorded as a member of their house in tax documents dating back to 1457, when he was five years old.

Ser Piero's second marriage, concluded a year after he became a widower, was to another fifteen-year-old daughter of a fellow notary, Francesca Ser Giuliano Lanfredini. Although the marriage helped consolidate his wealth,

**This "Carta della Catena" shows a panorama of Florence, circa 1490. Leonardo served his apprenticeship here, and it was also where his father's career as an influential notary was played out.** The 'Carta della Catena' showing a panorama of Florence, 1490 (detail), Italian School, (15th century) / Museo de Firenze Com'era, Florence, Italy / The Bridgeman Art Library International

it did little to expand his family. Francesca died before she had the chance to produce a child.

## LEONARDO WAS BORN INTO THE TUSCAN MIDDLE CLASS, WHERE THE OPPORTUNITIES FOR BASTARDS WERE FEWER THAN IN OTHER SOCIAL CIRCLES. BEING A BASTARD, LEONARDO WAS PREVENTED FROM ENTERING THE UNIVERSITIES AS WELL AS HIS FATHER'S GUILD.

The failure of Ser Piero to produce a legitimate heir over the course of Leonardo's childhood no doubt kept Ser Piero more interested in his illegitimate offspring than he otherwise might have been. Leonardo was fortunate to be born in an era where illegitimacy carried only a moderate stigma. This was no more apparent than in the highest echelons of the Catholic Church, where the vow of chastity was worn very lightly indeed. Two of Spanish Pope Alexander VI's (1492–1503) illegitimate children were the controversial brother and sister, Cesare and Lucrezia Borgia, around whom rumors of murder, incest, and lewdness swirled. Some popes themselves were bastards. Leonardo's fellow Tuscan, Pope Clement VII, who reigned as pope from 1523 to 1534, was the bastard son of Giuliano de' Medici and was raised by his uncle, Florentine ruler and patron of the arts Lorenzo the Magnificent.

However, Leonardo was born into the Tuscan middle class, where the opportunities for bastards were fewer than in other social circles. Occupying the social strata between poverty and wealth, and eager to assert the moral foundations for their developing social status, the emerging bourgeoisie of the fifteenth and sixteenth centuries, were somewhat more stringent in patrolling the boundaries of propriety. Being a bastard, Leonardo was prevented from entering the universities, as well as his father's guild.

### DISINHERITED

Ser Piero, on the cusp of his half century, subsequently married another child bride in 1475, seventeen-year-old Margherita di Guglielmo, who came with a large dowry. This time Ser Piero was in luck, and little more than a year after the wedding a son named Antonio arrived, to be followed by Giuliano in 1479.

For Leonardo, this was something of a blow because with the birth of Antonio, he was effectively deprived of his inheritance. His importance to his father was dramatically lessened. The timing could not have been worse. In 1476, the same year Antonio was born, Leonardo became the subject of scandal when he was accused of engaging in sodomy. One of the tactics the Medici, the powerful family who dominated Florence for much of the Italian renaissance, used to keep Florence under their control was to encourage citizens to inform on each other. People were able to make accusations against others by anonymously dropping written allegations of improper behavior into boxes, which were referred to, not necessarily that accurately, as *buchi vella verita*, meaning "holes of truth."

Homosexuality was so widespread in Florence that the German word for homosexual at the time was *Florenzer*. However, it remained illegal and thus accusations of such behavior were prime territory for blackmail and grudges. In 1476, an accusation reached the Office of the Night, whose function was to investigate homosexuality, that Leonardo, a tailor, a goldsmith, and a relative of Lorenzo de' Medici, had been sleeping with a male prostitute. After several months of hearings, the case was dismissed for lack of evidence. The truth of the accusation remains unknown.

Leonardo probably was homosexual, but was unlikely to have practiced it often. One entry in his notebooks observes that "the art of procreation and the members employed therein are so repulsive, that if it were not for the beauty of the faces and the adornments of the actors and the pent-up impulse, nature would lose the human species."

Ser Piero's response to the situation was to distance himself from his illegitimate son. It's easy to imagine the conservative notary—his life devoted to the accumulation of wealth and status, and thus acutely sensitive to shame and scandal—turning against his own offspring because of his homosexuality. With the birth of his half-brother Antonio, Leonardo, still a young man and yet to acquire the social insulation afforded by his reputation as a genius, was disinherited by his father.

Ser Piero had another son by Margherita. Soon after she died, he married his fourth wife, Lucrezia di Guglielmo Cortigiani, who came without much of a dowry but gifted her husband with seven sons and two daughters in fairly quick succession. When Ser Piero died in 1504, Leonardo was the only one of his twelve children to get nothing.

## FROM NATURAL CHILD TO CHILD OF NATURE

It would be a mistake to assume that being a bastard was all bad for Leonardo. The lack of parental love was compensated by the freedom it gave him, especially from the expectations of his father. It also allowed his superior mind to develop independently of the more prosaic ambitions of his parents.

Another name for a bastard is a "natural son," and in the case of Leonardo this has a particular resonance. Although he enjoyed the affection of his grandfather Antonio and uncle Francesco, they were busy running the family's farm; young Leonardo, who received only elementary level formal schooling, was largely left to his own devices. His time was spent wandering through the countryside around Vinci, observing and drawing the landscape and the animals and plants that existed in it. It was a beautiful landscape, hilly and dotted with small farms. There were grapes and olive groves that sat above the houses on terraces that climbed the hills. Above the olive groves, the land was thickly wooded with a variety of trees, including pine and chestnuts.

If Leonardo had been legitimate, he would have been compelled to undertake the classical education that made it possible for him to follow in his father's footsteps. A lack of formal education was instrumental in the development of Leonardo's philosophical system. Instead of trusting received wisdom, Leonardo believed in the primacy of knowledge that was acquired from nature via the eye. Throughout his life, he would remain skeptical of people who bolstered their views by quoting the experts who had gone before them, as was the tradition in a classical education. He believed it was knowledge gained from direct experience that counted.

"No one should ever imitate the style of another because he will be called a nephew and not a child of nature with regard to art," he wrote in his notebooks. Leonardo often used familial metaphors to express the primacy of nature,

**An anatomical sketch from Leonardo's notebooks. The artist was on a quest to understand all kinds of nature, including that of the human form.**

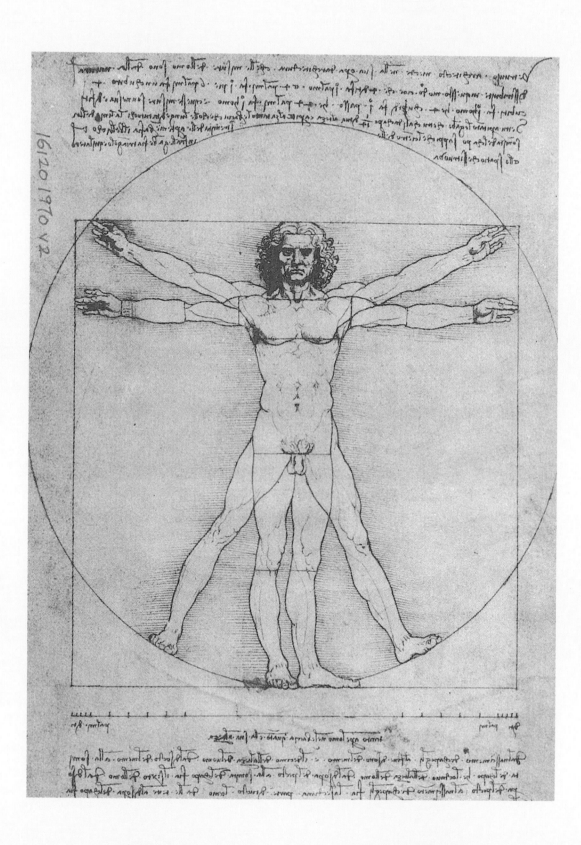

expressing both the extent to which the insecurity of his familial predicament bothered him throughout his life and how nature functioned as the cure.

## TWO GENIUSES: THE GENIAL AND THE GROUCH

Even if his talent had prevailed, it would likely have come at great personal cost. A comparison can be made to Michelangelo, who was legitimate. His family was impoverished minor aristocracy and his father worked as a magistrate.

**IF LEONARDO HAD BEEN A LEGITIMATE FIRSTBORN SON, THERE WOULD HAVE BEEN ENORMOUS PRESSURE ON HIM TO BECOME A NOTARY RATHER THAN AN ARTIST, AND HIS GENIUS MIGHT HAVE BEEN LOST TO THE COOKING OF THE BOOKS.**

To change the family's fortunes, Michelangelo's father gave him and his brothers a classical education and hoped to place his sons in the lucrative silk or wool merchant guilds. When Michelangelo showed a preference for drawing, his father beat him. Ultimately his talent prevailed, but the battle with his father cost him greatly; for the rest of his life Michelangelo would be known for his furious temper, his obsessive will, and his inability to get any real joy from his creations.

Leonardo, on the other hand, was known as a genial if absentminded spirit, a perfectionist who nonetheless enjoyed the world. Although troubled by the indifference of his father, he received sufficient male affection from his grandfather and uncle. Being a bastard meant that Leonardo didn't have to fight his father to prove his talent. The self-imputed respectability of the notary's guild was such that bastards couldn't be admitted. When Leonardo expressed his inclination to become an artist, his father helped him get an apprenticeship with a member of a lower, less exclusive guild, the painter Andrea del Verrochio in Florence. Most likely this happened at the same time as Leonardo's grandfather Antonio died, leaving Ser Piero head of the family and responsible for his son, bastard or not.

## BASTARD FANTASIES

When looking at the lives of artists and thinkers, it is the shape of their imaginations rather than their actions that gives us an understanding of their brilliance.

Leonardo was famous for not finishing many of the commissions he received. He would often stare for hours at his paintings, attempting to work out how best to replicate nature using oil paints and canvas.

In many ways, nature functioned as a surrogate parent for Leonardo. Where his father was a troubled and fleeting presence in his life, and his mother affectionate but harried by the needs of her younger children, nature was a constant source of wonder and satisfaction for him. Later, it would be the founding principle for his pursuit of art and invention. The artistic tension embodied in Leonardo's perfectionism came from trying to be as close to nature as he possibly could.

The evidence for this surrogate parenthood is circumstantial but collectively convincing. The love he developed for nature during the gamboling freedom of his childhood remained with him throughout his life. As an animal lover, he became a vegetarian. At other times, he would walk through the markets of the towns where he lived, buying birds in cages that were bound for the dinner table and then setting them free. Watching them make their escape, he may well have dreamed of being able to do the same himself.

Leonardo's paintings, some of the first to replace the medium of tempera with oil paints, were remarkable for their natural realism. Through his pioneering of *sfumato*—a technique where layers of translucent color are painted over each other to create perceptions of depth and volume—he was the first painter to capture the Tuscan landscape as it is filtered by Tuscany's peculiar light. His desire to get as close as possible to nature informed many of his intellectual and artistic activities, such as the dissection of human cadavers to further his understanding of human anatomy.

Leonardo, who never had a long-term romantic partner, replaced the urge for love with the urge to learn as much as possible about the physical natural world. The effects of this were present in Leonardo's fantasy life, too. In his fifties, Leonardo famously recounted what he believed was his first memory. He was lying in his crib when a kite bird landed on his face and fluttered its tail around inside his mouth. In Sigmund Freud's book on Leonardo, *A Childhood Memory of Leonardo Da Vinci*, which is largely based on this particular dream, Freud, the father of psychoanalysis, wrote of how this memory was probably a fantasy interpreted by Leonardo as a memory. Freud's interpretation was that Leonardo had substituted the tail feathers of the bird for his mother's breast.

For Freud, the fantasy of the bird also had a phallic connotation. His interpretation was that the relationship between mother and child was threatened by the possible reappearance of the father.

Another possible interpretation of the "memory," which at the very least harbors an ambivalent attitude toward his mother's breast, is that Leonardo, in displacing his mother for the bird, is asserting himself as a child not of parents but of nature. Leonardo recorded this "memory" in 1505. At the same time he was deeply engaged in experiments to achieve flight. His notebooks of the period contain the statement "the big bird will take its first flight above the back of the Great Cecero, filling the universe with amazement, filling all the chronicles with its fame, and bringing eternal glory to the nest where it was born."

Leonardo was talking here about his proposed trial flight of his flying machine from Mount Cecero, north of Florence. Perhaps by flying the "big bird," Leonardo hoped to bring glory to the nest where either the bird or its creator was born. It is possible that part of this might have been to transcend the stigma of his illegitimacy. In July of the year before, Ser Piero had died, leaving him nothing. It was a final act of filial rejection. His father's attitude to Leonardo's work was one of admiration tempered with willed indifference and some jealousy at his son's abilities. Paradoxically, Leonardo, who spent his life with kings and dukes at courts throughout Europe, had vaulted his father's middle class status. Yet throughout his life, Leonardo struggled to gain the love of a parent whose affection came in occasional droplets. Ironically, Ser Piero may well have felt outclassed by his talented bastard of a son.

While Leonardo was still an apprentice, Ser Piero came and visited his son with a wooden shield he had offered to get painted for a friend. Leonardo decided that a shield should be a frightening thing. He collected parts of a variety of animals and used them to create a hybrid dragon, which he then painted onto the shield. Having sent word to his father that the shield would soon be ready, Leonardo placed it in a shadowy corner of the room for maximum effect. When Ser Piero entered the studio and saw it he was frightened. When he regained his

**This alleged portrait of Leonardo, showing him with piercing eyes and a long beard, was discovered in 2009. The painter is unknown, as is the date that the image was created.**

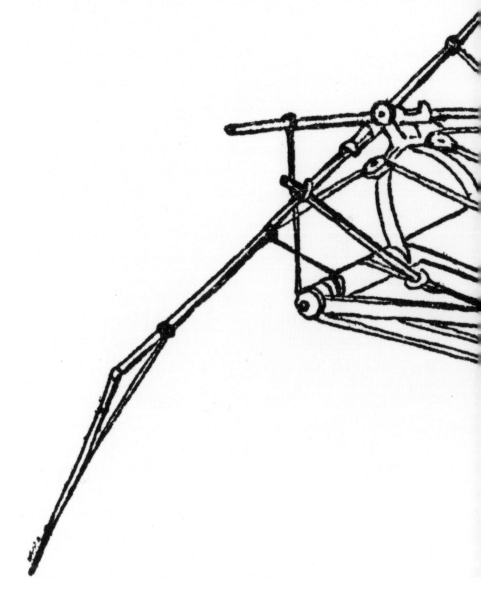

**One of Leonardo's designs for an ornithopter. The possibility of human flight was one of the overriding if ultimately unsuccessful obsessions of his inventive spirit.** One of Leonardo da Vinci's designs for an Ornithopter, copy of a diagram from Manuscript B, 1488-89 (pen & ink on paper) (b/w photo), Vinci, Leonardo da (1452-1519) (after) / Bibliotheque de l'Institut de France, Paris, France / The Bridgeman Art Library International

composure, however, he was impressed enough to buy another shield. But he did not keep the shield for himself as a proud father might. Instead, he sold it to an art dealer for a tidy sum.

If Leonardo hoped to find compensation in becoming the first man to fly for the irretrievability of his father's love brought about by the finality of Ser Piero's death, he would be disappointed. When he hauled his bird (which in some ways resembled today's hang gliders) to the top of Mount Cecero, harnessed himself in, and launched himself off the mountain into the atmosphere, the result was unspectacular. Leonardo crashed.

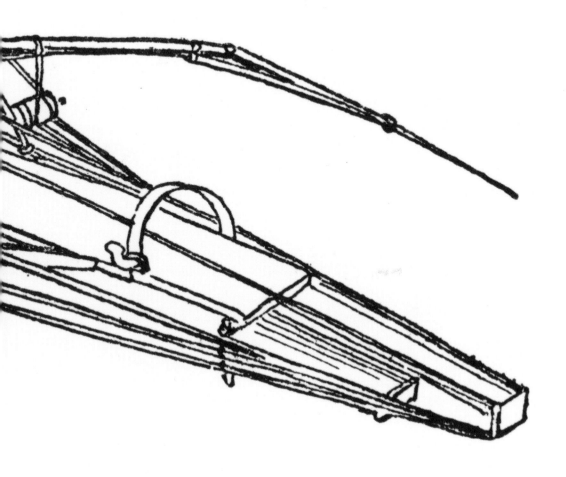

Leonardo da Vinci—painter, engineer, inventor, philosopher—was the embodiment of the Renaissance Man. His sublime paintings such as *Mona Lisa* and *The Last Supper*, and his brilliant ideas and inventions (including advances in the understanding of human anatomy, flying machines, and a submarine), cemented his reputation as one of the smartest, most enigmatic, and original thinkers in history. It is unlikely his achievements would have been so spectacular if he weren't trying to overcome the stigma caused by being a bastard.

# CHAPTER 3

# FRANCISCO PIZARRO

## A BRUTAL BASTARD
### 1475-1541

THE PRODUCT OF AN OFFICER'S DALLIANCE
WITH A PEASANT GIRL, FRANCISCO PIZARRO OVERCAME
A POOR CHILDHOOD AND ILLITERACY TO BECOME ONE OF THE
MOST FEARSOME AND SUCCESSFUL SPANISH CONQUISTADORS. HE
CONQUERED THE INCA EMPIRE CENTERED IN MODERN-DAY PERU,
ONLY TO BE UNDONE BY THE CONSEQUENCES OF
HIS GREED AND INABILITY TO READ.

LIFE FOR THE LOWER RUNGS OF THE SPANISH NOBILITY BEFORE COLUMBUS was almost as harsh as it was for the peasants. Captain Gonzalo Pizarro Rodríguez de Aguilar's estates in and around the town of Trujillo gave him a roof over his head, but were insufficient to provide him with the kind of income a nobleman desired. Like the younger sons of impoverished noblemen throughout history, the choices for Gonzalo were mainly two: the army or the church. Gonzalo Pizarro chose the army.

A life in the church wouldn't have suited his appetites. When not serving in the army, fighting in places such as Grenada and Navarre, Captain Pizarro was something of a local Lothario. Francisco, born in 1475, was the first fruit of his seed, but certainly not the last. Of his four male children, only one, Hernando, was legitimate. Francisco's mother was most likely a convent servant named Francisca González, whose peasant parents were responsible for looking after the nun's clothes. Although the nuns may have remained off limits to the soldiers, their servants apparently were not. It's unlikely the coupling that produced the future conquistador was one of

**Pizarro and former colleague Diego de Almagro swearing peace before a priest. The truce didn't last, and Almagro was captured, humiliated, and executed by the Pizarros.** Library of Congress

**1475:**
Francisco Pizarro is born in Trujillo, Estremadura, Spain, to Captain Gonzalo Pizarro Rodríguez de Aguilar and most likely a convent servant by the name of Francisca González. The two never marry.

**1513:**
Pizarro is right-hand man to Vasco Núñez de Balboa on an expedition that crossed the Isthmus of Panama and discovered the Pacific Ocean.

**1524:**
First expedition south in partnership with Diego Almagro. They set sail with eighty men, but expedition founders.

**1502:**
Sails to the New World for the first time.

**1519:**
Pizarro betrays Balboa to Pedro Arias de Ávila, Spanish governor of Panama. Balboa is found guilty of trumped-up treason charges and beheaded.

**1526:**
Second expedition south with twice as many men.

great or enduring love. Once she'd had the baby, Francisca was married off to a man of her own class known to history only as Martin.

Francisco Pizarro's childhood was harsh. He was shuttled between his parents' houses and felt like an outcast. Because he was a bastard, his father made no effort to educate him. Pizarro remained illiterate, something that would cost him dearly in his conflict with the Almagrists in Peru.

## BECAUSE PIZARRO WAS A BASTARD, HIS FATHER MADE NO EFFORT TO EDUCATE HIM. PIZARRO REMAINED ILLITERATE, SOMETHING THAT WOULD COST HIM DEARLY IN HIS CONFLICT WITH THE ALMAGRISTS IN PERU.

The area around Trujillo is famous for its pork products, and according to one account of Pizarro's childhood, in lieu of receiving an education, he was sent to be a swineherd. Francisco's closest brother, Hernando, wasn't born until more than twenty years later, but there was little consideration before then that Francisco might take over the family's estates. Impoverished and at the bottom rung of the aristocracy, hidalgos possessed little more than titles and valued them with a pride well beyond utility. Captain Gonzalo Pizarro had no intention of sullying the family seat by willing his title to his bastard son.

**1529:**
Emperor Charles of Spain grants Pizarro permission to make additional expeditions. He receives the title governor and captain general, which carries absolute authority in all the territories he might discover.

**1532:**
Lands in Tumbes and begins the conquest of the Inca. Captures the Inca Atahuallpa.

**1538:**
Civil War effectively ended by the Battle of Salinas in which Almagro is defeated by Pizarro's brothers and killed.

**1530:**
On January 18, he sails from Seville in Spain to Panama, with a couple of hundred men including his brothers, Hernando, Juan, Gonzalo, and Martín, and then embarks for Peru on December 27.

**1534:**
Atahuallpa ruthlessly strangled despite providing the promised ransom of a room full of gold.

**1541:**
Pizarro assassinated in revenge for the death of Almagro.

If it weren't for the opportunities of the New World, Francisco may have remained an insignificant character, perhaps a minor footnote to a European battle. The New World offered the opportunity for honor, riches, treachery, and outrageous cruelty in addition to social respectability.

## A NEW WORLD FOR OLD WOUNDS

Francisco first traveled to the New World in 1502, ten years after its discovery by Christopher Columbus. He was one of 2,500 colonists who sailed on a fleet of thirty ships with the newly appointed governor of Hispaniola, Nicolás de Ovando y Cáceres. There was no point in his remaining in Spain. By this time, his father had married and a legitimate heir, Hernando, had been born. Considering that many of the colonists were the legitimate sons of impoverished noblemen, Francisco's place in the pecking order was not auspicious. Although the details are unclear, it's likely the young swineherd was dispatched to Hispaniola to help his uncle, Juan, who had migrated there to establish his own fortune some years before.

Francisco didn't remain long with his uncle, who seems to have maintained little avuncular affection for his nephew. When Juan died without legitimate issue of his own, he left his estate to his brother, Gonzalo, without mentioning Francisco. Like his father, Francisco found his true facility was as a soldier. Uneducated and easy to rage, he found a surrogate family in the structures of the military. Francisco's childhood had accustomed him to hardship and also inured him to the suffering of others.

They were useful skills for a conquistador, and Francisco climbed the ranks. By 1509, he was a lieutenant under Alonso de Ojeda in Santo Domingo. When Ojeda led an expedition to the Urabá peninsula near the junction of contemporary Panama and Colombia, he trusted Pizarro to hold the fort with a detachment of starving men while he returned to Hispaniola for supplies. However, Pizarro's leap to prominence in the pages of history didn't really begin until he set out for the Panama isthmus with Vasco Núñez de Balboa in 1513 on the expedition that discovered the Pacific Ocean. By this time, Francisco's stock had risen considerably. In the list of conquistadors for this expedition, he came directly after Balboa (not that he could have read this), suggesting he was the expedition's second-in-command. Balboa clearly placed great faith in his underling, and Francisco was with him when he waded into the Pacific Ocean.

Balboa's faith in Pizarro and the friendship he bore him were not rewarded. Balboa was an extravagant character, a maverick whose charms and brilliance

**PERHAPS BECAUSE OF HIS SHUTTLECOCK CHILDHOOD, PIZARRO HAD AN ACUTE SENSE OF WHICH SUPERIOR FIGURE TO ATTACH HIMSELF TO. FOR HIM, LOVE AND FRIENDSHIP WERE LUXURIES HE COULD ILL AFFORD. HE MEASURED LIFE IN TERMS OF POWER AND GOLD.**

earned him great riches and the admiration of his soldiers, but incited the envy of his superiors. One of these was Pedrarias, the nickname for Pedro Arias de Ávila, a Castilian who had married a close friend of the queen. He had been sent to Panama to replace Balboa as its governor. Perhaps because of his shuttlecock childhood, Pizarro had an acute sense of which superior figure to attach himself to. For him, love and friendship were luxuries he could ill afford. He measured life in terms of power and gold.

Pedrarias, who was nearly seventy when dispatched to the New World, was jealous of Balboa's charisma and stamina. From the moment Pedrarias arrived in Panama there was an uneasy rivalry between Balboa, a natural talent, and Pedrarias, the governor's royal imprimatur. The tension was eased when

Pedrarias married his daughter off to Balboa. Balboa accepted the marriage as a political necessity but aroused his father-in-law's ire by continuing to live with his native mistress.

Rising tensions were alleviated when Balboa, after much waiting, received permission from Pedrarias to continue exploring to the south of Panama. But Pedrarias worried that Balboa would establish his own colony and usurp him. Returning in 1518 to his town of Acla on the northeast coast of Panama from an adventure along the Pacific Coast of Central America, Balboa received warm letters from Pedrarias asking him to meet him as soon as possible.

About halfway to the meeting, Balboa encountered his fellow conquistador and former right-hand man, Francisco Pizarro. His initial joy soon turned to

**When they didn't get their way, the Spaniards often set their dogs on South America's natives. This engraving shows this tactic at work in Balboa's expedition to Panama, of which Pizarro was second in command.**

rage and indignation when Pizarro told him that he had come on the orders of Pedrarias to arrest him on charges of treason. Balboa, outraged by the treachery of Pizarro as well as the trumped-up charges leveled against him, insisted upon returning to Spain for his trial. Pedrarias set up a show trial, and Balboa was found guilty and decapitated on January 12, 1519.

Francisco profited handsomely from his treachery. Pedrarias rewarded his Judas by appointing him as adjutant to Captain Luis Carillo, a young conquistador with excellent financial and social connections. By this time, Francisco was in his forties and valuable as an experienced hard nut, whose moral sensibilities had adapted to the Darwinian conditions of the New World, just as they had to the equally harsh circumstances of his childhood. Pizarro joined Carillo in the assault on the Carib Indians.

Pizarro's contemporary, historian González Fernando de Oviedo, described the conquistador as "valiant in his person . . . but uncouth." He remarked of this expedition that "Luis Carillo and Pizarro, and those who went with them, brought back many Indians and slaves, and very good gold, and they also used their cruelties on the Indians, for this evil habit was frequently deployed, and Pizarro knew it by heart, having used it for years before." His cruelties included burning the locals alive until they revealed where they had hidden their stashes of gold and other valuables. Sometimes he fed them to his dogs.

From these expeditions, Pizarro grew rich. He formed an alliance with another illiterate bastard conquistador who had a sharp business sense, Diego de Almagro. It was an alliance of many facets that included owning gold mines, supplying ships, and trading with Spain, while the two men also gained valuable concessions on the Isla Taboga, otherwise known as the Island of Flowers, off Panama, where they set the local Indians to work on the land.

When Pedrarias founded Panama City in August 1519, Francisco was given a seat on the municipal council, even though he was absent at the time. The bastard and former swineherd had clearly arrived, and a middle age of relative ease and luxury unimaginable back in the days of Trujillo was there for the taking. The cost had been high. He had killed hundreds of people and double-crossed one of his best friends. Despite the new social standing, he was known as a brave fighter, but not as a man of honor.

## TOWARD THE INCA

Francisco's newfound fortunes only left him hungry for more. His appetite was as insatiable as that of the pigs he had herded as a child. It was further exacerbated by the success of his second cousin, Hernán Cortés, who had become unimaginably rich from the conquest of the Aztecs in Mexico. Before Balboa's untimely demise, he had brought back to Panama rumors of a fabulously wealthy civilization to the south.

In 1522, Pascal Andagoya was sent on a mission in search of a tribe near a river known as Biru in the vicinity of the Bay of San Miguel in Panama. When Andagoya became too ill to carry out the mission, Pizarro and Almagro used their leverage with Pedrarias to take over. That same year, Pizarro's father died, from a wound received fighting in Navarre, leaving him nothing, although Pizarro at this point was richer than his father had ever been. He was almost fifty years old, never married, and with no acknowledged children of his own. He had traveled to the other side of the world and made a success of himself, but his success could not erase his childhood.

In 1524, Pizarro and Almagro sailed with eighty men and four horses south, only for Almagro to lose an eye in a skirmish and the expedition to founder in mosquito-ridden mangroves. Less determined men would have abandoned the project entirely, but despite difficulties in raising more money, in November, 1526, they set out again with two ships and twice as many men. At one point the expedition split up. Almagro returned to Panama for provisions, Pizarro camped on an uninhabited island off the mangrove coast of Colombia, while his pilot, Bartolomé Ruiz, sailed farther down the coast. Ruiz crossed the equator, then encountered a balsa wood cargo raft under sail, whose items to trade included gold, silver, and jewels.

Meanwhile, Pizarro and his men were not getting on. Camped on their island, they were dying two or three a day from disease. The starving survivors were reduced to eating snakes and shellfish. Only fear of Pizarro and a lack of any idea how to get themselves out of their predicament prevented a mutiny. Some of Pizarro's men had, however, managed to sneak a message on board Ruiz's ship asking to be rescued from their leader and the grip of his obsession. When Ruiz returned to Panama, Pedrarias ordered that those who wanted out be allowed to return.

When Ruiz's boat returned to the island, he carried this news to his boss. Pizarro's response was legendary. He unsheathed his sword and used its point to draw a line in the sand and said, "Comrades and friends, on that side lies the part that stands for death, hardship, hunger, nakedness, and abandonment. This side here represents comfort. Here you return to Panama to be poor. There you may go on to Peru to be rich. You choose which best suits you as brave Spaniards." Pizarro implored his men to stay for the adventure, arguing that any hardships they had been exposed to, he had been exposed to, too. He was ruthless and avaricious, but his bastard origins had taught him some humility, and he knew how to talk to his soldiers on their level.

Most of his men were eager to escape the dangers of being under the command of such a monomaniacal leader. Only thirteen chose to stay, and with their leader, they were dropped off on another island while Ruiz returned to Panama with the rest. Pizarro and his thirteen men stayed there in a tropical torpor for another seven months until a ship piloted by Ruiz and funded by Almagro came and picked them up. This time he succeeded. They sailed down the mangrove coasts of contemporary Colombia and Ecuador, past the Peruvian desert, to the northern Inca town of Tumbes. The first encounter between the two civilizations took place with both sides impressed by the other's rationality, though the Peruvians in retrospect would have done better to slay the Spaniards on the spot.

## RETURN TO SPAIN

When Pizarro returned to Panama from Tumbes, he decided to sail to Spain to get a Royal License to explore and conquer Peru. He was helped in achieving this goal by the presence of his second cousin, Hernán Cortés, who smoothed the way for the gruff and uncouth soldier to gain an audience with the king. Having been made rich by Cortés, Charles V was impressed by the prospect of getting even richer and granted the license.

The Royal License was not the only reason for Francisco's return to Spain. His hometown of Trujillo also featured prominently in his plans. It was a sweet feeling to return as a rich man, a conquistador of power and influence. Like many of his fellow wealthy conquistadors, Francisco had been sending money back to Spain, which he had used to buy land and erect buildings that displayed this newfound prestige. Yet the main reason he returned was not to rub it in the face of the family that had rejected him, but to enlist his half-brothers and fellow townsmen for the conquest that was to follow.

All of his half-brothers, including his father's legitimate heir, Hernando, decided to join their much older half-brother in the conquest of Peru. Francisco had outwitted his origins and become the effective head of his family.

## THE BULLY'S BULLION

In 1530, Pizarro and his half-brothers, Hernando, Juan, Gonzalo, and Martín, sailed from Seville with a small detachment of soldiers mainly drawn from his childhood neighbors. They sailed to Panama, where the final contingent set sail for Peru on December 27. There were 180 men, including 38 gentlemen, 90 men of moderate rank, and 20 of the lower classes. Only a third of them could read.

After slow progress down the coast, Pizarro and his men arrived in Tumbes in April 1532, where they found the conditions almost ideal for conquest. Since their last visit, the great Inca, Wayna Capac, had died from the smallpox that had preceded European invasion, as had many of his subjects. Pizarro's heart leapt when he heard that the power vacuum caused by his death had resulted in

**Atahuallpa, pictured here, was engaged in civil war with his brother, Huáscar, when Pizarro arrived in Tumbes. Pizarro quickly exploited the situation to his benefit.**

ATHABALIBA
*ultimus Rex Peruanorum*

civil war between two of his sons, Huáscar and Atahuallpa. Based on his cousin's experience with the Aztecs, it was the perfect opportunity to divide and rule.

As Pizarro traveled toward the army of Atahuallpa, he collected allies from tribes that had resented the rule of the Inca. He pushed his army over the Andes with pitiless discipline and arrived at Cajamarca in the northern highlands of Peru, where Atahuallpa was camped with his army of 30,000. Vastly outnumbered, Pizarro pursued his campaign by skullduggery. When Atahuallpa told the Spaniards that he would meet them in one of the large halls of the deserted town the armies were camped outside, Pizarro hid some of his men in the colonnades of the hall while the others waited for the Inca. When Atahuallpa was carried into the hall on his magnificent gold throne, Pizarro sent a message via one of his priests, Friar Vincente de Valverde, to tell Atahuallpa that he was an ambassador from a great king across the seas who desired friendship with the Inca. Atahuallpa replied that he didn't doubt this, but that being a great ruler in his own country he was under no obligation to conclude a pact of friendship.

The priest called for the natives to renounce all forms of God other than the Christian God whom the Spanish king worshipped. Hearing this, Atahuallpa asked the priest for the authority on which this was based and was shown a copy of the Bible. He demanded the priest hand him the Bible so that "it could speak to him." He put the Bible to his ear, then mockingly threw it to the ground. On the pretext of this insult to their God, the Spanish hidden in the colonnades began to fire their guns, causing havoc among the Incas. Up to 10,000 Indians were killed that day and another 5,000 were taken captive. Among them was Atahuallpa, who was later executed by Pizarro, even after he delivered the famous roomful of gold for which he had bartered his freedom. Most of his queens and many other women were raped by the same men who had acted on the insult against the Bible. Of course, if Pizarro had been in the equivalent position as Atahuallpa, he might have done the same, because the bastard couldn't read.

## BLOOD IS THICKER THAN BUSINESS

Having dispatched Atahuallpa to his maker, Pizarro marched on to Cuzco in southern Peru, the capital of the Inca empire, which the Spanish took uncontested. Manco Cápac, son of Wayna and half-brother of Atahuallpa, was

appointed Inca (leader) by the Spanish. At Cajamarca, Atahuallpa had given some of his queens to the Spanish conquistador. Francisco was given an eighteen-year-old beauty, Quispe Cusi, one of Wayna's many children, to take as a wife. At the age of fifty-six, Francisco found himself with a wife, and soon after, a family. Having had no proper family in his youth, Francisco was now surrounded by his half-brothers, his wife, and his children. Increasingly his thoughts became dynastic.

When projected into the future, greed can become limitless. The wealth on display at Cuzco was astounding, and the Spaniards set about reducing the tons of Incan artifacts into bullion with gusto, much of which was shipped back to Spain. All of a sudden, the Pizarro brothers and Almagro, who was also an illiterate bastard—he didn't even know who his parents were because

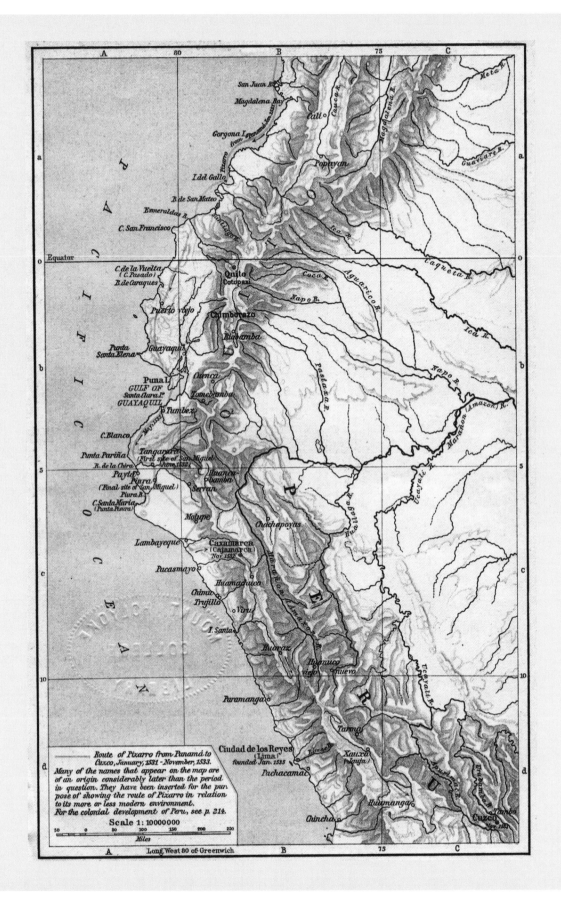

A · 80 · B · 75 · C

Meta R.

San Juan R.

Magdalena Bay

Gorgona I.

I. del Gallo

B. de San Mateo

Esmeraldas R.

C. San Francisco

Equator

C. de la Vuelta
(C. Pasado)
B. de Caraques

Puerto viejo

Punta
Santa Elena

Guayaquil

Puna I.
GULF OF
Santa Clara I.
GUAYAQUIL

Tumbez

C. Blanco

Tangarara
(First site of San Miguel
June 1532)

R. de la Chira

Payta

Piura
(Final site of San Miguel)
Piura R.

C. Santa Maria
(Punta Pisura)

Motupe

Lambayeque

Pacasmayo

Chimu
Trujillo

Viru

I. Santa

Paramanga

Ciudad de los Reyes
(Lima)
founded Jan. 1535

Pachacamac

Chincha

Cali

Popayan

Quito
Cotopaxi

Chimborazo

Riobamba

Cuenca

Lombebamba

Huanca-
bamba

Serran

Chachapoyas

Caxamarca
(Cajamarca)
Nov. 1532

Huamachuco

Huaraz

Huanuco
viejo   nuevo

Tarma

Rimac  Xauxa
(Jauja)

Huamanga

Tambo
Nov. 1533

Cuzco

Cauca R.

Magdalena R.

Guaviare R.

Ica. R.

Caqueta R.

Coca R.

Aguarico R.

Napo R.

Napo R.

Pastaza R.

Maranon (Amazon) R.

Huallaga R.

Ucayali R.

Ucayali R.

Purus R.

Beni R.

Madre de Dios R.

Route of Pixarro from Panama to
Cuzco, January, 1531 - November, 1533.
Many of the names that appear on the map are
of an origin considerably later than the period
in question. They have been inserted for the purpose of showing the route of Pixarro in relation
to its more or less modern environment.
For the colonial development of Peru, see p. 214.

Scale 1 : 10000000

50   0   50   100   150   200   250
Miles

A · Long West 80 of Greenwich · B · 75 · C

he had been dumped on the church door as a baby—were some of the richest men in the world. Unfortunately, it wasn't enough. Tensions soon began to appear between the two business partners over which part of the Inca empire belonged to whom.

The legitimate and thus best educated Pizarro, Hernando, was sent to Spain to handle relations between the Pizarros and the Spanish court. Partly this was to make sure that the Almagrists, as they became known, did not exact preferential conditions from Charles V. Spain was several months' journey away from Peru, and news was slow to travel. Rumors, however, were rife. One of them was that Charles had split Peru in two: The northern part was to go to the Pizarros, and the southern part, including the capital of Cuzco, was to go to Almagro.

This rumor particularly upset Juan and Gonzalo Pizarro, who, at the time, were happily camped in the city, destroying its treasures and raping women. When they heard of this division they protested, and even though Francisco must have known that his two half-brothers were thuggish and troublesome, his new status as pater familias caused him to take their side. Trouble was averted by another rumor, of an even richer civilization farther to the south in what is today Chile. Partly funded by Francisco, Almagro put together an expedition to conquer this rumored civilization. After eighteen months and 3,728 miles (6,000 kilometers) of hard travel, Almagro returned to Cuzco in early 1537 without having found a society on par with the Incas or Aztecs to conquer.

When Almagro returned, he was surprised to discover that the Inca had revolted against the Spanish. The Pizarros and the underlings who copied their swinish behavior had insulted the Incas to the extent they had decided it would be better to die fighting against the Spanish than submit to them. In a speech to his subjects, the Manco Inca said of the Spanish:

> They preach one thing and do another. They have no fear of God, and no shame, they treat us like dogs. Calling us no other names. Their greed is such that there is no temple or palace left they have not plundered. Indeed if all the snow turned to gold and silver it

**Pizzaro's route over land and sea to the conquest of the Incas is shown in red.**
Courtesy of University of Texas Libraries, the University of Texas at Austin

would not satisfy them. They keep our daughters and sisters as their concubines, behaving in this like animals. They have already begun to divide the provinces among each other so that they can loot them. They will enslave us and reduce us to the point where we are only fit as a source for livestock, women, and precious metals.

The Inca revolt was fiercely fought, and for a while it seemed that the Inca had the upper hand. Juan Pizarro was killed in the siege of Cuzco, and Francisco was forced to send for reinforcements by sea. However, the rebellion eventually failed. European microbes and weapons proved too strong for the Indian forces, as they did in many other parts of the world. The Pizarros were also helped by the mass of reinforcements from Spain, new conquistadors keen to cash in on the riches of Peru.

Eventually, the Manco Inca was forced to flee over the Andes toward the Amazon basin. He hoped to maintain his civilization where the Spanish wouldn't follow. In 1539, Gonzalo Pizarro chased the Inca down to the jungles of Vilcabamba, but failed to catch him; the Incan society survived there independently until 1572, although the Manco Inca was assassinated in 1544. Francisco was furious at the failure of his half-brother Gonzalo, but rather than punish his own blood, he engaged in a cruel and selective massacre of the Inca elite who had remained in the territory under his control.

With the Incan threat out of the way, the Pizarros and Almagrists were free to resume their struggle for control of Peru. This time there were no diversions, and the struggle soon became a war, which effectively ended in 1538 at the Battle of Salinas, where Almagro's forces fought against Gonzalo and Hernando Pizarro for control of Cuzco and lost. On the orders of Hernando, Almagro was tried for treason and beheaded.

This action would have grave consequences for his older brother. By 1540, with most of the crucial battles for control of Peru seemingly fought and won, Francisco had returned to his house in Lima, the port city he had built to facilitate maritime connections with Spain. His attention increasingly turned to governance rather than battle. It was an area in which his illiteracy put him at a distinct disadvantage, and Francisco was forced to rely heavily on his secretary, Antonio Picado, a prickly and arrogant character, who took this opportunity to enrich himself by taking advantage of his boss. His actions caused considerable disenchantment, particularly among the remaining Almagrists, whom Picado was fond of goading.

Francisco paid a high price for his dependence on his secretary. Although warned on several occasions that the son of Almagro was planning to kill him, Francisco failed to adequately protect himself. One Sunday afternoon after lunch, he was at home with a half dozen friends when twenty men led by Almagrist Juan Herrada rushed his house. In the fracas, Pizarro's half-brother Martín was killed. Although Pizarro drew his sword and held off the attackers for some time, his defense was foiled when his assailants pushed one of his allies onto Francisco's sword. With a man weighing down his blade, Pizarro was rendered defenseless and was slaughtered where he stood.

# CHAPTER 4

# ELIZABETH I

## FROM BASTARD DAUGHTER TO VIRGIN QUEEN
## 1533-1603

BORN A PRINCESS BUT LATER CAST OUT BY HER FATHER, HENRY
VIII, AND BRANDED A BASTARD, ELIZABETH PATIENTLY TAUGHT
HERSELF THE ARTS OF WISE GOVERNMENT AND SELFLESS
LEADERSHIP, THUS EARNING THE LOVE AND LOYALTY OF THE
ENGLISH PEOPLE AND TRANSFORMING HER NATION FROM A
BACKWARD ISLAND REALM INTO A GLOBAL EMPIRE.

THE WORLD INTO WHICH ELIZABETH TUDOR WAS BORN IN 1533 PICTURED
fortune as a great wheel. Depending on which spoke you happened to occupy, one day you were
on top, the next on the bottom—about to be crushed.

Did the twenty-one-year-old Elizabeth see the turning of the wheel when the men sent by her
half-sister, the queen known as Bloody Mary, came to take her from the spacious country manor
that had been her home to a dark, damp cell in the Tower of London? Terrified, Elizabeth became
so ill that her doctors told Queen Mary she could not, without risking her life, be moved, but Mary
would not relent. The distance to London from Ashridge was 30 miles (48 km), and Elizabeth was
so ill that the journey was frequently interrupted for rest, so that the progress spanned February
12 to February 22. She was lodged in the palace as a prisoner for nearly a month, before she was
carried in an enclosed litter through the London lanes down to the Thames. The young woman,
in a gesture of high theater, drew back the curtains of the conveyance so that all who thronged the
narrow, filthy streets could see how brutally this pale, sick, and frail girl was being treated.

**Known as *The Rainbow Portrait*, this painting by Taddeo Zuccari depicts Elizabeth in a cloak
embroidered with eyes and ears—emblematic of the Virgin Queen's formidable reputation for
having eyes and ears everywhere and for seeing and hearing everything.** Elizabeth I (1533-1603)
(colour litho), Zuccari, Taddeo (1529-66) (after) / Private Collection / Ken Welsh / The Bridgeman Art Library International

**1533:**
**September 7** Elizabeth is born at Greenwich Palace, England, to King Henry VIII and Anne Boleyn.

**1554:**
Seized on orders of her half-sister, Queen Mary I, Elizabeth is imprisoned in the Tower of London and subsequently held under house arrest at Woodstock.

**1559:**
Elizabeth is crowned queen of England on January 15.

Parliament passes the Second Act of Supremacy, which definitively does away with Catholicism as the state religion and makes Elizabeth "Supreme Governor" of the Anglican Church; she enforces uniformity of religious worship across England but also institutes a policy of religious tolerance.

**1560:**
Masterminds the recall and revaluation of "base coinage," a massive and brilliant effort to revitalize the English economy.

**1536:**
Anne Boleyn is beheaded on May 19, and Parliament proclaims Elizabeth a bastard the following day.

**1558:**
Mary I dies, childless, of ovarian cancer on November 17, leaving Elizabeth heir to the throne.

**1559-1560:**
Sends troops to Scotland to help local forces eject French soldiers stationed there and averts a threatened French invasion of England.

**1562:**
Sends troops to France to aid the Huguenots (French Protestants) in their fight against persecution by Catholics.

But this drama was no stage play. In what now became a hard rain, Elizabeth was deposited on a river wharf and transferred to a boat that would ferry her to the Tower's infamous Watergate, traditional portal of the condemned. She was painfully aware that she followed the very course her mother, Anne Boleyn, who had traveled on *her* way to the Tower eighteen years before to await an appointment with the headsman's axe. As the miserable Elizabeth stepped from the boat into the rain and onto the flagstones before the Watergate and water's edge, she held back any tears, protests, or plaints, and declared instead with calm composure, "Here landeth as true a subject, being prisoner, as ever landed at these stairs."

With these words, she seated herself on the stones in the prison's looming shadow, made all the darker by the lowering clouds, and let the torrent pour down upon her. To the plea of the Tower lieutenant that she come in out of the rain, Elizabeth answered: "It is better sitting here than in a worse place."

The sight of the pale beauty drenched and seated at the entrance of the place of her almost certain execution drove one of the "gentleman ushers" who had accompanied her to tears. She turned to him sharply and admonished the tearful guard that she "knew her truth to be such that no man would have cause to weep for her." That said, she consented at last to be shown to the cell that was only the latest of many cruel and abrupt changes in her fortunes. For she had not been *born* a bastard, without family and loyal friends. Her father, Henry VIII, and his Parliament *made* her one. That was the first turn of the great wheel.

**1577-1580:**
Commissions Sir Francis Drake as a privateer (state-sanctioned pirate) against the Spanish; he circumnavigates the globe, opens up parts of the New World to England, and conducts crippling (and highly profitable) raids on Spanish and Portuguese colonies and shipping.

**1588:**
Eloquently rallies her troops at Tilbury Camp to resist invasion by the Spanish, whose Armada is defeated at sea on August 8.

**1590–1599:**
Edmund Spenser writes *The Faerie Queene*, an epic verse allegory celebrating the reign of Elizabeth.

**1603:**
Elizabeth dies at Richmond, England, on March 24.

**1587:**
As Spain prepares to invade England, Elizabeth leads preparations for the defense of her realm.

After both confining and protecting her since 1568, Elizabeth reluctantly orders the execution of Mary, Queen of Scots, on February 8.

**1590:**
Shakespeare's first play, *The Comedy of Errors*, premiers. Twenty-three more Shakespeare plays are written and premiered during Elizabeth's lifetime, and thus he is known as an "Elizabethan" playwright, though he writes and premieres another dozen plays during the reign of James I.

**1601:**
The Earl of Essex, long Elizabeth's favorite, stages an uprising against her; the queen orders his arrest and trial for treason, and he is executed on February 15.

## A TWISTED TALE

Elizabeth's story begins more with her father than her mother. Shortly before he succeeded Henry VII to the English throne in 1509, Henry VIII married Catherine of Aragon, widow of his brother Arthur. For nearly twenty years, it was a happy union between the cultivated Spanish *infanta* and the strappingly handsome English king, who was learned in English, Greek, Latin, theology, and philosophy; a poet and a fine musician, he was a strikingly athletic horseman and hunter of renown. Although Catherine gave birth to a daughter, Mary (the future Queen Mary I), in 1516, the marital landscape darkened beginning about 1527, as Henry despaired over what he pronounced her failure to give him a *male* heir.

The king's eye wandered and then lit upon Anne Boleyn—probably in her late twenties (the year of her birth is not known for certain) when he met her—a tall and slender huntswoman with auburn hair, a fine aquiline nose, and full lips the color of rose petals. The attraction between the two was powerful and carnal, and Henry saw in her the fresh fertility Catherine no longer possessed.

The king summoned his lord chancellor, Thomas Cardinal Wolsey, and pointed to a page in the Old Testament, Leviticus 20:21, which forbids as a form of incest a man's taking his brother's widow as a wife. Arguing that the Lord would never allow a future monarch to be born of so obviously sinful a union as his with Catherine, Henry commanded his lord chancellor to petition Pope Clement VII

THE ENDVR
WORDE ETH
OF THE FOR
LORD EVER

SVPERSTICION

IDOLATRY

ALL FLESHE
IS GRASSE

FEYNED
HOLINE

This painting by an unidentified artist shows Henry VIII on his deathbed designating his son, Edward VI, already enthroned, heir to the kingdom. Among others pictured are the Dukes of Somerset and Northumberland and Thomas Cranmer, the Archbishop of Canterbury. The Pope is depicted crumpled impotently at the feet of the England's second Protestant monarch.

to annul the marriage, thereby making way for him to marry Anne. When the Pope refused (after all, the Holy Roman emperor on whom he relied for protection was also Catherine of Aragon's nephew, the king of Spain), Henry nevertheless proceeded with a divorce trial in 1529. Absent a papal decree, the trial ended without a decision, and a wrathful Henry removed Wolsey from office and then summoned him to answer royal charges of high treason. Wolsey had the good fortune to drop dead before suffering the consequences of those accusations.

In 1532, Henry elevated to his circle of advisors the masterfully devious Thomas Cromwell, who proposed that the king solve his dilemma by altogether breaking with Rome and creating a Church of England, replacing the authority of the Pope with that of the Archbishop of Canterbury, a figure beholden to the king and therefore certain to grant the divorce. By this solution, Henry cast off

**A WRATHFUL HENRY VIII REMOVED LORD CHANCELLOR THOMAS CARDINAL WOLSEY FROM OFFICE AND THEN SUMMONED HIM TO ANSWER ROYAL CHARGES OF HIGH TREASON. WOLSEY HAD THE GOOD FORTUNE TO DROP DEAD BEFORE SUFFERING THE CONSEQUENCES OF THOSE ACCUSATIONS.**

Catherine the following year and acquired his new bride. The establishment of the Church of England, however, was destined to propel the realm to the precipice of civil war.

Anne Boleyn became pregnant in the shortest possible time and, between three and four in the afternoon on September 7, 1533, in the Chamber of Virgins at Greenwich Palace, brought into Henry's world the terrible disappointment of a daughter. The king nevertheless proclaimed the newborn—she was christened Elizabeth—heir to the throne in place of Catherine's daughter, Mary. That marriage having been annulled as sinful and illegal, Mary was also summarily declared a bastard by act of Parliament.

As for Anne Boleyn, her failure to deliver a male heir appeared to the king all the proof necessary that she was suffering God's punishment for the sin of adultery, an act of treason under English law. Tried on the flimsiest of evidence—for there was in fact none—Elizabeth's mother was sent to the Tower of London and, on May 19, 1536, to the block. The night before her execution, she remarked to Anthony Kingston, constable of the Tower, "I heard say the executioner was very good, and I have a little neck." With that, according to Kingston, she encircled her throat with her hands and laughed, he reported, "heartily."

Following Anne Boleyn's execution, Parliament passed a law making Elizabeth a bastard and reducing her from princess to lady. She was two years, eight months old. On May 20, the king was betrothed to Jane Seymour, another young noblewoman in her late twenties, whom he married ten days later.

Elizabeth would spend most of the rest of her childhood in Hatfield Palace, which Henry had seized from the Catholic Church; situated 21 miles (34 km) north of London, it was remote from the royal court. As for the king's latest wife, Jane became pregnant early in 1537, delivered a son on October 12, and died less than two weeks later. The infant, Edward, was sickly and not expected to live long. Determined, therefore, to gain a sturdier male heir, the widower married on January 6, 1540, a bride Cromwell had recruited, the German princess Anne of Cleves. As soon as she arrived, however, Henry moaned that she was "nothing so fair as she hath been reported" and quickly persuaded her to accept an annulment on July 9, 1540. (Cromwell's flawed taste in women prompted the king to contrive a charge of treason, and the lord chancellor was duly tried and beheaded.)

Nineteen-year-old Catherine Howard, whose youthful beauty appealed greatly to Henry, became his fifth wife on July 28, 1540. Not surprisingly, she strayed from the aging and increasingly corpulent monarch and was beheaded for the treasonous crime of adultery on February 13, 1542. Catherine Parr, whom Henry wed on July 12, 1543, was destined to achieve what none of the previous five wives had: widowhood. Her husband the king died on January 28, 1547, but for the nearly four years of her marriage, Catherine welcomed Elizabeth back to the court and proved a kind and caring stepmother. Shortly after Henry died, however, she married England's dashing lord high admiral, Thomas Seymour, who secretly embarked on a plot to oust his own brother, Edward Seymour, whom Henry had appointed "protector" (regent) over Edward VI, just ten years old at the time of his succession to the throne. Always wary of his brother, Edward Seymour waited until the death of Catherine Parr in January 1549 to charge Thomas with a long rap sheet of high crimes, foremost among them a plot to marry Elizabeth in a conspiracy to gain control over the realm. Thomas Seymour was quickly convicted and executed, leaving Elizabeth vulnerable to the suspicions of all and sundry at court, many of whom believed she had actively colluded with Thomas Seymour, who, they also believed, had been her secret lover. The complete absence of actual evidence did nothing to dispel the dangerous cloud that hung over Elizabeth, and her every move and utterance was closely observed. After all, as a bastard by law, she had little to lose (other than her life) and much to gain from scheming with the wily lord high admiral.

### STAYING ALIVE

Elizabeth adapted to this latest climate of peril. She learned to give voice only to those thoughts she wanted others to hear. She learned to win friends among the influential, but never to give herself wholly to any one friendship. And because the people of greatest power in court circles were men, she learned to ingratiate herself with them, for she was growing into a beautiful woman, who was also the product of Europe's finest tutors and therefore full of charming conversation that showed wisdom beyond her tender years. Yet she refused to give herself wholly to any man.

## THUS ELIZABETH THE BASTARD, WITH NEITHER PARENT NOR ROYAL LEGACY TO PROTECT HER, LEARNED TO PROTECT HERSELF, TO SURVIVE, AND EVEN TO FLOURISH.

Thus the bastard, with neither parent nor royal legacy to protect her, learned to protect herself, to survive, and even to flourish. But on July 6, 1553, fifteen-year-old Edward VI, after a brief life of chronic suffering, having been feverish since the beginning of the year, wracked with a cough that brought up thick, discolored gouts of blood, whispered to his kindly tutor John Cheke "I am glad to die," and died.

**An unidentified English artist painted England's treacherous and dashing Lord High Admiral Thomas Seymour, executed for the certain crime of plotting against his brother to obtain the regency over young Edward VI and for the highly improbable offense of plotting to marry Elizabeth to gain absolute control over the English realm.** Portrait of Thomas Seymour (1508-1549) Baron Seymour (oil on panel), English School, (16th century) / National Portrait Gallery, London, UK / The Bridgeman Art Library International

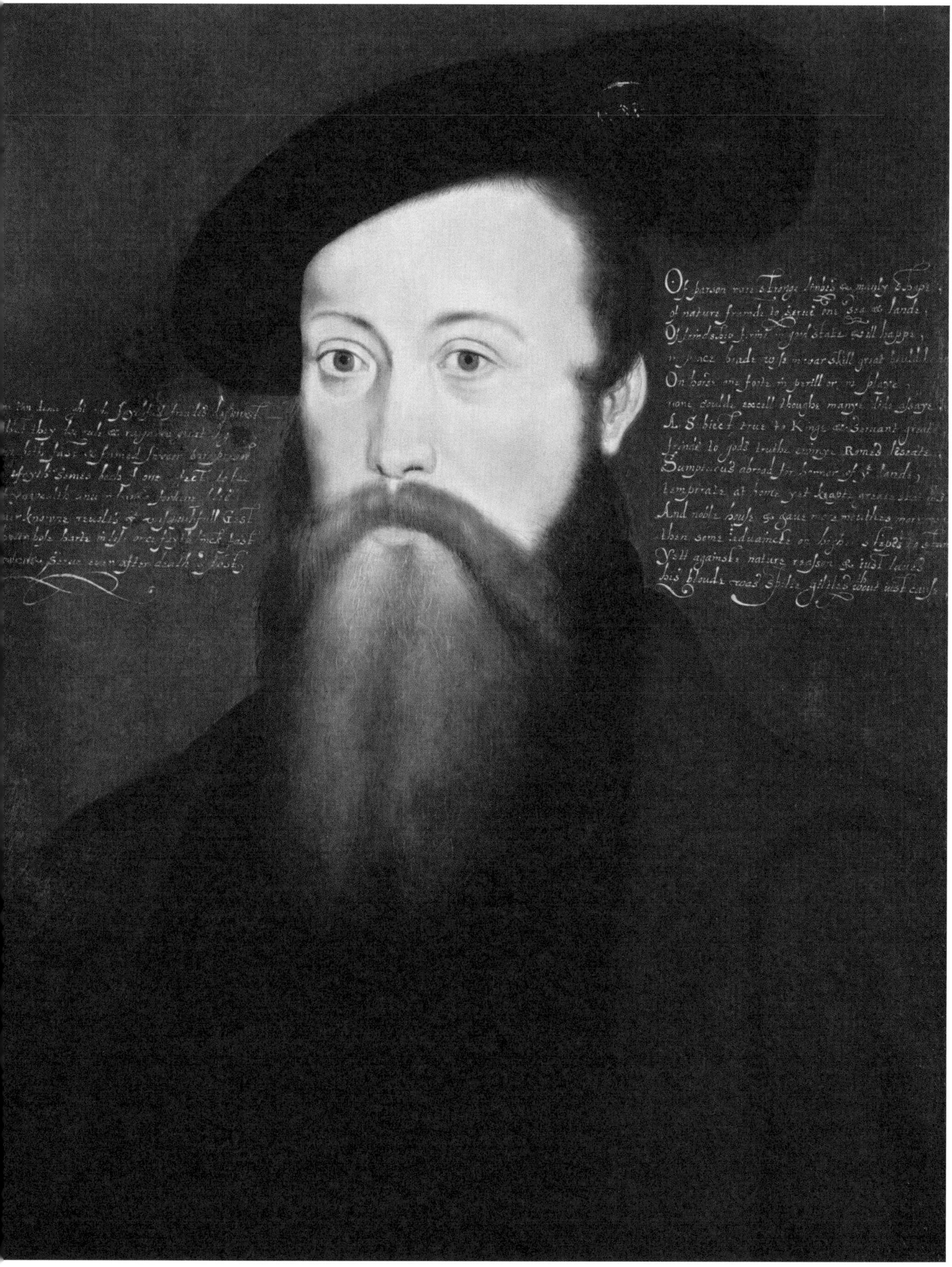

Aware that Edward was not destined to a long life, Henry VIII in 1543 had prevailed on Parliament to pass a new law restoring both Mary and Elizabeth to the line of royal succession (the act did not explicitly alter their legal status as bastards, however). Young King Edward, before he died, had expressed fears that Mary would undo the Reformation by restoring Roman Catholicism to England if she ascended the throne; he wanted, therefore, to disinherit her, so that Elizabeth, who embraced the Protestant faith, would be certain to succeed him. Informed that the Succession Act barred removing one sister from the line without also disinheriting the other, Edward was talked into backing a dark horse candidate, Lady Jane Grey, daughter-in-law of the influential 1st Duke of Northumberland, to succeed him. She assumed the throne on July 10, 1553, but was deposed just nine days later, leaving Mary, as Henry's eldest daughter, the new queen of England.

Elizabeth knew that her half-sister would always regard her as a potential rival, especially given their profound religious differences. She understood that her life was now in more peril than ever before and decided, therefore, to make a show of worshiping in the Catholic manner and expressing at every opportunity both loyalty to and love for the queen.

It was to no avail.

One year after she succeeded to the throne, Queen Mary I wed Spain's Philip II, the son of the Holy Roman emperor and, of course, a Catholic. The union rocked all of England—creating discontent among the Protestant majority, who now feared persecution at the hands of a powerful Catholic minority, but also among the realm's Catholics, who did not trust Spaniards, regardless of their religion. Into this turmoil, Sir Thomas Wyatt—a courtier whose father had loved Anne Boleyn and whose mother may well have been an object of Henry VIII's lustful attentions—fomented in Kent an uprising against the crown and led 4,000 rebels to London Bridge and Ludgate, where forces loyal to Mary

**On the death of Henry VIII's short-lived heir, Edward VI, in 1553, young Elizabeth follows her half-sister, Mary, into London to witness Mary's coronation. Within a year, "Bloody Mary" would order the arrest of Elizabeth. This historical fresco was created in 1910 to decorate the British Parliament.** Queen Mary (1516-1558) and Princess Elizabeth (1533-1603) entering London, 1553, 1910 (fresco), Shaw, John Byam Liston (1872-1919) / Houses of Parliament, Westminster, London, UK / The Bridgeman Art Library International

turned them back. As his army instantly dissolved about him, Wyatt surrendered, throwing himself on the queen's mercy. He found none. But worse for Elizabeth, he was charged with plotting to overthrow Mary for the purpose of putting her half-sister on the throne. It was for this reason that Mary ordered her conveyed to the Tower of London.

Though bastardized, exiled, and stripped of any official power, Elizabeth had devoted much of her childhood and young womanhood to winning the sympathy and loyalty of influential figures in government. They now rallied to her support, prevailing on Mary for her release. The queen yielded to the extent of setting her free from the Tower, but she exiled her to Woodstock in Oxfordshire, where the young woman was housed in a gatehouse of Woodstock Manor, because the main residence was too broken down to accommodate her. Here Elizabeth spent nearly a year under house arrest.

During her youth, Elizabeth learned that, save for the friends she might contrive to win, she was ultimately alone and finally dependent most upon herself. Nevertheless, as she was conveyed from the Tower to Woodstock, she was amazed to see crowds thronging the streets and country lanes to get a look at her and cheer her. If the love and loyalty of kings, queens, and courtiers could not be relied upon, it may have been at this moment that she began to believe that her greatest strength might lie with the common people of England, who saw in her her father's daughter and a faithful champion of the Protestant cause.

## THE WHEEL TURNS—AGAIN

On April 17, 1555, riders called at Woodstock to summon Elizabeth to attend what all assumed was to be the birth of a child; the queen's belly had been growing prodigiously for nearly nine months. Doubtless, Elizabeth was moved by Mary's desire to have her present, and doubtless Mary knew that she now needed all the support she could get. Her efforts to restore the realm to Catholicism entailed England's involvement in a ruinous military alliance with Spain and, at home, a reign of persecution against those Protestants who protested the rollback of the Reformation. By the time Elizabeth had been summoned to her side, the queen had already earned the epithet of Bloody Mary for having sent some three hundred souls to burn at the stake for heresy.

Pregnancy came to Mary as a joyous relief—for she had thought herself barren—but days became weeks and weeks months, and she neither delivered nor miscarried, yet her belly continued to swell. After some time, Elizabeth returned to Woodstock, but now as the presumptive heir to the throne. For two things were clear to everyone at the court of Mary I. She would have no children, and what grew in her womb would certainly kill her. On November 17, 1558, the queen died of ovarian cancer.

Legally still the bastard child of an adulterous traitor, Elizabeth was crowned on January 15, 1559. On the eve of this event, she was greeted and cheered by the people of London, who were (an eyewitness wrote) "wonderfully ravished" by their graceful and charismatic twenty-five-year-old monarch.

## THE VIRGIN QUEEN

Three days after becoming queen, Elizabeth confessed, "The burden that has fallen upon me maketh me amazed." Years of distractions during the tumultuous reign of her father, added to more years of misrule under her half-sister, created an England that was (in the words of a contemporary observer) "most afflicted, embroiled on the one side with the Scottish, on the other side with the French war; overcharged with debt . . . the treasury exhausted; . . . the people distracted with different opinions in religion; . . . bare of potent friends, and strengthened with no alliance of foreign princes." The realm that was now Elizabeth's to rule was a marginal power compared with most of the rest of Europe, poor, possessed of virtually no army or navy, verging on religious civil war, menaced by Scotland (at the time a foreign country), burdened by Irish rebellion, and greedily watched by the monarchs of France, Spain, and the Holy Roman Empire, all of whom regarded it as something of an overripe fruit ready to fall from the branch and into the hands of whomever was quickest to catch it.

But Elizabeth the bastard queen was accustomed to adversity and long odds. She was determined not only to restore England to the road of the Reformation but also to carry it to preeminence in trade and influence among nations. Her long, lonely, perilous political apprenticeship had taught her the necessity of strategic patience. Far too long, England had been jerked violently to and fro on fortune's wheel, and she resolved to work the transformation of the kingdom slowly, always retaining enough of the familiar to provide her subjects with an

ample measure of confidence. Although she correctly counted herself among the best-educated monarchs in Europe, she aggressively sought the advice of the best minds she could find, stocking her Privy Council with these men and only these, and taking care to retain on the Council the best people from the reigns of her predecessors, including a few Catholics, while gradually adding her own nominees, foremost among whom were William Cecil, Lord Burghley, who served as secretary of state and, subsequently, lord treasurer, and the dashing Robert Dudley, 1st Earl of Leicester, who was master of the horse and lord steward of the royal household as well as a privy councilor.

Illegitimacy had severed Elizabeth from the luxury of taking anything for granted. Purported friends were often enemies, and family members were the most treacherous enemies of all. Her survival had depended on cultivating a savvy understanding of individual character, and so she came to the throne an avid and skilled reader of people, possessed of an uncanny faculty for separating actual from feigned motives, true loyalty from counterfeit, as when she saw through the protestation of loyalty made to her by her first cousin and principal rival, Mary, Queen of Scots, or recognized the dangerous military incompetence of Robert Devereux, 2nd Earl of Essex, who had long been a favorite of hers.

The modern science of anthropology is founded on the belief that a given culture may be best understood by a well-trained outsider. The circumstances of Elizabeth's birth and upbringing had made her an outsider in her own culture, and she came to the throne with a profound, objective understanding of the people over whom she would now reign. She understood that she was a queen in a culture that valued and respected men far more than women, yet she also understood that men respected and valued—indeed, worshiped—two idealized images of womanhood: the virgin of chivalric lore, pale, fair, nearly ethereal, and the Virgin of Christianity, a holy intercessor whose love for her people was as pure as it was unbounded. It was from this understanding that Elizabeth I presented herself as the "Virgin Queen," simultaneously courtly and worthy of quasi-religious adoration.

◄ **In 1588, the English fleet drove the Spanish Armada into a storm, thereby preventing what seemed an inevitable invasion against which Elizabeth had eloquently and courageously rallied her troops at Tilbury Camp, pledging, if necessary, to die by their side.** Photo by MPI / Getty Images

Part of the presentation was physical. Elizabeth had the good fortune to possess the fair hair and willowy stature essential to the image, but she was also an enthusiastic horsewoman and hunter. Rather than give this up, she shielded her face from the tanning rays of the sun by wearing a mask on clear days, holding it in place by a button clamped between her teeth. She enhanced her fairness of complexion with makeup powders compounded of finely ground alabaster, and she applied unguents and lotions of beeswax, ass's milk, and the ground-up jawbones of hogs. Other steps were almost certainly more extreme. Renaissance women were known to work into their skin compounds of white lead dissolved in vinegar or borax combined with sulfur, setting off the lips with an application of red ocher and red mercuric sulfide or cochineal, a red dye prepared from the ground-up bodies of the red cochineal insect. As for freckles, these were assiduously bleached with birch-tree sap and sulfur dissolved in a solution of turpentine and mercury sublimate. All such preparations were expensive, but the true cost was eventual semi-mummification of the skin.

The other component of the presentation was the queen's very way of life. Despite the persistent entreaties of Parliament that she wed—producing an heir was paramount—Elizabeth persistently refused. A virgin, after all, does not marry, and Elizabeth argued that neither does a true queen. To place a husband above herself would diminish her power. Moreover, if she married a foreign prince (as Mary had), her loyalty would be divided between her country and her husband's, and the union might (as was the case in Mary's reign) lead to entangling alliances. If instead she wed an Englishman, all those at court who were not chosen would find themselves driven by jealousies and suspicions. To Parliament and others who begged her to marry, Elizabeth finally and firmly replied that she *was* married: wedded to England.

## FROM POWERLESSNESS TO POWER

A modern psychologist would almost certainly dismiss all of the queen's strategic and political explanations of her refusal to marry and point squarely to the portrait of marriage her childhood had painted for her—of women serially discarded or, like her own mother, discarded and killed.

And who could deny that Elizabeth's journey from bastard daughter to Virgin Queen was deeply scarred by searing psychic wounds? Yet equally undeniable is that a girl who had suffered the most devastating rejections imaginable found the strength and wisdom in her early experience of life to lead her people safely through diplomatic, economic, religious, and military crises with foreign powers in Scotland as well as continental Europe; to heal the religious divisions that threatened to tear England apart; to steer the nation from economic stagnation to growth that would eventually build the kingdom into a global empire; to send intrepid men in explorations of the New World; and generally to set England on a course that would transform it from an island backwater into a center of culture, commerce, and imperial power whose influence has made itself felt not only across geographical distances but also throughout time itself.

Among the many crises conquered and achievements made during Elizabeth's forty-five-year reign—1558 to her death in 1603—one instance stands out as emblematic of Elizabeth at her finest. On July 19, 1588, some 130 ships of the Spanish Armada were sighted in the English Channel. With invasion clearly imminent, Elizabeth parried the pleas of Privy Council and courtiers that she remain under guard in London and instead went to Tilbury, where England's small army prepared to repel the anticipated Spanish landings. There were those among her advisers who warned of the danger of exposing herself among so many armed men in so perilous a time. "I do not desire to live to distrust my faithful and loving people," she declared, and as she freely walked through the encampment, to a man, the army fell on its knees before her. The next day, having donned the shining steel cuirass of a cavalry officer, she rode among her soldiers astride "a prancing steed attired like an angel bright." She spoke to the troops:

> Let tyrants fear, I have always so behaved myself that under God I have placed my chiefest strength and safeguard in the loyal hearts and good will of my subjects. And therefore I am come amongst you as you see at this time not for my recreation and disport, but being resolved in the midst and heat of the battle to live or die amongst you all. To lay down for God and for my kingdom and for my people my honour and my blood even in the dust.

Betrayed by family, menaced by scheming rivals at court, Elizabeth placed her reliance on herself—and on her people. This was enough. She proclaimed to her soldiers the fearlessness and defiance founded in the bond, stronger than family, stronger than marriage, she had forged between herself and England, its people, and its defenders:

> I know I have the body of a weak and feeble woman but I have the heart and stomach of a King, and of a King of England too, and think foul scorn that Parma or Spain or any Prince of Europe should dare invade the borders of my Realm to which rather than any dishonour shall grow by me, I myself will take up arms, I myself will be your General, Judge, and Rewarder of every one of your virtues in the field.

In the end, it was the Royal Navy, which Elizabeth had nurtured and financed, that prevented the mighty Spanish Armada from delivering the thirty thousand invaders it carried. Driven by the British fleet into the teeth of severe storms, half the Armada was lost at sea and never again returned to menace the realm. That the men of the army gathered at Tilbury did not have to fight came to them almost as a disappointment, for their queen had inspired them to a greatness far beyond their meager numbers. Elizabeth's example at Tilbury endured far beyond the vanished danger posed by the Armada, however. It was to her that Prime Minister Winston Churchill turned some 350 years later when it fell to him to lift Britain on the wings of sublime oratory through its darkest days in World War II to what he himself called the nation's "finest hour."

# CHAPTER 5

# JAMES SCOTT

## 1ST DUKE OF MONMOUTH
## THE BASTARD WHO WOULD BE KING
## 1649-1685

**BARRED BY HIS ILLEGITIMATE BIRTH FROM REIGNING OVER WHAT HAD BEEN HIS FATHER'S KINGDOM, THE DASHING DUKE OF MONMOUTH FASHIONED HIMSELF INTO A POPULAR MILITARY HERO WHO SOUGHT BY SKILL AT ARMS AN ALTERNATIVE PATH TO THE ENGLISH THRONE.**

HE WAS THE BASTARD SON OF CHARLES II, LATE THE KING OF ENGLAND, Scotland, and Ireland, and like his father, Monmouth was a tall man, powerfully built, and made for a life in the saddle, yet with good looks perpetually boyish in their delicacy. All of this made his abject pleas for mercy and his protestations (quite false) that he had converted to the Catholic religion of the new king, his uncle James II, all the more heart wrenching. Well, heart wrenching to some, but to those who had known him as a fearless military hero, unseemly, even disgusting. As his neck was forced down upon the block stained black with years of bloodshed, he cried out the name of William Russell.

The sweating crowd pressing close around the scaffold on London's infamous Tower Hill, some weeping, others jeering, fell suddenly silent. All understood what the condemned man meant by invoking Lord Russell. And none understood better than the man holding the axe, Jack Ketch, executioner in the service of James II Rex. On July 21, 1683, he had executed a sentence of death upon Russell at Lincoln's Inn Fields. On that occasion, Ketch wielded the instrument

**James Scott, 1st Duke of Monmouth. A born military leader, he quickly raised an army to seize the English throne—and even more quickly saw that army dissolve around him.** Portrait of James Scott KG (oil on canvas), Wissing or Wissmig, William (1656-87) (school of) / Private Collection / © Philip Mould Ltd, London / The Bridgeman Art Library International

of death either with such sadistically nuanced skill or with such lack of simple dexterity—nobody could tell which—that the victim suffered horrifically under blow after blow, each excruciating but not one in itself lethal.

Even among the bloodthirsty throngs that habitually attended English beheadings, the gory and agonizing display had created such outrage that Ketch felt moved to write and publish a pamphlet titled *Apologie*, in which he excused his performance with the claim that Lord Russell had failed to "dispose himself as was most suitable" and that he was therefore distracted while taking aim on his neck.

Monmouth's reminder of Russell's execution either unnerved or angered Ketch. Even as the first blow fell upon the duke, those who counted themselves connoisseurs of the headsman's art knew the axe had missed its mark. Ketch stood back, regarding his botched handiwork, and dealt another blow, then another, as Monmouth writhed, screamed, and moaned.

According to the official record of the Tower of London, there were five blows in all, though some onlookers counted seven and others eight. Whether five, seven, or eight, none proved sufficient to sever the man's head from his suffering body, and Ketch pulled a butcher's knife from the sheath on his hip, which he drew across the last cords of sinew and flesh that prevented the head from dropping to the scaffold floor. With that, the life of James Scott, 1st Duke of Monmouth, ended on July 15, 1685.

**1678:**
Commands the Anglo-Dutch brigade
in the Battle of Saint-Denis, near Mons,
Belgium, during August 14–15, and emerges
as a popular military hero.

**1683:**
Implicated in the so-called "Rye
House Plot" to assassinate Charles
II and James, Duke of York.
Monmouth flees into Dutch exile.

**1679:**
Puts down the Covenanters Rebellion in
Scotland, defeating rebels under Robert
Hamilton at the Battle of Bothwell Bridge
on June 22.

**1685:**
Charles II dies on February 6, prompting Monmouth to hatch a rebellion aimed at
overthrowing the king's designated heir, James, Duke of York, and installing himself
on the English throne. Lands with a handful of supporters at Lyme Regis on June 11 and
commences his rebellion, crowning himself king of England at Chard and then again,
on June 20, at Taunton. On June 27, is defeated by royal troops under Louis de Duras,
second earl of Feversham, at Philips Norton; withdraws to Wells on July 1, which his men
sack, then attacks Feversham's forces near Bridgwater on July 6, suffers a disastrous
defeat, and is captured. Monmouth is convicted of treason and beheaded on July 15.

## ONE OF TWELVE

His life began on April 9, 1649, in Rotterdam, Netherlands, to which his
father, the future King Charles II, had taken refuge after the Puritans
beheaded *his* father, King Charles I, in the English Civil War. Charles would
be crowned on April 23, 1661, in what history calls the Restoration, the
return to monarchy from the Interregnum, an eleven-year experiment in
Republican government.

The English people soon learned to call their new king "the Merrie
Monarch" because he so heartily enjoyed strong drink and pretty women, lots
of pretty women. Before Charles's life and reign ended in 1685, he had fathered
no fewer than twelve children out of wedlock and none at all by his wedded wife,
Catherine of Braganza.

Charles's principal mistress in the late 1640s was Lucy Walter, described
by the celebrated English diarist John Evelyn as "brown, beautiful, bold but
insipid"; she was nineteen when she gave birth to James Crofts. (He would not
be called James Scott until his fourteenth year.) By the time of the baby's birth,
Lucy had long since acquired a reputation as a bad girl from a good Welsh family,
having been the mistress of a Roundhead (Puritan) officer, Algernon Sydney,
and subsequently of his younger brother, Robert, who was a Cavalier (Royalist).
It was probably Robert who introduced her to Charles. In any case, Lucy's liaison with the future king was off and on again until the fall of 1651, when she

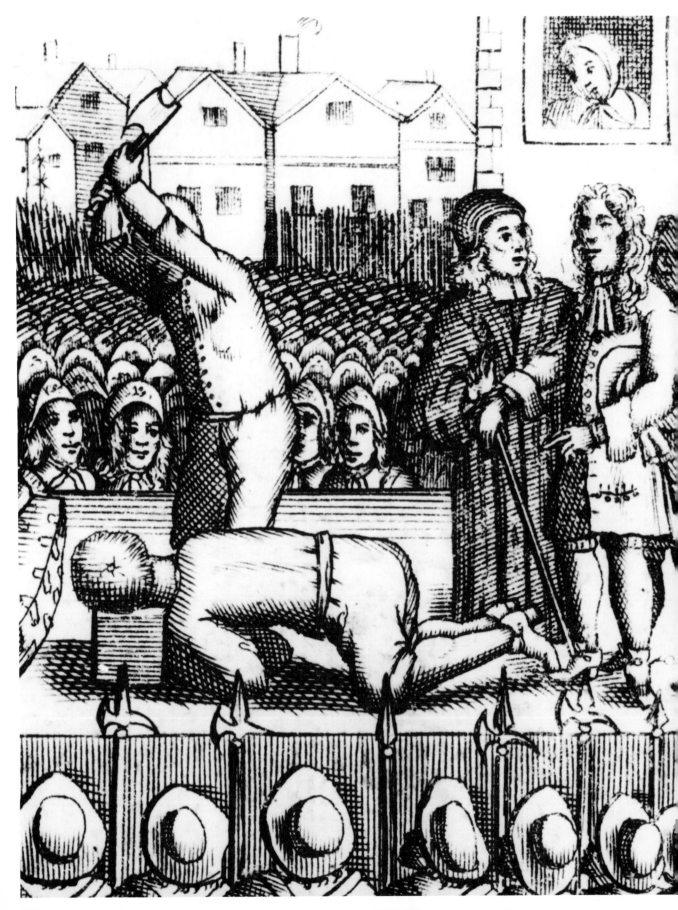

dropped out—or was sent out—of his life, sank into obscure poverty, and died from unknown causes in Paris in 1658. She was twenty-eight.

James Crofts fared far better than his mother. In an era that dismissed children born out of wedlock as "bastards" and "by-blows," Charles freely acknowledged James as his son, though not his heir, but he did create him, at age fourteen, the 1st Duke of Monmouth, which carried the subordinate titles of Earl of Doncaster and Baron Scott of Tynedale. That very year, Monmouth also acquired, by royal arrangement, a wealthy wife, Anne Scott, 4th Countess of Buccleuch, and, the day after the nuptials, yet another title—Duke of Buccleuch, the king having elevated his daughter-in-law from countess to duchess. Add to these acquisitions the surname by which James would become known to history. Until James's marriage, he had used the family name of William Crofts, 1st Baron Crofts, to whom Charles II had entrusted his care. Once married and laden with titles, James discarded that name for his wife's.

**IN THE RESTORATION EPOCH, GIVEN LUCK, INDULGENCE, AND SOME NATURAL ABILITY, EVEN A BASTARD COULD COME TO WIELD A GREAT DEAL OF LEGITIMATE POWER IN THE WORLD. THE ONE THING MONMOUTH COULD NOT BECOME, HOWEVER, WAS KING OF ENGLAND.**

All in all, it was a very good start for any young man, especially a bastard—and, even more, just one of a dozen illegitimate offspring. But, then, as young Monmouth himself must have understood, legitimacy was something of a relative commodity in seventeenth-century England, more a subject of interpretation than of fact. Supposedly, the nation's kings ruled by divine right, irrevocable and absolute, but Charles I had been deposed and executed by an act of Parliament on January 30, 1649.

**The Duke of Monmouth was beheaded by one John Ketch, an executioner some thought consummately sadistic and others believed simply very clumsy. In either case, the rebellious duke suffered no fewer than five and perhaps as many as eight blows of the axe before Ketch finished him off with a stroke of a butcher knife.** The Beheading of the Duke of Monmouth (1649-85) at Tower Hill, 15th July 1685 (woodcut) (b/w photo), English School, (17th century) / Private Collection / The Bridgeman Art Library International

From 1653 to 1658, the Parliament's champion Oliver Cromwell wielded a relatively enlightened dictatorship as "Lord Protector" of the English realm, his rule passing to his son, Richard, who proved so weak that Charles II was invited in 1660 to return to England and in 1661 to the throne. Unlike previous English monarchs, who held religion—*their* religion—as absolute and immutable, Charles II unsuccessfully contended with Parliament to bring religious tolerance to England, hoping to make room for Puritans and Catholics as well as Anglicans. Later, when Charles II wanted the aid of France in the Third Dutch War, he secretly promised his cousin King Louis XIV that he would discard his Anglican faith and become a Catholic—by and by.

No doubt, the concept of "legitimacy" was to a remarkable degree negotiable in the Restoration epoch, and, given luck, indulgence, and some natural ability, even a bastard could come to wield a great deal of legitimate power in the world. The one thing Monmouth could *not* become, however, was king of England—and that stuck more and more insistently in his craw.

## MARTIAL MASTERY

From an early age, Monmouth must have recognized that he was a very popular figure. Because Catherine of Braganza had failed to furnish a legitimate heir to the throne, Charles II was forced to acknowledge his brother James, Duke of York, as the heir apparent. Trouble was that James embraced Catholicism and was therefore scorned by the majority of English men and women, who were Protestants. This situation of instability made it all the harder for Monmouth to abandon his own evolving royal ambitions. He seems increasingly to have weighed the fact of his illegitimacy against the future of a throne that, more and more, looked to be up for grabs.

Not that he exhibited any flair for government, but he did possess a passion for all things savoring of martial glory. Beginning in 1665, at age

**Monmouth was one of a dozen bastards sired by Charles II, the "Merrie Monarch" whose restoration to the English throne ended the Puritan interregnum. The king is depicted here in a seventeenth-century Dutch painting by Gerrit van Honthorst.** Charles II (1630-85) (oil on canvas), Honthorst, Gerrit van (1590-1656) / Ashdown House, Oxfordshire, UK / National Trust Photographic Library / John Hammond / The Bridgeman Art Library International

sixteen, Monmouth set about becoming a hero. He sailed with his uncle the Duke of York, who commanded the English fleet in a contest for supremacy in trade known as the Second Dutch War. Soon concluding that life at sea was not for him, he returned to England and was given command of a cavalry troop; however, war weariness among both the English and the Dutch, combined with the disastrous effects of the Great Plague then sweeping Europe, sent the belligerents to the negotiating table before young Monmouth saw action.

Nevertheless, Monmouth knew that he had found a vocation in the army, and in 1669, when he was just nineteen, he was commissioned colonel and commanding officer of the elite King's Life Guards. With the death of George Monck, the 1st Duke of Albermarle, the very next year, Monmouth effectively became, at twenty-one, the most senior officer in the English army (although he would not be officially named captain general of the army, commander in chief of all English land forces, until 1678). Within two years, in 1672, he also had at long last a new war to fight.

The Third Dutch War saw an unusual alliance between England and France (based largely on Charles II's secret promise to Louis XIV that he would turn Catholic) against the Netherlands and four other countries. Monmouth led six thousand men into battle and in June 1673 was part of a French assault on the formidable Dutch fortress town of Maastricht. After brutal siege fighting, French troops broke through to the town's principal fort, a crescent-shaped edifice protected by a moat. They did not hold this prize for long, however, as Spanish troops drove out all but about thirty men before nightfall.

Determined to rescue the holdouts and retake the fort in force, Monmouth made a major assault against the Spaniards defending a covered road that guarded the moat and fort. The battle was intense, but the defenders were so well protected by their positions along the covered road that the English attack soon turned suicidal, and Monmouth, always leading from the front, ordered a withdrawal after counting some three hundred of his men killed.

With the defeat of this assault, the Dutch retook the fortification, whereupon Monmouth personally rallied his fearful, disheartened, and exhausted troops for a second try against what was now an even stronger enemy position. Inevitably, Monmouth was beaten back—it would take Louis XIV's massed artillery to neutralize Maastricht—but he had earned renown as an inspiring, driven leader to whom fear was a stranger.

## GREATER GLORY

Although Monmouth became a popular military hero, this latest war against the Dutch soon turned highly unpopular, and, prodded by Parliament, Charles II withdrew from the fray in 1674 and turned against his erstwhile ally, France.

Monmouth took command of the Anglo-Dutch brigade that was part of the army led by Holland's William III of Orange against Marshal Luxembourg's Frenchmen at the Battle of Saint-Denis, near Mons (a town in what today is Belgium), on August 14 and 15, 1678. Provoked by the French four days *after* Louis XIV's minister had signed the Treaty of Nijmegen but before France and Spain had made peace, the battle was a naked French attempt to grab one last prize, Mons, before the fighting ended for good. Feeling the pressure of peace, Marshal Luxembourg drove his troops to an especially bloody effort, which cost the lives of no fewer than two thousand soldiers on each side.

From this slaughter, two heroes emerged: William himself and the Duke of Monmouth, who was seen wading valiantly into the melee just as it became a hand-to-hand contest of pikes and swords.

Monmouth returned to England after Saint-Denis and the very next year led an army that had been mustered to quell the rebellion of the Covenanters, rebels who championed the Scottish people's desire for Presbyterian government of their national church as opposed to the Episcopal church government imposed by the English crown. To his credit, Monmouth marched into Scotland with the intention of leavening military might (though at only five thousand men, his army was just barely mighty) with offers of leniency, tolerance, and outright amnesty. Negotiations broke down, however, when Robert Hamilton, commanding the Covenanters, refused to order his men to surrender their arms, as Monmouth demanded.

The refusal was a tragic decision. Hamilton failed to back his personal defiance with adequate preparation for a major battle. Indeed, by the morning of June 22, 1679, with Monmouth's five thousand troops formed in perfectly disciplined ranks on the north bank of the River Clyde at Bothwell

Bridge, the Covenanters, who assembled on the south bank, had dwindled from the nearly seven thousand who had gathered on the river two weeks earlier to a mere four thousand.

Worse, they were poorly armed—many bearing nothing more lethal than pitchforks and other farm implements—and badly positioned, some deployed on the edge of a moor near the bridge and others stationed just outside of the town of Hamilton. Robert Hamilton had assigned the smallest number, just three hundred men, to defend the bridge, which was, of course, the critical prize of battle. Small though the party was, it was armed with muskets as well as a modest brass cannon.

Monmouth commenced the attack with an artillery barrage aimed at the crude wooden stockades the Covenanters had erected to protect their position at the bridgehead. They returned fire with their single cannon—which, astoundingly, was sufficient to send Monmouth's artillerymen running for cover. Had Hamilton been a far better captain, he would have seized the moment either to turn the abandoned English cannon against the attackers or to spike the barrels of the weapons, rendering them useless. Instead, he ordered a stand-up fight, during which his unprepared army exhausted all its ammunition and powder within two hours.

For his part, Monmouth wasted no time, but rode his horse through the ranks, rallying his infantry and personally leading his shaken artillerists back to their weapons. They resumed the barrage—with devastating effect.

As the Covenanters' return fire died away, Monmouth tugged sharply on the reins of his horse, rearing it back. Drawing his sword, he pointed toward Bothwell Bridge, over which he led his army across the Clyde.

Confronted by Monmouth's force at close quarters, the Covenanters panicked and thereby gave themselves up to slaughter. When it was over, at about ten o'clock, four hundred of them lay dead and another twelve hundred had

◀ **This battle scene is believed to be a depiction of the 1st Duke of Monmouth at the heroically doomed Siege of Maastricht, 1673. Outnumbered, his men reeling from catastrophic casualties, Monmouth refused to give up, stood always at the head of his troops, and thereby earned renown as an inspiring martial leader who knew no fear.** A Battle Scene: possibly James Scott, Duke of Monmouth at the Siege of Maastricht in 1673 (oil on canvas), Wyck, Jan (1640-1700) / © Victoria Art Gallery, Bath and North East Somerset Council / The Bridgeman Art Library International

become prisoners of war. The rest scattered, with Hamilton (in the words of the Reverend John Blackadder, an eyewitness) "among the foremost that fled."

Yet again, the Duke of Monmouth was hailed by the English people, and it was increasingly clear that the masses, in the absence of a legitimate heir born to Charles II and Catherine of Braganza, far preferred that Monmouth be anointed successor to the throne than the king's Catholic brother James.

## THE PLEASURES OF EXILE

Unlike Catherine, Monmouth's father's wife, Anne Scott was anything but barren. When her husband was not occupied with war, he was engaged in procreation, Anne giving the Duke of Monmouth seven children, four of whom would live to adulthood. With his mistress, the dark-haired, ivory-skinned Eleanor Needham, daughter of Sir Robert Needham of Lambeth and reputed to have on occasion shared the bed of none other than Charles II, the duke had three illegitimate children; a son, James Crofts, who became a major general, and two daughters, one of whom lived to marry well and the other who died in youth.

Later, Monmouth also managed an affair with Henrietta, Baroness Wentworth, who, unlike his wife, his mistress, and his progeny, both legitimate and non, faithfully followed him into his self-imposed exile in the Netherlands (then called the Dutch United Provinces) after he was implicated in an abortive 1683 conspiracy known as the Rye House Plot to assassinate both Charles II and his brother James, Duke of York. It remains unclear whether Monmouth was actually involved in the Rye House Plot or even whether any such plot actually existed. Many historians believe the conspiracy was largely fabricated by Charles and his loyalists as the pretext for a political purge, which included the bastard son who, in the eyes of Charles II, was becoming far too popular with the English people.

Not that the duke suffered in Holland. In fact, he occupied his hours most agreeably in company with Henrietta as he patiently awaited the passing of his father—who, in his fifties, was hardly a young man by seventeenth-century standards—whereupon he intended to rely on his popularity and Protestant credentials to elevate him peacefully to the throne, bastard though he was.

Yet when Charles II's death came on February 6, 1685, four days after an "apoplectic fit," it was instantly clear to Monmouth that, unless he sought the throne by force of arms, the people would not of their own volition demand that he be crowned, and therefore James II would rule. Monmouth turned for support to his former comrade at arms, William III of Orange, who swallowed hard and explained to his friend that, loath as he was to see a Catholic ascend the English throne, he was treaty-bound to James and could therefore offer no support to one who would challenge him. Believing that no good would come of any attempt to contest the throne by force, William counseled Monmouth to forget England and throw himself instead into the glory of distant battle as a commander in the Holy Roman army of Austria's Leopold to fight against the infidel Turks.

Monmouth pondered this. But he was hardly the only Englishman who had been touched by the Rye House Plot, and the small, tight-knit exile community in Holland spoke in a voice that drowned out the counsel of William of Orange. They urged a fight for the crown.

## MONMOUTH LAUNCHES HIS REBELLION

In Holland, Monmouth and his supporters managed to hire three small vessels, purchase a cache of fifteen hundred muskets and four small field cannons, and recruit an "army" of eighty-two men. Monmouth's friends assured him that his presence in England would instantly produce a military force more than sufficient to enable him to seize the throne. To hedge this bet, Monmouth decided to make his landing at Lyme Regis, a West Dorset town on the southwest coast of England known for two things: the Cobb—a walled harbor that made for a safe landing—and a population of zealous Protestants.

Monmouth sailed in May 1685 and landed at Lyme Regis on June 11. There was no army waiting for him, but he was able to recruit about three hundred willing supporters right away, and, believing his arrival to be unknown beyond Dorset, he assumed that he could march to London unopposed, picking up more followers en route. Soon learning, however, that a pair of local customs officials, who owed their livelihoods to the king, had galloped to London to warn James II of his arrival, Monmouth decided to delay his assault on London and advance instead into Somerset, where he could win over the West Country and grow his army.

On June 14, at Bridport, a Dorset town down the coast from Lyme Regis, famous for producing the rope that royal executioners traditionally used for hangings, Monmouth encountered the Dorset militia and fought a short, sharp exchange that won over many militiamen to his cause. The next day, at the Devonshire carpet-making town of Axminster, Monmouth brushed aside another force of militiamen—and picked up even more recruits. In the space of just four days, his army had grown to six thousand. The militia deserters had brought their own firearms, and Monmouth distributed the fifteen hundred muskets he carried. This left at least four thousand of his followers armed with nothing better than pitchforks and other farm implements—the very weapons the Covenanters had wielded against him in 1679 at Bothwell Bridge.

At Chard, a Somerset town on the Devonshire border, Monmouth briefly paused to pick up another 160 followers and crown himself king of England, introducing himself as "James Scott, 1st Duke of Monmouth and the son of His Royal Majesty Charles II." Apparently willing to regard truth the way he

**AT CHARD, A SOMERSET TOWN ON THE DEVONSHIRE BORDER, MONMOUTH BRIEFLY PAUSED TO PICK UP 160 FOLLOWERS AND CROWN HIMSELF KING OF ENGLAND, INTRODUCING HIMSELF AS "JAMES SCOTT, 1ST DUKE OF MONMOUTH AND SON OF HIS ROYAL MAJESTY CHARLES II."**

regarded legitimacy, as subject to pragmatic interpretation, Monmouth went on to brand James II as guilty of both fratricide and regicide: "All those who join me in my quest against the Catholic Usurper, James Duke of York, my father's brother and his murderer, will gain Royal favour when I take my rightful place as England's Ruler."

On June 20, at nearby Taunton, Monmouth crowned himself again—this time, in a bid to impart the odor of greater legitimacy to the event, ordering his army to use their pitchforks to "persuade" the Taunton Corporation (town council) to "officially" witness the ceremony, which was conducted outside of the White Hart Inn.

As Monmouth led his army on a meandering course north, then northeast, then northwest, toward the major city of Bristol, which he intended to capture, the Royal Navy arrived at Lyme Regis and took possession of the duke's three ships. He now had no way off the English isle.

## THE REBELLION FALTERS

On June 24, Monmouth set up camp at Keynsham, between Bath and Bristol. From here, on the 25th, he made his move toward Bristol, but was quickly discouraged by clashes with his old regiment, the King's Life Guards, now under the command of Louis de Duras, 2nd Earl of Feversham. Rather than fight it out, Monmouth turned 180 degrees away from Bristol and began to march instead southeast toward Bath, only to find it occupied by a large Royalist contingent. He therefore made camp at Philips Norton (modern Norton St. Philip), a few miles south of Bath, to ponder his next move.

He did not have long to ponder, because Feversham brought the battle to him, attacking the Philips Norton camp on June 27. This drove Monmouth and his army to Frome, just south of the camp. He wanted to avoid a major battle, desperate to buy time for what he believed was an imminent and massive rebellion in Scotland, led by the 9th Earl of Argyll, which would surely force James to divide and deplete the army now arrayed against him. Indeed, Argyll had begun to muster a rebel army at Campbeltown late in May, but it disintegrated on the march to Glasgow; Argyll was captured on June 19 and, as of June 27, he had just three days to live before he would be beheaded, drawn, and quartered at Edinburgh.

There were other rebellions in the offing. Monmouth was confident that both Cheshire and East Anglia would rise up. But they did not. And what with much running and little fighting, Monmouth's army began to dissolve as well. At Trowbridge in Wiltshire, Royalists intercepted his line of march, prompting him to retreat back through Somerset. Retreating into Wells on July 1 and in desperate need of bullets, Monmouth's men stripped the lead from the roof of the town's famed cathedral to melt down, and then, in a frenzy of frustration over battles avoided, they became a mob of vandals, breaking out the stained glass windows and smashing the organ into kindling. The cathedral's nave was transformed into an impromptu stable.

Still, the Royalist forces pressed their pursuit, and on July 3 Monmouth and the four thousand men left to him holed up in the Somerset town of Bridgwater, which they fortified as best they could. Just three days later, however, the duke decided to risk a surprise night attack on Feversham's forces. He must have concluded that time was on the Royalists' side. They could starve out his army, forcing desertions, whittling it down to nothing. Hunkering down, therefore, was a losing proposition.

## THE BITTER END

Monmouth led his men out of Bridgwater at about 10 p.m. on July 6. His guide was one Richard Godfrey, servant to a local farmer, who knew the country well— or so he said. He led the army into a dismal moor, which was traversed by deep, watery ditches in which man and horse might easily drown. Valuable time wasted away as the rebels stumbled across the difficult and uncertain ground. Then one of Monmouth's cavalry was unexpectedly jostled by his mount or imagined he saw the enemy. In either case, a musket shot rang out. It hit nothing and no one, but it nevertheless killed the element of surprise.

Monmouth's small cavalry vanguard found itself at first confronted and then surrounded by the King's Regiment of Horse. The superb horsemen of the regular English army literally ran circles around the mounted rebels, quickly routing and defeating them—with plenty of time for a rider to break away to alert Feversham and the main body of Royalist infantry. What followed was a fight too lopsided to be called a proper battle. Although Monmouth outnumbered Feversham four thousand to three thousand, the Royalist troops constituted a professional army, whereas the rebels were a motley collection of militiamen and farmers, the majority of them armed with nothing more than farm implements. In a remarkably short span, a thousand of them fell in battle, and half that number was captured. The rest scattered into the night.

Among those who fled were Monmouth and Lord Grey of Warke, his cavalry commander. The man who would be king shed his ornate greatcoat and other regal military equipage. He and Warke donned the drab, shabby dress of the local peasantry and made for the southern coast. The two got as far as Ringwood, a Hampshire town along the River Avon. Exhausted, they lay down in a ditch overgrown with ferns and underbrush.

A party of Feversham's men, hot on their trail, seized an old woman of the neighborhood, who told them she had seen a tall man filling his pockets with peas, and she pointed toward the Avon. Night fell, and the troops resumed the pursuit at daybreak. As they marched along the river, one of the soldiers saw the skirt of a man's coat just above the rim of a ditch. The 1st Duke of Monmouth,

The Duke of Monmouth, captive, pleads with his uncle James II to spare his life. In this scene by the nineteenth-century Scottish-born historical painter John Pettie, the king's body language clearly conveys the absence of avuncular forgiveness. The Duke of Monmouth Pleading for his Life before James II (oil on canvas), Pettie, John (1839-93) / © South African National Gallery, Cape Town, South Africa / The Bridgeman Art Library International

sodden with filth and hollow with hunger, was taken into custody along with Warke, who was found moments later.

## AN AFTERMATH OF BLOOD AND GLORIOUS REVOLUTION

The beheading of Monmouth was not the end of it. The Parliamentary "Act to Attaint James Duke of Monmouth of High-Treason" not only condemned the would-be usurper to "suffer Paines of Death," but also to "Incurr all Forfeitures as a Traitor Convicted and Attainted of High Treason," which meant that his dukedoms of Monmouth and Buccleuch would be lost to his family—though some lesser titles were later restored to them. Fortune and noble station, so easily conferred by Charles II on his bastard son, were even more easily taken from him and his heirs. It required but the stroke of a pen on a parliamentary act.

Far worse was the fate that befell Monmouth's supporters. Those of his army who escaped death or immediate capture were relentlessly hunted down in the aftermath of the battle. Some of those located were dispatched with musket balls wherever they lay in hiding. Many, however, were hanged from impromptu gibbets along the Somerset roads—examples to all those who would covet a throne not theirs by right.

James II, an unforgiving monarch, assigned Lord Chief Justice George Jeffreys to ensure that all of the duke's partisans were rounded up and tried. More than eleven hundred individuals were convicted in proceedings held at Taunton Castle, a process destined to be known to history as the Bloody Assizes. Three hundred and twenty of those found guilty were sentenced to the full mode of execution imposed on traitors.

Unlike their leader, Monmouth, who was only beheaded, they were first *drawn and quartered*, lashed to a timber frame called a hurdle and roughly dragged to the scaffold. Here they were hanged with sufficient skill to bring them to death's doorstep without crossing the threshold. While still living, each condemned prisoner was disemboweled and castrated, the guts and genitals thrown into a fire so that the man might see them burn as he drifted in and out of consciousness. This completed, the body was quartered—butchered into four parts—and then beheaded. Some eight hundred convicted by the Bloody Assizes escaped death and were instead sentenced to "transportation," meaning exile to the West Indies, where they were worked as slaves.

As threatened heads of state had done before and would do in the future, James II seized what today would be called "emergency powers," suspending habeas corpus—so that anyone could be arrested and held at any time and for any reason. He built up his army and placed loyal Catholics in all of the important government offices. When Parliament objected, condemning many of his actions as illegal—which is to say, illegitimate—James II prorogued Parliament on November 20, 1685, until it was dissolved altogether in July 1687.

This drew England to the verge of revolution. What pushed it over was the birth in 1688 of James Francis Edward Stuart, which thrust upon the Protestant nation a Catholic heir apparent. That same year, at the behest of the anti-James faction known as the Parliamentarians, no less a figure than William III of Orange was invited to overthrow James II and assume the throne in his place. It would be called the Glorious Revolution, and, like all revolutions, it would challenge assumptions of legitimacy, asking and answering the question, *Who by rights should rule?*

Fittingly, before William of Orange offered his challenge, the Duke of Monmouth, whose very birth lay beyond the boundaries of conventional legitimacy, presented his and suffered on account of it the terrible fate that befalls those whose version of truth and right—legitimacy—fails to win acceptance.

# CHAPTER 6

# ALEXANDER HAMILTON

## AN ILLEGITIMATE SON BECOMES A FOUNDING FATHER OF A NEW NATION
## 1757-1804

BORN OUT OF WEDLOCK IN 1757 AND SHAPED BY GRINDING POVERTY,
ALEXANDER HAMILTON RELIED ON HIS INNATE INTELLIGENCE
AND AMBITION TO OVERCOME THE STIGMA OF HIS BIRTH—AND
ULTIMATELY HELP FOUND A NATION.

YOUNG ALEXANDER HAMILTON HAD COME TO LOATHE GOING INTO TOWN. The locals were always watching him, judging him. He pretended not to notice that his presence caused a stir. The adults usually glanced quickly at him before shaking their heads in disapproval, or worse yet, pity. The children—especially the older boys—could be particularly cruel, staring blatantly, snickering, and even pointing at him. The boy averted his eyes from theirs, looking down at his shoes. Well worn, but clean, his clothes hung loosely on his thin frame.

Eight-year-old Alexander, or Alex, as he was known, was an exceedingly precocious child with a quick wit and a maturity that surprised those around him. He was extremely respectful to his elders and seemed eager to impress with an astute observation about the weather or a well-turned phrase picked up from a book he had read. He was painfully aware that his family was an object of derision on the island of St. Croix, where they resided. Although his parents lived together, they were not married. Born out of wedlock, Alex and his older brother James were labeled "obscene children" in official court documents and census records. The stigma was especially difficult for Alex, the more sensitive of the two, to bear.

**Alexander Hamilton transformed himself from a poor, illegitimate boy from the West Indies into an accomplished, brilliant politician who was instrumental in shaping a new nation.** Portrait of Alexander Hamilton (1755/57-1804) (litho), Chappel, Alonzo (1828-1887) (after) / Private Collection / Ken Welsh / The Bridgeman Art Library International

## 1757:
**January 11** Is born on the island of Nevis in the British West Indies to Rachel Fawcett Lavien and James Hamilton, who lived together but did not marry. His mother is married to John Michael Lavien at the time.

## 1765:
James Hamilton abandons the family after they move to St. Croix.

## 1773:
Arrives in New York.

## 1776:
Is appointed captain of the Provincial Artillery.

## 1780:
Marries wealthy socialite Elizabeth Schuyler.

## 1758:
Lavien divorces Rachel Fawcett.

## 1772:
A hurricane tears through St. Croix, destroying hundreds of homes and killing several residents. Fifteen-year-old Alexander composes public letter seeking aid and assistance for the island. Impressed with the letter, prominent figures on the island finance his education.

## 1775:
The American Revolution breaks out in the thirteen colonies; Hamilton enlists for military service.

## 1777:
Is appointed aide de camp to George Washington.

As Alex made his way through town, a teenage boy muttered something derogatory under his breath about Alex's mother. A small, frail child, Alex was no match for the older and bigger antagonist. His heart beat faster and his fair complexion flushed red with humiliation. He hastened his pace, eager to get home. His family lived on the second floor of a small, modest, two-story house; the first floor had been converted into a shop where Alex's mother sold produce and other staples. The Hamiltons owned only one bed; the boys slept on the floor. Alex longed to return to the nearby island of St. Christopher, where the Hamiltons spent several uneventful years in welcome obscurity.

## FOR ALEXANDER HAMILTON, ST. CROIX WAS THE PLACE WHERE HE LEARNED THE DISTRESSING TRUTH ABOUT HIS BIRTH—AND ABOUT HIS MOTHER'S PAST.

Because they were illegitimate, the boys were barred from attending the government-sponsored schools on the Caribbean island. Their mother taught them to read and write. Young Alex was sent to study at a local Jewish school, where he learned to speak Hebrew. He became an avid reader, poring over the classics his mother kept at home.

It was 1765 and St. Croix was under Danish rule. English was the predominant language spoken, followed by Creole, French, Dutch, and Spanish. The

**1782:**
Earns his law degree, is appointed tax receiver for New York, and is elected as a representative to the Continental Congress.

**1784:**
Helps found the Bank of New York.

**1789:**
September 11 Is appointed first U.S. Secretary of the Treasury by President George Washington.

**1795:**
Leaves cabinet, but remains influential.

**1781:**
Leads a victorious charge against the British in Virginia, resulting in the surrender of the enemy commander.

**1783:**
The American Revolution ends.

**1787-1788:**
Writes the majority of the *Federalist Papers*, a series of 85 essays published in newspapers in defense of the Constitution and republican government. The essays are widely influential and considered classic political literature.

**1790:**
Persuades Congress and the president to create the Bank of the United States, America's first national bank.

**1804:**
July 11 Sustains a fatal wound in a duel with Aaron Burr. Dies the next day.

island was a busy port for trade; locally produced sugar and tobacco were the most popular exports. Christiansted, the center of island commerce, was a boomtown with a steady influx of merchants and prospectors hoping to strike it rich. A picturesque island, St. Croix boasted sloping hills and numerous plantations and was surrounded by brilliant blue water. Physically, the island looked like paradise. For the many African slaves forced to work the fields and plantations, it was little more than a tropical prison. For Alexander Hamilton, it was the place where he learned the distressing truth about his birth—and about his mother's past.

## A FOUNDING FATHER'S TRAGIC CHILDHOOD

Rachel Hamilton was no stranger to St. Croix, having lived there as a child and later as a young bride. At sixteen, Rachel married John Michael Lavien, a thirty-eight-year-old merchant whose large, fashionable wardrobe misled people (including Rachel's mother, Mary Fawcett, who encouraged the union) into thinking he was financially well-off.

From the start, the Laviens' marriage was a disaster. John Michael proved to be a bully who mistreated his teenage bride. He was also far less solvent than Mary Fawcett had believed him to be. Rachel was desperately unhappy. A year into the marriage, the couple had a son whom they named Peter. Motherhood did little to raise Rachel's spirits. She ran off to stay with friends on the island.

Rumors of assignations followed her. Lavien had her arrested and thrown in jail for adultery. He hoped the time in jail would teach her a lesson and make her more accepting of domestic life. However, when Rachel was released several months later, she fled the island, leaving Lavien and Peter behind.

Rachel landed on St. Kitts, just a few miles away from St. Croix. There she embarked on another ill-fated relationship, this time with James Hamilton. A Scot who was estranged from his wealthy, aristocratic family, Hamilton had come to the West Indies to improve his finances. Feckless and flighty, he jumped from job to job and struggled to eke out a living. Although still legally

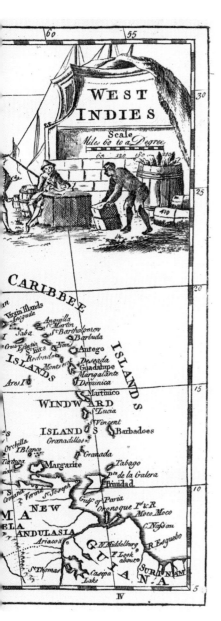

wed to Lavien, Rachel lived with Hamilton as his common-law wife. Together they had two sons: James and Alexander. The family was poor and moved frequently as Hamilton sought new employment.

Nearly a decade after Rachel left St. Croix, Lavien sued her for divorce, accusing the "shameless, rude and ungodly woman" of abandoning her duties as a wife and mother and "whoring with everyone." He also pointed out that Rachel had given birth to two bastard children. Rachel did not answer the summons to appear in court. Lavien was granted the divorce. According to Danish law at the time, Rachel was prohibited from remarrying; Lavien, however, was free to do so.

Although stigmatized as a "fallen woman," Rachel was relieved to be officially free of Lavien. She was understandably upset when, in 1765, James Hamilton's employer transferred him indefinitely to St. Croix. It was with great apprehension that Rachel agreed to move the family to the place where she had experienced such misery—and where she might encounter her ex-husband again. Her sons soon experienced their own unhappiness when they discovered that they were illegitimate. (It is unclear whether Rachel broke the news to the boys herself or whether they heard it from the locals.)

On St. Croix, the relationship between Rachel and James Hamilton unraveled. Just months after the move, Hamilton abandoned the family, never to return. He did not send Rachel any financial assistance. Despite this fact, Alexander, then eight years old, remained inexplicably fond of his father, recasting him as a sad, bemused aristocrat who had fallen from fortune's favor. In his revised history, he portrayed his father as more victim than victimizer.

Perhaps this fantasy helped soften the pain of rejection. As an adult, Alexander sought out his wayward father. The two men communicated through mail, but the older Hamilton refused to meet with the son he had abandoned, even though Alexander helped support him financially.

Rachel was forced to turn to her sister's family for assistance. The Lyttons had fallen on hard times, but patriarch James Lytton did his best to help her. With Lytton supplying the seed money, Rachel opened a small country store, selling produce and necessities to local residents. She barely made ends meet. James Jr. was sent to apprentice with a carpenter. Alexander remained at home, working in the family store, filling orders and serving customers.

Alexander had barely recovered from the abandonment of his father when Rachel succumbed to yellow fever in 1768. Her former husband, Lavien, immediately swooped in to claim her meager belongings for his son Peter. Peter Lytton was appointed guardian of the Hamilton boys. A year into his guardianship, Lytton committed suicide, leaving no provisions for James and Alex. James Lytton, their uncle, died soon afterward. James Hamilton, living in pov-

## ALEXANDER HAMILTON MAY WELL HAVE BEEN CONFINED TO A LIFE AS A CLERK HAD MOTHER NATURE NOT INTERVENED.

erty on another island, had neither the means nor the inclination to assume custody of his sons. He left them to their own devices. The boys were forced to rely on the mercy and generosity of strangers. Fortunately, James Jr. was faring well in his apprenticeship and was able to remain on with his employer.

A local family took Alex in, treating him like one of their sons. Intelligent and quick-witted, Alex impressed the adults around him. Cruger, a businessman from New York, saw potential in Alex and employed him as a clerk in his trading company, trusting him to run the business while he was away. For five months, fourteen-year-old Alex served as de facto head of the company, dealing directly with other merchants, importers, exporters, ship captains, and customers.

Alex quickly learned how to juggle various responsibilities, negotiate effectively, and communicate with people from different socioeconomic classes. The experience would later prove invaluable. He was deflated when Cruger returned and he had to resume his position as a simple clerk.

Alex worried about his future. The memories of his father's failed business endeavors haunted him. He expressed his fears in a letter to a friend. "My ambition is so prevalent that I disdain the groveling conditions of a clerk to which my fortune condemns me. I would willingly risk my life, though not my character, to exalt my station," he said. Alex concluded the letter by wishing for a war. Although peaceful and nonviolent by nature, he realized that war was an equalizer. War presented a young man with the opportunity to prove his mettle and make a name for himself, regardless of his social class.

Alex knew that his illegitimacy and poverty were tremendous obstacles to the success and respectability he yearned for. He possessed the intellect and drive needed to achieve his dreams, but his background held him back. Alexander Hamilton may well have been confined to a life as a clerk had Mother Nature not intervened.

On August 31, 1772, a devastating hurricane tore through St. Croix, destroying hundreds of homes, killing several residents, and injuring dozens more on the 22-mile-long (35 km) island. Then fifteen, Alexander composed a heartfelt account of the tragedy, urging the wealthy to help feed and house the many people left homeless by the hurricane. "[D]o not hold your compassion," he wrote. "Act wisely [and] Succour the miserable and lay up a treasure in heaven." He also praised the governor of the island for his valiant relief efforts. The letter, which was published in the local newspaper, so impressed some of the more prominent residents on the island that they decided to finance the young man's education. Alexander was sent to the thirteen colonies to study medicine. Upon completion of his studies, it was assumed that he would return to St. Croix to serve as the island's doctor.

## REVOLUTION AND REINVENTION

Alexander never received his medical license, nor did he return to St. Croix. Instead, the man whom John Adams called the "bastard son of a Scottish peddler" became one of the founding fathers of a new nation. The thirteen colonies were straining under the tyranny of British rule when the young man from the West Indies arrived. Commercial restrictions and exorbitant taxes imposed by the Crown had the colonists in a state of unrest; talk of revolution filled the streets. Tensions were particularly high in New York, where pro-British Loyalists clashed with the Patriots (or Whigs), revolutionaries who wanted independence from England. America was on the brink of becoming a nation and establishing

its presence in the world. It was a fortuitous time for Hamilton—a man looking to make his own mark on the world—to arrive.

Arriving in New York in 1773, some 200 nautical miles (322 km) from St. Croix, Hamilton was awed by the burgeoning metropolis. The city seemed to beckon to him, and the young immigrant quickly adapted to his new home. Armed with letters of recommendation from his benefactors, he was granted access to the finest homes and establishments in New York. Most of his new contacts were unaware of his illegitimacy, and Hamilton did his best to distance himself from his roots. He strove to present the image of a cultured, well-bred gentleman, never mentioning the hardship he had endured on St. Croix.

Still, however, much as Hamilton tried to forget his childhood, it remained with him, tugging always at the corners of his memory, fueling his drive for social and professional success and, more important, respectability. With each new achievement, each contact, and each prestigious appointment, Hamilton moved further away from the pitiful, scorned child he had been.

When the American Revolution broke out in the colonies in 1775, Hamilton's teenaged wish for war came true. Two years later, George Washington, then commander in chief of the Continental Army, met Hamilton in New York and was impressed by the confident, resolute young man in the impeccable uniform. He offered him the position as his aide de camp. Hamilton was one of the very few members of Washington's inner circle who did not hail from a wealthy, aristocratic family. It was a tremendous coup for a man with such humble beginnings.

His marriage to Elizabeth Schuyler in 1780, a socialite from a wealthy and influential New York family, elevated his status even more. He had transformed himself from an "obscene" child into a gentleman and major player in the political arena. Hamilton's career was remarkable—the first U.S. secretary of the Treasury, he was a brilliant Constitutional lawyer and, along with James Madison and John Jay, wrote the *Federalist Papers*, the primary source for Constitutional interpretation. Hamilton was the sole New Yorker to sign the Constitution.

**As George Washington's aide de camp, Hamilton worked closely with the commander-in-chief, drafting his correspondence, sharing his confidence, and advising him on political decisions.** First meeting of George Washington and Alexander Hamilton, from 'Life and Times of Washington', Volume I, published 1857 (litho), Chappel, Alonzo (1828-87) (after) / Private Collection / Ken Welsh / The Bridgeman Art Library International

In 1781, Hamilton led a victorious charge against the British in Virginia, resulting in the enemy commander's surrender. As a civilian, Hamilton continued blazing a path to glory. In 1782 alone, he earned his law degree, was appointed tax receiver for New York, and, most important, was elected as a representative to the Continental Congress. The Hamiltons' first child, a son named Philip, was also born that year.

In 1784, the up-and-comer helped establish the Bank of New York, the first bank in the new country. It was clear that Hamilton possessed the financial acumen that had eluded his father. On St. Croix, Alexander learned that money led to power and respectability. As a young child, he witnessed James Hamilton fail miserably in one business endeavor after another. Determined not to repeat his father's mistakes, and terrified of being doomed to life as a clerk, the boy had watched his employer with hawk eyes, eagerly absorbing the intricacies of business. As a boy with no family to rely on, Alexander understood the value of a solid grounding in financial matters.

Hamilton used this hard-earned experience and knowledge in the latter part of his life, shaping the new nation into an economic and military power. He believed that America should be controlled by a strong, centralized republican government. Growing up on St. Croix tremendously affected his outlook on what he once described as a "selfish, rapacious world." Hamilton learned early on that people could be capricious and cruel. Although ambitious and diligent, he was deeply critical of human nature and had difficulty trusting others. His hardscrabble childhood undoubtedly influenced his politics. He believed that man could not be trusted to govern himself; left to his own devices, man would always succumb to avarice and corruption.

Despite Hamilton's success, he was unable to fully escape his miserable, humiliating childhood. His single-minded quest for success had earned him a number of enemies—enemies who made inquiries about his background. It wasn't long before rumors of his illegitimacy began to spread. Although Hamilton ignored them, the rumors would dog him throughout his career—and his life. He confided the truth about his birth to his wife, but not to his children or friends. His political rivals used his illegitimacy as a weapon against him, trotting out the facts of his birth to defame him.

**Alexander Hamilton was one of the very few members of George Washington's inner circle who did not hail from a wealthy, aristocratic family. He's seen here with Washington's first cabinet.** Getty Images

Tensions between Hamilton
and his longstanding rival
Aaron Burr came to a head
in 1804, when Burr fatally
shot Hamilton in a duel.
Indicted for murder in New
York and New Jersey, Burr
fled to Washington to escape
prosecution. His ploy worked:
The case never went to trial;
he remained unpunished.

HOOPER SC.

## POLITICAL SABOTAGE AND SELF-DESTRUCTION

Despite Hamilton's many talents and considerable intelligence, he was remarkably socially inept. He was stubborn and often abrasive and mercurial. He made many enemies during his career, including political rival Aaron Burr.

It could be argued that the socially mobile Hamilton carried a chip on his shoulder from his days on St. Croix. He was easily offended and preoccupied with personal honor, not surprising for a man who had been routinely dismissed and disrespected as a child.

Hamilton's career was marked by a series of perplexing, self-destructive acts. He foolishly severed his ties with his most powerful ally, George Washington, over a petty reprimand in 1781. Although Washington apologized, Hamilton refused to speak to him and even disparaged him to others. Elizabeth Hamilton eventually persuaded her husband to reconnect with Washington.

In 1787, Hamilton helped pass a law that granted divorce only in cases where adultery could be proved—and forbade the guilty party from remarrying. It was a curious decision for someone with his particular background. His parents *would* have married—had they been allowed. For all his life, Hamilton had been trying to escape the stigma of the circumstances of his birth. Yet he enacted a law that perpetrated the cycle of misery.

Several years later, Hamilton was publicly outed as an adulterer himself. He carried on an affair for several years with a young woman named Maria Reynolds. Unhappily married, the twenty-three-year-old Reynolds ardently pursued Hamilton. Inexplicably, he published the details of his affair for all to read. Hamilton seemed to genuinely regret the indiscretion. "[T]here is nothing worse in the affair than an irregular and indelicate armour," he wrote. "I have paid pretty severely for the folly and can never recollect it without disgust and self condemnation."

Perhaps Hamilton's gravest political misstep was the circulation of a pamphlet criticizing incumbent president and fellow Federalist John Adams of being unfit for office. The two men did not get along, and Hamilton deeply disliked Adams, who refused to appoint him as George Washington's replacement as commander in chief. In his scathing *Letter of the Public Conduct and Character of John Adams*, Hamilton wrote, "Not denying Mr. Adams' patriotism and integrity, and even talents of a certain kind, I should be deficient in candor, were I to conceal the conviction, that he does not possess the talents adapted to the *Administration* of Government, and that there are great and intrinsic defects in his character, which unfit him for the office of Chief Magistrate." Hamilton shared the pamphlet with a few allies, foolishly believing they wouldn't pass it around. *The Letter* fell into the hands of Aaron Burr, who had it published and distributed.

Hamilton's unwitting smear campaign ultimately undermined the Republican Party and helped Democratic-Republican Thomas Jefferson win the presidency; Aaron Burr became his vice president. Hamilton's anti-Adams screed turned many of his allies against him and earned him more enemies, including Burr.

The two had a long history of animosity, with each disparaging the other. Hamilton believed Burr to be morally corrupt and felt it was "his religious duty" to oppose him. He was instrumental in thwarting Burr's bid for the vice presidency, and then for the governorship of New York. "I fear Mr. Burr is unprincipled, both as a public and a private man," he wrote to a colleague. "In fact, I take it he is for or against nothing but as it suits his interest and ambition." Burr blamed his political failures on Hamilton, and when he learned his rival had insulted him at a dinner party, he seized the opportunity to avenge himself.

Early in the morning on July 11, 1804, Hamilton faced off in a duel against Burr in Weehawken, New Jersey, where Hamilton's oldest son, Philip, had died in a duel three years before. Hamilton fired his pistol into the air, but it is unclear whether he accidentally misfired or did so deliberately, in an attempt to call off the duel. Burr aimed for and hit his rival. Hamilton died the next day. He was forty-seven years old.

Coauthor of the supremely influential *Federalist Papers*, secretary of the Treasury, delegate to the Continental Congress, founder and director of the Bank of New York, and creator of the *New York Evening Post*, Hamilton was the ultimate overachiever, and one of the most dedicated civil servants the nation has ever seen. Today his image graces the ten dollar bill. An airport in his home of St. Croix, where he had been ridiculed as a child, is named after him.

The "obscene" child from the West Indies accomplished so much in such a short span. He lived long enough to watch his dreams come to pass . . . and then slip away from him. "When America ceases to remember his greatness," said Calvin Coolidge of Hamilton, in 1922, "America will no longer be great."

# CHAPTER 7

# JAMES SMITHSON

## A MYSTERIOUS BASTARD BECOMES BENEFACTOR OF AMERICA'S MOST PRESTIGIOUS MUSEUM 1765-1829

THE ILLEGITIMATE, UNACKNOWLEDGED SON OF AN ENGLISH DUKE,
JAMES SMITHSON FEARED DYING IN OBSCURITY.
AN UNPRECEDENTED PHILANTHROPIC ENDOWMENT TO
THE NEWBORN UNITED STATES OF AMERICA, HOWEVER,
SECURED HIM A PLACE IN HISTORY.

IN 1835, MEMBERS OF THE U.S. CONGRESS WERE AT ODDS OVER HALF A million dollars that had been bequeathed by a mysterious Englishman named James Smithson. Smithson had willed his estate (the equivalent of $9 million today) "to the United States of America, to found at Washington [D.C.], under the name of the Smithsonian Institution, an establishment for the increase and diffusion of knowledge."

The debate was not over how to use this generous gift but whether to accept it at all. Some officials feared the endowment would spark a public backlash, coming as it did from a foreigner. Others, such as South Carolina Senator William Campbell Preston, objected to naming an American institution after an apparently self-aggrandizing philanthropist. He complained that "every whippersnapper vagabond might think it proper to have his name distinguished in the same way." Senator John Calhoun, also from South Carolina, bluntly declared it was "beneath [America's] dignity to accept presents from anyone."

**Although born illegitimate, James Smithson lived the life of a typical aristocrat. He attended the finest schools and mingled with upper class Britons.** National Portrait Gallery, Smithsonian Institution / Art Resouce, NY

**1765:**
Is born James Lewis Macie in Paris, France, to Hugh Smithson, Ist Duke of Northumberland, and the aristocratic Elizabeth Hungerford Macie. Both English, Smithson is married to another woman at the time, and Macie is a widower. Smithson does not acknowledge his illegitimate son.

**1786:**
Receives a master of arts from Pembroke College, Oxford.

**1800:**
Changes his surname to Smithson to reflect his true parentage.

**1784:**
Tours the Hebrides Islands and nearly drowns trying to collect geological specimens under water.

**1787:**
Is elected the youngest fellow of the Royal Society of London for the Improvement of Natural Knowledge

Complicating matters even more, President Andrew Jackson was unsure whether he even had the authority to accept the gift on behalf of the country. A congressional committee was formed to deal with this most curious situation. Congressman and former president John Quincy Adams argued that Smithson's endowment could be used to advance the scientific knowledge of the fledgling nation.

"If the Smithsonian Institution, under the smile of an approving Providence, and by the faithful and permanent application of the means furnished by its founder, should contribute essentially to the increase and diffusion of knowledge among men, to what higher or nobler object could this generous and splendid donation have been devoted?" Adams asked the committee.

He argued persuasively that Smithson's gift be put to good use. In the end, sensible minds prevailed. Even Senator Preston had a change of heart. In England, one of Smithson's relatives contested the will. Richard Rush, former secretary of the U.S. Treasury, was entrusted with the job of representing the country's claim to the estate in an English court.

"A suit of higher interest and dignity has rarely, perhaps, been before the tribunals of a nation," Rush said of his mission. "Benefits may flow to the United States and the human family not easy to be estimated." After two years, the case was decided in favor of the United States. It took another eight years before construction began on the Smithsonian Institute because of an inability of Congress to agree on how to spend the money. Smithson

**1826:**
Draws up his last will and testament, naming his nephew as his beneficiary, but stipulating that if his nephew dies without heirs, the estate be bequeathed to the United States to found "an establishment for the increase and diffusion of knowledge among men."

**1846:**
**August 10** The Smithsonian Institution is established in Washington D.C.

**1802:**
Proves zinc carbonates were true carbon minerals, rather than zinc oxides, as had previously been thought. The mineral smithsonite (carbonite of zinc) is eventually named after him.

**1829:**
Dies after a prolonged illness. His nephew dies six years later, without heirs.

**1904:**
Smithson's remains are brought to the United States, chiefly through the efforts of Alexander Graham Bell. He is buried in the original Smithsonian building.

had been vague in his will, neglecting to specify how his endowment should be used. He merely requested that the funds go toward the advancement of knowledge.

Adams lobbied for an astronomy observatory, Massachusetts Congressman Rufus Choate wanted a "grand" library, while others favored a botanical garden or a university. Finally, a decision was made. On August 10, 1846, James K. Polk signed a bill that affirmed the creation of the Smithsonian Institute.

## AN IDENTITY CRISIS

Who was this mysterious English benefactor? And what had inspired him to such an act of generosity? A naturalized English citizen, James Smithson never set foot on American soil, nor did he have any connection to the country. Smithson was a reticent man, and the motives behind his philanthropy, for the most part, remain a mystery. In 1865, a fire blazed through the Smithsonian Institute, destroying nearly all of Smithson's journals, private papers, and personal effects. Historians can merely speculate as to why he chose to leave his estate to a strange, unknown country.

James Smithson was the illegitimate son of Hugh Smithson and Elizabeth Hungerford Macie. A handsome social climber with a head of thick, wavy brown hair, Hugh Smithson had married into one of Britain's most distinguished families. The union elevated his status and his fortunes. He took on his wife's more

Hugh Smithson Percy, 1st Duke of Northumberland, was a social climber who married into one of England's wealthiest families.

prestigious surname, calling himself Hugh Smithson Percy. The marriage also granted him a number of titles, and he became the 1st Duke of Northumberland.

A descendent of an aristocratic family, Elizabeth Hungerford was an attractive woman who counted Sir Thomas Hungerford, the first speaker of the House of Commons, among her distant relatives. She was a widow when she embarked on a love affair with Hugh Smithson. Such indiscretions were not uncommon among the aristocracy. However, for the sake of propriety, Elizabeth Macie traveled to France to give birth to the couple's son in 1765. She named the boy James Lewis Macie. For the first half of his life, James Smithson was saddled with the surname of his mother's dead husband. It was a peculiar situation for the young man, who was aware that the 1st Duke of Northumberland was his real father. He was forbidden from referring to himself as the son of John Macie, and his biological father refused to acknowledge him. This double rebuff deeply pained

Smithson, who years later would describe himself as "Son to Hugh first Duke of Northumberland, & Elizabeth, heiress of the Hungerfords of Studley & niece to Charles the proud Duke of Somerset."

James Smithson lived the life of a typical aristocrat, but never quite fit in. He was slight of build, with a strong nose, and wavy hair like his father. Smithson spent his early years in Paris, where he was raised by a nurse. His mother visited infrequently, spending her time socializing and eventually remarrying. Elizabeth Macie brought the boy to England when he was nine years old. He was enrolled in the finest schools and associated with wealthy Britons. Material things were his for the asking. His mother was well-off, and they lived among the upper class in Weston, a suburb of Bath in the southwest region of the country.

Hugh Smithson Percy financed the boy's education, enabling Smithson to attend Pembroke College at Oxford University. Financial support was all that Smithson Percy ever offered his son—and even that was done covertly, so as not to incur the wrath of his well-connected wife. Yet, when the duchess died, leaving Smithson Percy a widower, he chose not reach out to his son. There is no evidence that the two ever met.

## SMITHSON PERCY'S BEHAVIOR TOWARD HIS ILLEGITIMATE SON WAS COMMON. THE LIAISONS OF THE ARISTOCRACY FREQUENTLY PRODUCED BASTARD CHILDREN; THESE CHILDREN WERE OFTEN PRESENTED AS "COUSINS" OR DISTANT RELATIVES.

Smithson Percy's behavior toward his illegitimate son was common. The liaisons of the aristocracy frequently produced bastard children; these children were often presented as "cousins" or distant relatives. Indeed, Smithson appears to have escaped the stigma usually associated with illegitimacy. His status as bar sinister was known; fortunately, such matters were not discussed in polite society. However, the inner turmoil Smithson experienced was considerable, and he spent much of his life searching for his own identity.

Living with a borrowed name, and lacking full English citizenship, Smithson felt groundless and unsettled. He also maintained a slight French accent from his years in Paris, which further underscored his strangeness. Because of his illegitimacy, his prospects and opportunities were limited. Considering his parentage, this was

especially frustrating for Smithson. His father was a duke and lived in a castle. "The best blood of England flows in my veins; in my father's side I am a Northumberland, on my mother's I am related to kings, but this avails me not," he noted.

## IN NAME ONLY

When James Smithson was eight years old, he became a naturalized English citizen. But his naturalized status was not equivalent to full English citizenship, and he was ineligible for many rights afforded other young men of his social class. According to the crown, Smithson was not entitled to be "of the Privy Council or a member of either House of Parliament or take any office or place of trust either civil or military or have any grants of lands, tenements, or hereditaments."

It was a stinging pronouncement for a boy who already felt like an outsider. His half-brother—Smithson Percy's legitimate son—was lauded as a hero for his service during the American Revolutionary War. Many of Smithson's peers embarked on careers in government service, careers that increased their social standing. Smithson could only watch from the sidelines.

**JAMES SMITHSON UNDERSTOOD THAT HIS SUCCESS OR FAILURE LAY WITHIN HIS OWN HANDS. NO HELP WOULD BE FORTHCOMING FROM HIS FAMOUS FATHER, A MAN KNOWN FOR HIS LAVISH SPENDING AND LOVE OF EXCESS.**

After his mother's death, he applied to the crown for permission to legally change his surname to Smithson, publicly acknowledging his true heritage for the first time. "Since her death," Smithson told a friend, "I make little mistery [sic] of my being brother to the present Duke of Northumberland."

Although he had already established a reputation in the scientific world as James Macie, he was eager to use the name Smithson. His request was granted, but the crown declared that he had no right to any titles held by his father, the duke—a right that his legitimate half-brother did have. Smithson Percy's

**Smithson's biological father, Hugh Smithson Percy, funded Smithson's education, but did so covertly, and never acknowledged him as his son.**

James Smithson was a diligent young student, dedicated to scientific research, who even risked drowning to gather geological observations.

wealth and power had increased twofold; as a bastard, however, Smithson was deprived of the honors conferred to the son of a duke. He understood that his success or failure lay within his own hands. No help would be forthcoming from his famous father, a man known for his lavish spending and love of excess. The duke was fond of hosting huge parties that writer Horace Walpole dubbed "pompous festino." More than a thousand guests at a time attended these famous extravaganzas, where the grounds were lit up with "arches and pyramids of light."

When Smithson Percy died, he was one of the richest men in England; his numerous properties made up 1 percent of the country. He left nothing to his illegitimate son. Smithson's mother, however, willed him a great deal of valuable property when she died. He was a savvy businessman and made quite a bit of money from selling and renting properties he owned. He managed his finances well, leaving an estate worth more than £100,000 (though it was just a fraction of the value of his father's estate).

## SEDUCED BY SCIENCE

While attending Oxford, Smithson developed a passion for science and research. He was a diligent and studious young man who was intensely focused on his work. He was the finest chemist and mineralogist in the class, according to his classmate Sir David Gilbert. He received a master's degree in arts in 1786. A year later, he was accepted into the esteemed Royal Society of London for the Improvement of Natural Knowledge. Smithson was the youngest fellow in the organization.

"It is in his knowledge that man has found his greatness and his happiness, the high superiority which he holds over the other animals who inherit the earth with him, and consequently, no ignorance is probably without loss to him, no error without evil," Smithson wrote in his journal. His quest for knowledge took him on dozens of research expeditions. At nineteen, he joined a group of scientists on an expedition to Scotland and the Isle of Staffa in the Hebrides. He was the youngest, but most enthusiastic, member of the group. Bravely standing on a pail supported by a rope, Smithson was lowered into a mine to search for minerals. On another occasion, he nearly drowned trying to collect geological specimens under water.

Smithson maintained a nomadic lifestyle, moving frequently throughout Europe. He never married and never remained in one place for very long. "The man of science is of no country, the world is his country, all mankind his countrymen," he often remarked. A lonely man, Smithson channeled his energies into his work, examining thousands of specimens of minerals, plants, and vegetables. He designed his own portable laboratory, and he carted the kit with him wherever he went. He had an insatiable hunger for knowledge; for Smithson, no observation was insignificant, and no discovery too small.

"Chemistry is yet so new a science," he wrote, "that what we know of it bears so small a portion to what we are ignorant of; our knowledge in every department of it is so incomplete, consisting so entirely of isolated points, thinly scattered, like lurid specks on a vast field of darkness, that no researches can be undertaken without producing some facts that extend beyond the boundaries of their immediate object." An associate recounted Smithson "happening

**A photo of the Smithsonian Institute from 1898. Today, the Smithsonian is the largest museum complex in the world, housing a zoo, library, and nine research centers.**
Library of Congress

to observe a tear gliding down a lady's cheek, endeavored to catch it on a crystal vessel" to examine it.

Smithson was also a prolific writer, publishing nearly thirty scientific papers on everything from geology to chemistry to mineralogy. The gentleman scientist considered no subject too unimportant; one of his papers was titled *The Art of Making Coffee*, another, *Some Improvements in Lamps*. "Every man is a valuable member of society who by his observations, researches, and experiments procures knowledge for men," he wrote. In 1802, he upset popular science by proving zinc carbonates were true carbon minerals, rather than zinc oxides, as had previously been thought. Zinc spar was renamed smithsonite, posthumously, in his honor. It was an honor he would have cherished, as Smithson longed for recognition all his life.

**IN 1802, SMITHSON UPSET POPULAR SCIENCE BY PROVING ZINC CARBONATES WERE TRUE CARBON MINERALS, RATHER THAN ZINC OXIDES, AS HAD PREVIOUSLY BEEN THOUGHT. ZINC SPAR WAS RENAMED SMITHSONITE, POSTHUMOUSLY, IN HIS HONOR.**

Smithson died in the summer of 1829 after a prolonged illness. He was sixty-four and had accumulated a small fortune in his lifetime. He willed his estate to his nephew Henry James Hungerford, with the contingency clause that should Hungerford die without heirs—Smithson had taken care to specify "children, legitimate or illegitimate"—the proceeds of the estate were to be passed on to "the United States of America, to found at Washington, under the name of the Smithsonian Institution, an Establishment for the increase and diffusion of knowledge."

Smithson's heir died childless, six years after his uncle. Hungerford's mother contested the will, but an English court declared that the estate was to go to the United States, as Smithson had ordered.

## AN ILLEGITIMATE SON'S LEGACY

Rejected by his biological father, ignored by his homeland, and deprived of his birthright, Smithson was an island unto himself. His bequeath to America perplexed many. Perhaps Smithson identified with America—a new country striving to establish its identity and place in the world. The scientist had spent his life trying to accomplish the very same goals.

"Smithson always seems to have regarded the circumstances of his birth as doing him a peculiar injustice," stated former secretary of the Smithsonian Institute Samuel Langley. "[I]t was apparently this sense that he had been deprived of honors properly his which made him look for other sources of fame than those which birth had denied him, and constituted the motive of the most important action of his life, the creation of the Smithsonian Institution."

Alexander Graham Bell is shown overseeing the removal of Smithson's body in Italy. It was shipped to the United States and burried at the Smithsonian Institute.
Library of Congress

The institution that bears James Smithson's name is the largest museum complex in the world. Located between Independence and Constitution avenues in Washington, D.C., it houses the National Zoo, nineteen museums, nine research centers, an impressive research library, and the offices for *Smithsonian* magazine. Seventy-five years after Smithson's death, Smithsonian regent Alexander Graham Bell arranged to have the scientist's remains relocated to Washington. He is interred in a tomb inside the building that bears his name.

It was "entirely fitting that the man who never saw this country, but who nearly a century ago appreciated the potentialities of the American people, should find his last resting place among those he served so well," Bell stated.

In life, fame eluded the illegitimate Smithson. In death, he found immortality. Today, his name graces one of America's most vaunted institutions. "My name shall live in the memory of man when the titles of the Northumberlands and the Percys are extinct and forgotten," Smithson wrote. His words were prophetic.

# CHAPTER 8

# BERNARDO O'HIGGINS

## HOW THE VICEROY'S ILLEGITIMATE SON
## BECAME A NATIONAL HERO
## 1778-1842

**HIDDEN AND DISOWNED BY HIS GUILT-RIDDEN ROYALIST FATHER, YOUNG BERNARDO O'HIGGINS JOINED THE ANTI-MONARCHIST SIDE IN THE CHILEAN WAR FOR INDEPENDENCE AND ENDED UP AS THE COUNTRY'S DICTATOR.**

BERNARDO O'HIGGINS COULDN'T BELIEVE HIS EYES. FROM THE BELL TOWER of the village church in Rancagua that day in 1814, he looked with eager anticipation for the promised reinforcements that would bolster his embattled forces in the Chilean War of Independence and the whole revolutionary cause. And, yes, here they came, a cloud of dust announcing their approach. And then—what was this?—the advancing troops suddenly halted, turned, and marched away without joining O'Higgins's men struggling against the Royalist supporters of imperial Spain.

With a shout, he hurried down from the tower, mounted his horse, and sped off at full gallop to the front of his outnumbered and under-equipped force. It was to no avail. The clash went on briefly. Then O'Higgins, rising in his saddle, cried out, "*O vivir honor o morer con gloria! El que sea valiente que me siga!*—Live with honor or die with glory! He who is brave, follow me!"

With that rallying cry, the illegitimate son of the man who had been Spanish America's highest official was transformed into Chile's greatest revolutionary hero, outdoing the illustrious father who had alternately ignored him, kept him secret, provided for his upbringing and education, exiled him, disowned and disinherited him, and then, four days before the father's death, bequeathed to him the O'Higgins name and a legacy that made him the largest landowner in southern Chile.

**Ruddy complexion showing his Irish ancestry, Bernardo O'Higgins led Chilean Patriots in the overthrow of colonial rule in Chile.**

**1778:**

**August 20** Born near Chillan, Chile, to Isabel Riquelme, unmarried daughter of wealthy family.

Baptized as Bernardo Riquelme, under his mother's name. Father is listed as Don Ambrosio O'Higgins, "a bachelor" and high-ranking Spanish colonial official who would eventually become Viceroy of Peru, highest colonial rank in Spanish America.

Taken from his mother and installed at home of Don Albano Pereira, elderly friend of his father.

**1790:**

Bernardo is taken by father's friends to Lima, Peru, for education in a Jesuit school.

Sent to Spain, then transshipped to London for further education.

Meets Francisco Miranda, exiled revolutionary, and falls under his influence.

Accused with Miranda of plot to overthrow colonial governments in Spanish America. Flees to Spain.

**1802:**

Bernado returns to Peru and concentrates on developing new estate to agricultural showplace.

**1788:**

Ambrosio O'Higgins visits Bernardo, the first and only time father and son meet. They are not introduced.

**1801:**

**January** Now viceroy, O'Higgins renounces his son and cuts off all ties and financial support.
**March 14** O'Higgins dies of stroke after first writing will recognizing Bernardo as son and heir and leaving him large estate near Concepcion, in southern Chile.

**1807:**

Spanish overthrow King Carlos, replacing him with son Ferdinand. Napoleon of France offers to mediate, ousts both and installs Napoleon's brother Joseph as king. Civil war breaks out in Spain. Britain backs Ferdinand supporters against Napoleon and France, launching Peninsular War.

## A CELT COMES TO CHILE

Irish-born Ambrose Higgins (he added the "O'" prefix in later life to prove his lineage with the noble Irish Catholic clan that had been stripped of its ancestral lands in the seventeenth century by the Protestant Oliver Cromwell) came to South America by a roundabout route that is still uncertain. He once said that, like many Irish youths, he enlisted in the English army, only to be denied promotion because he was Catholic.

He then migrated to Catholic Spain in the 1740s where other Irish had fled, including a priest uncle with whom he settled in Cádiz. A bright young man, he trained as an engineer and soon was involved with the Spanish army in designing roads, bridges, and buildings across the country. He then either volunteered or was assigned to the developing Spanish domain in South America, arriving there about 1750.

He soon became known as "the man who brought the mail to Chile." Chile in the 1750s was part of the viceroyalty of Peru, a vast territory consisting of present-day Peru, Bolivia, Paraguay, Argentina, and Chile, and governed from Lima. Chile, a string bean of a country nearly 3,000 miles (4,828 km) long, was wedged between the Pacific Ocean and the forbidding 2-mile-high (3.2 km) Andes Mountains. Among the poorest of Spanish colonies, it was effectively cut off from the others during the Southern Hemisphere winter, unreachable except by arduous trek over the mountain passes or via the hostile Atacama Desert to the north.

**1810:**

**September 18** With colonial government in chaos, Chileans, including Bernardo, declare independence from Spain. Raises two troops of "patriot" cavalry in southern Chile and trains them against royalists. Takes part in first battle. Wounded but inspires troops with courage and leadership. Force under O'Higgins is defeated when other "patriots" fail to come to his aid. Retreats over the Andes to Argentina, where he remains three years. Merges his force with those of Jose de San Martín, liberator of Argentina, into Army of the Andes.

**1818:**

Meets Rosario Puga, a married Chilean. They become lovers and she bears him a son, Pedro Demetrio. Their household includes mother Isabel and two half-sisters by Isabel's marriage.

**1823:**

**January 28** Conservatives and clergy opposing his reforms stage successful coup. Goes into exile in Lima.

**1866:**

Body is returned to Chile with naval escort and full military honors and entombed in marble shrine in Santiago, the capital.

**1817:**

**January 18** Army of the Andes launches invasion of Chile.
**February 15** Royalist army in Chile surrenders to San Martín and O'Higgins. Chileans declare O'Higgins liberator and new head of state.
**February 16** Sworn in as "Director Supremo"—dictator—of Chile.

**1817-1823:**

Absolute ruler of Chile. Establishes schools, libraries, and hospitals; builds roads; and rebuilds cities. Installs courts and rule of law. Abolishes nobility and titles and restricts power of Catholic Church. Builds fleet that defeats Spanish at sea.

**1842:**

**October 24** Dies in Lima after heart attack.

Engineer Higgins conceived of a chain of shelters for travelers and mail carriers along the mountain passes and successfully campaigned to have them built. He then went on to build schools, bridges, churches, and government buildings and to construct roads linking the few cities. Leading military cam-

**BERNARDO'S BAPTISMAL CERTIFICATE LISTS "DON AMBROSIO O'HIGGINS, A BACHELOR" AS HIS FATHER AND HIS MOTHER AS "A LADY OF QUALITY, ALSO UNMARRIED, WHOSE NAME IS NOT GIVEN HERE FOR THE SAKE OF HER REPUTATION."**

paigns against the fierce Araucano People, he pushed them back into the more remote southern sectors of the country. He then rose through the colonial hierarchy to become captain-general of Chile, military commander, governor, and finally viceroy of all Peru.

## ONE THING LED TO ANOTHER

In his fifties, O'Higgins had never married. He was simply too busy. Then, as the governor inspecting his territories, he met a slender, black-haired, attractive young woman, whose father was one of southern Chile's leading landowners. Isabel Riquelme may have been eighteen at the time; some historians say she was as young as fourteen. O'Higgins was distinguished-looking, husky but with

a florid Irish complexion. Behind his back, he was called "El Camaron"—"the shrimp." He courted the pretty teenager, some forty years younger, until in the old expression "one thing led to another," and Isabel became pregnant.

O'Higgins declined to marry her, explaining that an officer of the crown could not marry a "criollo"—someone born in Chile rather than in Spain—without express consent of the Spanish king. He seems never to have requested the permission, however, and he never visited mother or infant after the child's birth on August 20, 1778. He did not dodge the issue, however.

Bernardo's baptismal certificate lists "Don Ambrosio O'Higgins, a bachelor" as the father and the mother as "a lady of quality, also unmarried, whose name is not given here for the sake of her reputation." The "conditional" baptism was performed in 1783, when Bernardo was already more than four years old.

Bernardo was given his mother's surname, Riquelme, but at his father's command, he was taken from his mother at an early age and placed in the care of Don Juan Albano Pereira, an elderly friend of O'Higgins, at Albano's country home near Talca, in Chile. Then one day in 1788, when Bernardo was ten years old, a heavy-set, florid-faced man came to the Albano home. He was treated with great deference by the family and introduced to the little boy. Bernardo solemnly shook the man's hand. He was not told the identity of this imposing figure, only that he was a representative of the king and the newly appointed ruler of the land. It was the only time father and son ever met.

Shortly afterward, in 1790, an emissary of the viceroy came and scooped up Bernardo and swept him off to Lima, not to the vice regal palace but to a Jesuit school for the education of the sons of high government officials. He wore the school uniform of black suit and cocked hat for four years. But word somehow crept out—or his father may have feared it would—of the boy's parentage. This would never do; O'Higgins's appointment was already being criticized by high-placed criollos loyal to Spain as "the English viceroy." Spain and England had been enemies since the days of the Armada in 1588.

Don Ambrosio now also referred to himself as the Baron Bollyready, the hereditary title to which the name O'Higgins entitled him. It would be a major

O'Higgins's father, the viceroy of Peru, "Don Ambrosio," wears the tricorn hat and embroidered coat of Spanish America's highest colonial office. © North Wind / North Wind Picture Archives— All rights reserved.

O'Higgins's mother, Isabel Riquelme, was considered a noted beauty in eighteenth Century Chile. She was still a teenager when her son was born.
La colección fotográfica del Museo Histórico Nacional de Chile

scandal if the viceroy, supposed upholder of truth and virtue, were disclosed to have fathered a bastard son whom he had kept secret. Bernardo, now sixteen, was once more unceremoniously picked up by a friend of the viceroy and this time placed on a ship to Spain. He was greeted in Cádiz by Albano's son-in-law, Don Nicolas de la Cruz, a wealthy merchant who had amassed a fortune in Spain and whom O'Higgins had appointed as the boy's guardian. Under the viceroy's instructions, de la Cruz transshipped him to England to complete his education.

**IT WOULD BE A MAJOR SCANDAL IF THE VICEROY, SUPPOSED UPHOLDER OF TRUTH AND VIRTUE, WERE DISCLOSED TO HAVE FATHERED A BASTARD SON WHOM HE HAD KEPT SECRET.**

### "MY DEAREST FATHER AND BENEFACTOR"

Exactly when or how Bernardo learned the true identity and exalted position of his unseen father is not certain, but now began a voluminous one-way correspondence. The viceroy had established an ample three-hundred-pound-a-year allowance for the young man, but much of the money apparently disappeared into the pockets of a pair of London clockmakers whom de la Cruz had named to look after Bernardo's affairs. Many of the letters addressed to "My dearest father and benefactor" complained of these financial problems, along with a cascade of letters to the supposed guardians.

Much of the correspondence, found in a copy book after Bernardo's death, dealt with the "moderate progress I am making here in my studies which are English, French, geography, history ancient and modern, music, drawing and the exercise of arms, in the last two of which I am tolerably proficient." He also apologetically asked for his father's guidance in choosing a career, pointing out that he was then twenty-one and not yet chosen a career path. A "career of arms," he wrote, perhaps prophetically, might bring him "advancement and honor." What did his father think "fit and proper"? He never received a reply.

Britain—and all Europe—was buzzing in the 1790s with revolutionary ideas, stirred up by the American and French Revolutions. Teachers and scholars preached antimonarchism, anticolonialism, and the rights of man over those of aristocrats. One charismatic and eloquent apostle was Francisco Miranda, a

Venezuelan exile who befriended the lonely Bernardo. Miranda called for the overthrow of kings like the Bourbons of Spain and the Hapsburgs of Austria and their replacement with governments of the people. Moreover, colonies should be abolished, totally abolished. People should be enabled to choose their own rulers. He urged Bernardo to be a courier carrying this radical gospel back to Chile.

Not surprisingly, word of this inflammatory rhetoric reached Madrid and thus the colonial functionaries in Spanish America, including the ears of the viceroy, a monarchist through and through who owed his eminence to the crown. By now Spain and England were at war, the offshoot of the ongoing conflict between Napoleon and Britain. Madrid warned the viceroy of possible English efforts to undermine Spanish rule in the colonies. Sure enough, another of Miranda's pupils came forward to reveal an alleged conspiracy against the Spanish colonial government, including a memorandum Miranda had supposedly written outlining the plot to the British government. The document named his fellow conspirators. One name was that of Bernardo Riquelme.

## ILLNESS AND DISAPPOINTMENT

By then, however, Bernardo had left England. Borrowing money from friends that he was unable to wrest from his supposed guardians, he sailed to Spain and returned to the household of de la Cruz in Cádiz. He sent a flurry of letters to his father describing the many horrors that had befallen him, the last of which was his unsuccessful attempt to return to Chile and the subsequent seizure as a prize of the Chile-bound, Spanish-flagged ship by the British, in which he lost all of his possessions, right down to his newly purchased trousers.

He returned to the de la Cruz home just as Cádiz succumbed to an epidemic of yellow fever. Bernardo, too, was soon stricken so severely that he was given up for lost, the last rites of the church administered to him. Then, after a miraculous recovery, he attempted to enlist in the army but was rejected because of his irregular parentage. De la Cruz grudgingly gave him a clerk's job.

Then came the worst blow of all. De la Cruz called him in one day in early 1801 and read from a letter received from the viceroy himself. Bernardo's father declared that he was most displeased with his ungrateful son, who had wasted his money, consorted with enemies, and failed to choose a career for himself. De la Cruz was directed to forthwith evict Bernardo from his house.

A flabbergasted Bernardo immediately sat down and wrote an imploring, beseeching letter to "My dear father and my only protector." He protested that he had been very careful with money, even doing his own sewing and mending, and had been wearing the same suit of clothes for four years. Why, there had been days when he had to go completely without food, and he had never asked his father for anything more than parental wisdom, guidance, and advice. "Sir, I will trouble you no further," he concluded. "May God still prolong your precious life for many years. Your Excellency's most humble and grateful son, Bernardo Riquelme."

The viceroy never read this last valedictory letter. By the time it reached Lima, another letter had passed it in the opposite direction. O'Higgins, eighty-one years old and now carrying the title of Marques de Osorno, had passed away. In late January 1801, he had suffered a debilitating stroke. After dallying with lawyers whom he feared might disclose his most closely guarded secret, on March 14, 1801, he dictated his will to his close friend Thomas Delfin. Apparently remorseful at his failure to acknowledge Bernardo in his lifetime, the will at last recognized Bernardo as his natural heir and granted him a large and valuable estate in southern Chile near the city of Concepcion. He left most other possessions to a favorite nephew, Tomas O'Higgins. Bernardo left immediately for Chile and in September 1802, after a stormy voyage around Cape Horn, arrived in Valparaiso to take possession of his new estate, a large and fertile tract of land known as Las Canteras.

## BUILDING HIS LEGACY

Bernardo spent the next years developing the property. He built up the cattle herds to three thousand head, planted ten thousand vines that launched the Chilean wine industry, and constructed new farm buildings and an imposing house for his now-married mother and his half-sister. But the winds of revolution had not subsided and now reached Spanish America. In 1807, the populace of Madrid rebelled and ousted the harsh and incompetent Carlos IV, replacing him with his son, who became Ferdinand VII.

Napoleon, pretending to referee the dispute, reestablished Carlos on the throne and sent troops into Spain and Portugal to reinforce his edict and also to prevent the two neutrals from supplying his enemy, Great Britain. He then jailed Ferdinand, persuaded Carlos to abdicate, and replaced him in 1808 with his older brother, Joseph Bonaparte, whom he had previously installed as the king of Naples. The Spanish rose up in protest at the French emperor's high-handedness, and guerrilla fighting broke out, later supported by English troops under the Duke of Wellington.

In all this turmoil, Chileans saw an opportunity. They had long grumbled about being ruled from afar or locally by "Peninsulares"—those born in Spain as opposed to Chilean-born "criollos"—Creoles.

O'Higgins had paid only scant attention to politics, but as a large land-owner he had been elevated to the *cabildo*, a local council whose duties were primarily consultative. Now, on the pretext of mustering support for the legiti-mate King Ferdinand, they persuaded the Chilean governor-general to enlarge the *cabildo* by a dozen members. The group, confused by the conflicting sig-nals from the two camps in Madrid, began to talk openly of obtaining greater power locally. Opinion split into three factions: diehards wanted to retain the monarchial ties just as they were; moderates wanted to continue the kingly role but with some self-government in a limited monarchy; and radicals wanted to throw the Spanish rascals out and strike for independence.

The three groups united long enough to persuade the governor to call a *cabildo abierto*, a kind of congress representing all citizens. Bernardo first allied himself with the pro-king moderates, but he gradually favored a more radical stance, with parliamentary self-government based on the English model that he had witnessed in London. Meanwhile, word reached Chile that the citizens of Buenos Aires had revolted and thrown out the viceroy. Thus inspired, Santiago voted overwhelmingly on September 18, 1810, to oust the Spanish-appointed governor of Chile and replace him with a junta of local citizens. That date was designated Chilean Independence Day. It also marked the date of a whole new career for Bernardo O'Higgins. He was to spend much of the ensuing decade fighting for that independence.

## THE RELUCTANT WARRIOR

For all his talk of a possible military career, O'Higgins had no military experi-ence and no real grasp of military strategy. (José de San Martín, the Argentine Patriot leader who fought alongside O'Higgins in the war for liberation, down-

played O'Higgins's military skills while praising his valor and sense of purpose.) He raised two units of cavalry from his workers and neighbors at Las Canteras, but he had no real idea of how to lead or train them.

He turned to another Irishman, his father's friend Juan Mackenna, who had served with the Don Ambrosio in the frontier wars against the Araucanian Indians. "I hope you will not think me a coward when I confide that I cannot bear the thought of ending my days in some obscure dungeon without being able to raise a hand to help liberate my country," he wrote Mackenna, in English.

Mackenna responded with a bulky memorandum of instruction, suggesting that he first enlist an experienced sergeant of dragoons, who could instruct him in the horseback use of sword and lance and the basic maneuvers of cavalry and infantry units. Bernardo's militia, Mackenna wrote, should be modeled on his father's old outfit, the Frontier Dragoons. "If you study the life of your father," Mackenna wrote, "you will find in it military lessons which are most useful and relevant to your present situation, and if you always keep his brilliant example before your eyes, you will never stray from the path of honor." Mackenna went on to compare Don Ambrosio's military skills to those of Frederick the Great.

The first major test of Bernardo's leadership and skills—as well as his willingness to compromise—came in one of his early major battles in 1813. A power-hungry and manipulative band of brothers, José Miguel, Juan José, and Luis Carrera (along with an equally fanatic sister Javiera), had insinuated themselves into the junta, José Miguel becoming chairman and then replacing the other members with his brothers. José Miguel, with grandiose dreams of military success but even less knowledge or command presence than O'Higgins, had named himself commander in chief of the Patriot armies. O'Higgins dutifully agreed to serve under him, even though other officers protested that José Miguel Carrera was not only ruthless but also incompetent.

In October 1813, after a series of skirmishes in southern Chile that left Las Canteras in ruins, the Royalist and Spanish troops surprised the Patriots as they were crossing the River Itata at El Roble ford. José Miguel abandoned the troops and fled on a fast horse. O'Higgins was badly wounded in the leg. He bandaged the

**The vast Spanish colonial domain in South America has developed into the modern states of Argentina, Chile, Paraguay, Uruguay, and Bolivia, as shown in this early map.** © Blueberg / Alamy

wound personally, then insisted he be carried to the front lines, where he lay in pain and under fire but nevertheless rallied the troops in a successful counterattack. Word spread of O'Higgins's courage but also of the ineptitude and cowardice of José Miguel, who had lost four times as many men as the enemy. O'Higgins became a hero. Still, he deferred to José Miguel as commander in chief.

The relationship was put to a further test in the 1814 bell tower incident at Racangua.

José Miguel had divided his Patriot army into three divisions; one commanded by O'Higgins, the others by his brothers. The Patriots numbered four thousand men, their enemy five thousand under the seasoned Spanish general Mariano Osorio. The Royalists were moving forward toward Racangua, which commanded a road leading to the Chilean capital, Santiago. O'Higgins advanced to confront them, expecting Luis Carrera to join him. Instead he received a frantic message from Luis. His force had taken refuge in Racangua, and he begged O'Higgins to come to his aid.

A savage two days of street fighting ensued, with O'Higgins momentarily expecting to be reinforced by Luis's Third Division. It was Luis's division that the bell tower lookout had seen retreating. Without reinforcements and bereft of supplies, O'Higgins recognized that the battle was lost. His men responded to his urgent appeal and manned a valiant cavalry charge, broke through the Royalist ranks, and escaped, badly bloodied but still in good order. O'Higgins decided the best option was to retreat over the Andes to the friendly northern province of Argentina.

## EXILE AND A NEW ALLY

O'Higgins was not to see Chile again for three years. He spent the time in Buenos Aires mustering more men, stocking up supplies, obtaining armaments, and, most important, allying himself with San Martín, who had led his own insurgents to victory in Argentina. San Martín dreamed of the complete expulsion of Spanish rulers from the southern part of the continent as Simón Bolívar was achieving in the north. San Martín gladly merged O'Higgins's forces with his own into an "Army of the Andes."

**José de San Martín, the Argentine Patriot leader who fought alongside O'Higgins, is seen here after crossing the Andes in 1817 to invade Chile.** General San Martín after crossing the Andes in 1817, 1865 (oil on canvas), Boneo, Martin (1829-1915) / Museo Historico Nacional, Buenos Aires, Argentina / Photo © AISA / The Bridgeman Art Library International

At this time, José Miguel Carrera resurfaced in Argentina and announced he should command the combined armies and the liberation of Chile. San Martín waved him off and appointed O'Higgins deputy commander. By the end of 1816 the two leaders, San Martín and O'Higgins, had built an invasion force of five thousand men, plus artillery and fourteen hundred cavalry horses and mules. On January 18, 1817, the height of the southern summer, the army began its arduous trek over the challenging passes and by February 1 had stepped into Chile.

The Royalists set a stout defense around the village of Chacabuco, guarding the approach to the capital. O'Higgins exhorted his men to charge with the bayonet. By February 12, 1817, the enemy had been disastrously routed, with one-third of the men killed or disabled and another one-third taken prisoner. A normally reserved San Martín triumphantly messaged Buenos Aires: "In the space of 24 days, we have crossed the highest mountain range in the world, overthrown the tyrants, and given freedom to Chile."

The two generals rode into Santiago to wild acclaim. On February 15, 1817, the leading citizens of Santiago gathered to choose a new head of state. The unanimous choice was San Martín, but the victorious general had a government in Buenos Aires to lead. He declined and said that, anyway, the position should go to a Chilean, a policy with which many Chileans agreed. He nominated O'Higgins in his place. The following day O'Higgins took the oath of office as Chile's "Director Supremo." The illegitimate son of the viceroy had now become the country's dictator, without opposition.

The war between the Patriots and the Spanish/Royalists continued until 1818, when an army commanded by San Martín overwhelmed the Royalists at the village of Maipú on the road to Santiago. O'Higgins, despite a serious arm wound, hurried to the battlefield, embraced his old comrade, and thanked him profusely for liberating his homeland.

O'Higgins served as Director Supremo until 1823. He fended off attempts by the Carreras to undermine him and faced down opposition by the powerful, Spanish-trained clergy and conservatives protesting his democratic reforms and abolition of nobility titles. He built a Chilean navy to protect the country's long coastline, which played a key role in the invasion of Peru, bringing Spanish colonial rule to an end once and for all. He established courts, colleges, librar-

ies, and hospitals; revamped the school system; and rebuilt the major cities. A conservative coup deposed him in 1823, and he went into exile in Lima, where he died in 1842.

Buried initially in Lima, his body was brought back to Santiago with great ceremony in 1866, escorted by the navy that he had established, and reinterred in the capital as Chile's foremost hero. The main street in Santiago was rechristened Boulevard O'Higgins, and it honored the once-outcast Bernardo, not the father who had turned his back on an unfortunate boy.

**The Battle of Maipu on the Chilean border, depicted here, subdued a Royalist uprising and cemented patriot control of Chile.** The Battle of Maipu on the 5th April, 1818, printed by Raffet (lithograph), Spanish School, (19th century) / Private Collection / Index / The Bridgeman Art Library International

# CHAPTER 9

# ALEXANDRE DUMAS FILS

## AN ILLEGITIMATE SON INHERITS
## HIS FATHER'S TALENTS—AND VICES
## 1824-1895

**AS THE BASTARD CHILD OF A BRILLIANT, FAMOUS WRITER AND A MODEST DRESSMAKER, ALEXANDRE DUMAS FILS EXPERIENCED RIDICULE, HEARTBREAK, AND DESPAIR. TODAY, HOWEVER, HE IS CONSIDERED ONE OF THE LEADING FRENCH DRAMATISTS OF THE NINETEENTH CENTURY.**

AT SEVEN, ALEXANDRE WAS NOT THE YOUNGEST BOY ATTENDING THE VAUNTED Institution Goubaux, near Paris, but he was the least sophisticated, and certainly the poorest. His classmates were the sons of nobles and aristocrats; they led lives of privilege and were accustomed to socializing with children, and adults, of their social class. They were also exceptionally precocious and could be cruel. The new boy in school was a convenient and attractive target. He used the wrong fork at dinner, didn't understand their jokes, and seemed perplexed in class. His worst offense was that he was an outsider.

Alexandre was clearly different from them—from his provincial accent, to his naïveté, to his questionable parentage, to the fact that he had Haitian blood. One of the boys recognized Alexandre's mother, Marie-Catherine Labay, when she came to visit the boy at school. It was with barely restrained glee that the boy identified Labay as his family's seamstress. As it turned out, Labay counted many of the boys' parents as customers. This discovery provided the bullies with even more ammunition to use against Alexandre.

**Dumas fils saw himself as a preacher, a man charged with showing society the error of its ways. His plays focused on morality, yet Dumas fils fathered an illegitimate child with another man's wife.** Alexandre Dumas Fils (1824-95) in his study (b/w photo), French Photographer, (19th century) / Private Collection / Ken Welsh / The Bridgeman Art Library International

**1824:**
**July 27** Alexandre Dumas fils is born in Paris. His father is well-known writer Alexandre Dumas pére and his mother is Marie-Catherine Labay, a local seamstress.

**1844:**
Moves to Saint-Germain-en-Laye, where he meets the courtesan who inspires his immensely popular novel *La Dame aux Camellias, The Lady of the Camellias*.

**1852:**
Adapts *La Dame aux Camellias* into a successful stage play.

**1859:**
*Un Père Prodigue* is published.

**1831:**
Is legally acknowledged by his father, who is granted custody of the boy. Forbids his son to see his mother and enrolls him in boarding school.

**1848:**
*La Dame aux Camellias* is published.

**1858:**
Publishes the autobiographical play *Les Fils Naturel*, in which an illegitimate son tries to convince his father to give him his name.

Labay had been supporting the boy to the best of her abilities when his wayward father, Alexandre Dumas, reappeared in their lives, years after abandoning them. One of the most celebrated authors in Europe, Dumas père was a man with an outsized personality. He began his career as a playwright, and was an integral part of the theater scene, writing and producing plays, dating leading ladies, and founding the Théâtre Historique in Paris, a venue that ultimately left Dumas bankrupt. He then immersed himself in fiction, writing a series of novels that followed the exploits of a musketeer named d'Artagnan. The first of these, the wildly popular *The Three Musketeers*, dazzled readers and established him as a master storyteller. The sequels, *Twenty Years After* and *The Vicomte of Bragelonne: Ten Years Later*, were enormous successes. His position in Parisian literary circles was elevated further by a string of successful plays he penned, including *Henri III et Sa Cour* and *Antony*, which were beloved by theater audiences and critics alike.

Dumas awoke one day and decided to claim Alexandre as his son. He feared losing his namesake and petitioned the court for custody. Labay, unmarried, poor, and without powerful contacts, opposed Dumas in court and lost. Despite the fact that Dumas had turned his back on his son when the boy was an infant, Dumas was awarded custody in the spring of 1831. Labay was devastated. Dumas, in an act of cruelty, forbade the boy from seeing his mother. He then immediately enrolled the seven-year-old in boarding school. Dumas did not take into consideration the impact such an upheaval would have on his

**1868:**
Mother Catherine Labay dies.

**1874:**
Is elected to the Académie Française, a prestigious organization devoted to the study and preservation of the French language.

**1894:**
Is awarded the Légion d'honneur, the highest award in France.

**1864:**
Marries his mistress, Nadeja Naryschkine. They have two daughters together. While married, has an affair with Henriette Régnier de la Briére.

**1870:**
Dumas père dies.

**1875:**
Actress Sarah Bernhart stars in the stage production of his play *L'Étrangère*.

**1895:**
Marries Henriette Régnier de La Brière, after his first wife dies.
**November 27** Alexandre Dumas fils dies.

son, who was until that time a sheltered, provincial, poverty-stricken young boy. The results were disastrous.

The students at Institution Goubaux taunted Alexandre mercilessly, hiding his books, tripping him in the hallway, stealing his food at mealtimes, and

**ONE OF THE BOYS RECOGNIZED ALEXANDRE'S MOTHER, MARIE-CATHERINE LABAY, WHEN SHE CAME TO VISIT THE BOY AT SCHOOL. IT WAS WITH BARELY RESTRAINED GLEE THAT THE BOY IDENTIFIED LABAY AS HIS FAMILY'S SEAMSTRESS.**

scribbling obscenities about his mother in their notebooks. The latest assault had been verbal. Laughing, the boys called him names—including a word he had never heard. Alexandre holed up inside an empty classroom. There he sat, crossed-legged on the cold floor with the heavy, leather-bound dictionary pilfered from the library perched on his lap. He browsed through the book until he found what he was looking for. It stared up at him, silently, from the yellowed pages: *bastard*. According to the dictionary, the word described a "natural" child, one who was born out of wedlock. The seven-year-old read the definition over and over. He knew his parents were not married, but he did not know, until that moment, that there was a name for what he, Alexandre, was. He remained in the empty room for a good hour, emerging, dazed and red-eyed, during din-

ner. A prefect ushered him into the dining room. Alexandre merely toyed with his food, unable to summon an appetite.

Alexandre was miserable and missed his mother terribly during his time at the Institute. He sometimes cried himself to sleep at night, pushing his face into his pillow to prevent his roommates from hearing him. He dreamed about returning home to his mother, where he felt safe and happy. He knew his absence pained his mother, and that she was desperately trying to regain custody of him.

For many years, Alexandre resented his father for whisking him away from Labay—and for leaving her for another woman after she gave birth to him. Although the two men would later become close, Alexandre admitted that he never truly forgave his father for the cruelty he unleashed on Labay. Dumas père's actions were inexplicable. He was not a vengeful man by nature, but he had a tremendous ego and viewed Alexandre as an extension of himself, as his creation. His conceit seems to have inured him to Labay's suffering.

## THE HEIR TO A LITERARY LEGEND

Alexandre Dumas II, also known as Alexandre Dumas fils, was born in Paris, France, on July 27, 1824. His father—often called Alexandre Dumas père—was a handsome, magnetic, womanizing raconteur, with laughing blue eyes who would go on to become a literary giant. The senior Dumas was the son of a general in Napoleon's army and the daughter of an innkeeper. His paternal grandmother was African, a Haitian slave, making Dumas one-quarter black.

Alexandre's mother was a Belgian dressmaker. Fair-skinned and slightly plump, she was a simple, uneducated, warm woman. Nothing is known about her parents, and it appears that she herself was born out of wedlock. To explain the existence of her son, Labay told people that she had been married to an unstable man from whom she had fled. For a brief time, Dumas lived with Labay and the infant Alexandre. However, the writer balked at the idea of monogamy. Unable to adjust to domestic life, he quickly moved on, leaving his family and taking up with another woman. It was a pattern that Dumas would repeat many

**"My father is a great baby, of mine—born when I was quite a little child," Dumas fils said of the senior Dumas, a charismatic, colorful, larger-than-life figure who spent much of his life fleeing creditors and spurned lovers.** akg-images

times in his life. Labay was heartbroken and did her best to raise Alexandre on her own. She was shocked and devastated when Dumas showed up out of the blue and claimed the boy.

In boarding school, the previously robust, cheerful Alexandre became sickly and cynical, and he was plagued by headaches and fits of anxiety. He worried constantly about his mother and obsessed about punishing his father for mistreating her. Being ostracized by his classmates further added to his distress. He got into frequent scuffles defending his mother's honor—and his own.

"One thought he had the right to point the finger of scorn at my poverty because he was rich; another to laugh at my hardworking mother because his own parents led a life of leisure; a third to mock me as a working-class boy, because he had a noble father; yet another to despise me because I had no father, whereas he, perhaps, had two," he later commented.

The experience left deep emotional scars, and Alexandre said that his mind "had never wholly recovered its balance." It was at boarding school that he learned how unfair the world could be. It was a lesson that informed and shaped much of his work. As an adult he remarked, "[T]he bitterness which I felt in those days has never been entirely at rest, even in the happiest days of my life."

The teenaged Dumas left boarding school and went to live with his father and his father's new wife, actress Ida Ferrier. Alexandre was furious over their union. Previously, Dumas had eschewed marriage, leaving Alexandre's mother in a perpetual state of disgrace. "I wonder whether the man who reduced her to the position of a poor, unmarried mother, forced her to provide unaided for the needs of his child, ever realized what he was doing?" Alexandre wrote. If his father wanted to marry, he owed it to Labay to marry *her*.

Alexandre was not the only one who was surprised when Ida snared the notoriously footloose Dumas. The writer was attached to Ida but did not seem particularly enamored with her. Rumors spread that Ida earned this Don Juan's gratitude by bailing him out of a financial jam. Alexandre and his stepmother clashed often. Caught in the middle, the elder Dumas sided with Ida.

**Catherine Labay was heartbroken when Alexandre Dumas was awarded legal custody of their son. Although Dumas had abandoned Labay and the child years earlier, the French court decided the case in his favor.** akg-images / Gilles Mermet

"It is not my fault, but yours, that the relationship between us is no longer father and son," Dumas wrote in a letter to Alexandre. "You came to my house where you were well received by everyone, and then, suddenly, acting on whose advice I do not know, decided to no longer recognize the lady who I regarded as my wife."

## FRIENDSHIP . . . AND FORGIVENESS

Father and son remained cordial but distant until 1844, when Dumas and Ida separated. Alexandre, then twenty, moved in with his father in Saint-Germain-en-Laye, some 20 miles (32 km) from Paris. The two became the best of friends and were nearly inseparable. They were frequently seen together in the trendiest Parisian salons and restaurants. The father often introduced Alexandre as his "finest work." He told him, "[W]hen you, too, have a son, love him as I love you, but do not bring him up as I have brought up you."

**THE FATHER OFTEN INTRODUCED ALEXANDRE AS HIS "FINEST WORK." HE TOLD ALEXANDRE, "[W]HEN YOU, TOO, HAVE A SON, LOVE HIM AS I LOVE YOU, BUT DO NOT BRING HIM UP AS I HAVE BROUGHT UP YOU."**

Dumas had grown wider, Alexandre, taller. The son had auburn hair and pleasant features. He dressed well and presented a fine figure. It was the elder Dumas, however, who received the most attention. Dumas was at the height of his career; a celebrity in Europe, he was received by French royalty. Alexandre had matured and come to accept his father for the brilliant, charming, and flawed individual that he was. He adored his father, but he loathed his propensity for boasting, his often-boorish behavior, and his inability to manage his finances. Dumas père went through money like water and was perpetually in debt, despite the fortunes he made off his books and plays. "If he does not supply me with a good example," Alexandre quipped, "he gives me a good excuse."

**Although Dumas fils disapproved of his father's bohemian lifestyle, he was extremely fond of the man, and impressed by his literary accomplishments. In turn, Dumas pére was a proud father who loved to boast about his son's successes.** Journey from Paris to Cadiz, 1846 (oil on canvas), Giraud, Eugene (1806-81) / Musee de la Ville de Paris, Musee Carnavalet, Paris, France / The Bridgeman Art Library International

Writer and confidante George Sand sympathized with Alexandre. "He needs a life of excesses if he is to keep the enormous blaze going," she wrote in a letter to Alexandre. "You will never change him, and you will always have to carry a double weight of glory, yours and his: yours with all its fruits, his with all its thorns. What do you expect? He has engendered your great gifts, and feels that he has discharged his duty to you . . . It is not a little hard and difficult, at times, to be one's father's father."

Larger than life, the senior Dumas was a force of nature, as enchanting as a sun shower, and as destructive as a hurricane. "He is at one and the same time, frank and dissembling," explained a countess who knew him. "There is no falsity in him. He very often lies, but he does not know that he is lying. He begins (as we all do) by telling some necessary, some careless untruth. He retells some apocryphal story. A week later, both the story and untruth have become, for him, the truth. He is no longer lying, but believes implicitly in the accuracy of what he has been saying. He persuades himself, and so persuades other people."

Although the two Dumas men enjoyed each other's company, they were very different. Alexandre, remarked the same woman, "is, primarily, a man with a sense of responsibilities. He is scrupulous about fulfilling them. You will not find in him the warm expansiveness, which is characteristic of his father. His childhood was tempestuous . . . His great defect is disenchantment, which is in him, the bitter fruit of experience."

## HIGH DRAMA—ONSTAGE AND IN REAL LIFE

Alexandre's first novel, *La Dame aux Camellias, The Lady of the Camellias*, was based on his passionate, tragic love affair with Marie Duplessis, a Parisian courtesan renowned for her beauty. Duplessis succumbed to tuberculosis a year after Alexandre broke with her. Filled with regret over ending the relationship, Alexandre was planning to beg Duplessis to take him back when he learned that she had died. He channeled his disillusion and heartbreak into a novel. Later, he adapted the novel for the stage, in the hopes of earning enough money to pay his—and his father's—bills. The play, which inspired Verdi's *La Traviata*, was a tremendous success; it launched Alexandre Dumas fils's career as a dramatist. French critic Théophile Gautier praised the play, noting in a review, "One is conscious, throughout, of a new and fresh mind at work, of a wit which does not hoard up its best sallies in a notebook for use when the right moment comes." The money Alexandre earned from the play allowed him to move his mother into a better apartment.

Alexandre was much more introspective, cynical, and brooding than his father. He was also deeply concerned about social mores and morality—a concern he was unable to reconcile with his personal life. He railed against adultery, yet engaged in a number of illicit affairs. He championed the family unit, yet ran off with another man's wife. He pitied abandoned, unwed mothers, and their unfortunate offspring, yet he fathered a child with a married woman.

Whereas Dumas père willingly, and unrepentantly, submitted to vice, Alexandre did so begrudgingly. But he submitted nevertheless, making his later works startling

## "MY FATHER IS A GREAT BABY, OF MINE—BORN WHEN I WAS QUITE A LITTLE CHILD," ALEXANDRE TOLD FRIENDS.

for their hypocrisy. The older Alexandre got, the less tolerant he grew of his father's many indiscretions and scandals. Dumas père fled France to avoid his many creditors. Dumas fils was left to settle his father's accounts. "My father is a great baby, of mine—born when I was quite a little child," Alexandre told friends.

Alexandre was obsessed with sexual ethics and the status of illegitimate children—obsessions obviously born of his own life. Taunted as a boy for being a "bastard," Dumas fils was unable to move past the circumstances of his birth, even as society embraced and showered him with accolades. His wealth and success surpassed that of many of his early tormentors, but Alexandre remained, very much, their victim. He was also a victim of his own moral weakness; an irony, given his foray into moralizing. Alexandre argued that female honor was a property, and as such merited legal protection. He encouraged the state to make wayward fathers claim and support their children. Oddly, the man who felt such compassion for his mother was a sexist, whose views often bordered on misogyny. Women were inferior creatures who must bend to the will of men. "Man can do nothing without God; woman can do nothing without man," he contended.

Dumas fils's self-righteousness increased with each year of his life. He came to see himself as a preacher, a man who must show an immoral society the error of its ways. "We are lost unless we hasten to place this great art in the service of important social reforms and the high hopes of the soul," he said of drama. "Let

JULES PELCOQ

us inaugurate, therefore, the useful theatre at the risk of hearing an outcry from the apostles of art for art, three words absolutely devoid of meaning."

Produced in 1853, his play *Diane de Lys* centers on a love triangle that ends with a wronged husband killing his wife's lover. *Le Demi-Monde* is populated with promiscuous, repentant women who attempt unsuccessfully to rehabilitate themselves through marriage. *Un Père Prodigue* follows the corruption of a son by his father. *Le Fils Naturel* hews most closely to Alexandre's real life. In this 1858 play, an illegitimate son tries to convince his reluctant father to give him his name. His later works were filled with characters whose immorality brings about ruin, despair, and occasionally death. Writer Gustave Flaubert objected to Dumas fils's constant moralizing, complaining, "What's his purpose? Does he want to change human nature, write good plays, or become a Deputy?"

In the winter of 1864, Alexandre married his mistress, Nadeja Naryschkine. A Russian princess, Naryschkine left her husband—and country—to live with

Dumas fils. When her husband died, she was able to remarry. Together, she and Alexandre had two daughters, Marie-Alexandrine-Henriette Dumas, born out of wedlock, and Jeanine Dumas, born in 1867. While still married, Alexandre began an affair with a woman named Henriette Régnier. Like Naryschkine, Régnier left her husband for Alexandre. After his wife's death on June 26, 1895, Alexandre married Régnier, who had waited patiently for him for eight years.

Despite his cynicism, Dumas fils never gave up hope of uniting his parents. His mother remained single and lived alone with a servant in a comfortable house. His father was broke and ill but still a dynamic personality. Dumas père, now divorced, was not adverse to the idea of reuniting with Labay. Labay, however, dismissed the idea, telling a friend, "I am over seventy. I am always ailing, and live simply with one servant. Monsieur Dumas would blow my small flat to smithereens. It is forty years too late." She died four years later in 1868. Dumas père died two years later, after a prolonged illness.

Whereas the senior Dumas infused his work with fantasy and high adventure, Alexandre chose to focus on realism. His preoccupation with love, sexuality, and morality is evident in almost all his works. His "dramas are remarkable for the fine drawing of characters, the pathos of many scenes, the skill with which he brings out the denouement," French critic Rosine Mellé remarked. "Few among the best psychologists have shown a more perfect knowledge of the customs of our times, a greater keenness of observation, and a deeper study of passions and of human nature."

As a result of his work in the theater, Alexandre was admitted to the Académie Française, a prestigious organization devoted to the study and preservation of the French language. In 1894, he received the Légion d'honneur, the highest award in France. Alexandre Dumas fils summed up his philosophy as such: "I start with the prophylactic assumption that all men are scoundrels, all women trollops. Then, if I find that I have been wrong about some of them, my surprise is pleasurable rather than painful." He died on November 27, 1895.

# CHAPTER 10

# HENRY STANLEY

## THE ILLEGITIMATE WELSHMAN
## WHO FOUND DR. LIVINGSTONE
## 1841-1904

A YOUNG BASTARD WHO GREW UP IN A WELSH WORKHOUSE LED
AN EXPEDITION INTO AFRICA TO FIND A MISSING MISSIONARY. HE
EMERGED A HERO AND BECAME BOTH AN ACCLAIMED EXPLORER
AND ONE OF THE NINETEENTH CENTURY'S TOP CELEBRITIES.

"DR. LIVINGSTONE, I PRESUME?" IT MAY HAVE BEEN THE MOST FAMOUS
greeting in history, learned, memorized, and mimicked by generations of schoolchildren in
America and Britain. One afternoon in 1871, two white men met in an African tribal village on
the shores of Lake Tanganyika, in what is now Tanzania. The older man, gray-haired and frail
looking, stepped forward and lightly lifted his cap. He held out his hand, nodded, and answered
the question in one word. "Yes," he said.

The other man swept off the pith helmet he had specially cleaned up for the meeting. He
bowed. He was much younger, just reaching thirty, short, stocky, with a carefully tended mus-
tache. Behind him waited a long line of native bearers, balancing packs and supplies. Speaking
with what Queen Victoria, with a contemptuous wrinkle of the royal nose, would later characterize
as "a strong American twang," the young man explained that the outside world had become concerned about the revered medical missionary who had devoted his life to exploring and charting
"darkest Africa," with an eye to identifying the most propitious locations for mission stations
and the peoples most in need of Christianity. The sainted Livingstone was feared lost in trackless
jungles, deathly ill of virulent tropical disease, maybe dead, perhaps even eaten by cannibals.

**Tipping his polished pith helmet under a billowing U.S. flag, Henry Stanley greets the revered
"missing" missionary David Livingstone, with the famous words, "Doctor Livingstone, I presume?"
in this 1872 engraving.** The Granger Collection, New York

## 1841:

**January 28** Born in Denbigh, Wales, to unmarried Elizabeth Parry, eighteen. "John Rowlands" is listed in parish register as father and boy as "John Rowlands Jr."

**Spring** Elizabeth departs for London, leaving her newborn with seventy-year-old father Moses.

## 1852:

Impoverished Elizabeth Parry is confined to workhouse along with two other illegitimate children. Mother and son meet, coldly, and do not converse.

## 1858:

Signs on as "ship's boy" on sailing vessel bound for New Orleans, where he jumps ship.

Clerks in groceries and stores in New Orleans and Arkansas, supposedly traveling with Henry Stanley, whose name he takes and whom he claims as adoptive father.

## 1862:

**April 4** Captured by Union troops at Battle of Shiloh and sent to military prison near Chicago.

## 1846:

Moses Parry dies, leaving five-year-old John in care of Moses's two grown sons. Sons place him with foster family, the Prices.

After sons fail to pay Prices for boy's care for six months, son Dick Price places tearful John in Denbigh workhouse.

## 1856:

Discharged from workhouse to live with cousin, a schoolmaster. Removed from cousin's custody and placed with aunt in Liverpool, where he works as errand boy.

## 1861:

**April 20** U.S. Civil War breaks out. Under peer pressure, enlists in Confederate army under name of Stanley.

## 1863:

Switches sides and enlists in Union army. Apparently deserts, and travels to Wales to visit mother, who rebuffs him. Back in United States, enlists in Union navy. Assigned to warship as "writer," to draft reports of ship's battles. Decides on career as journalist.

---

With the emphatic two-word command, "Find Livingstone!" the young man's employer, James Gordon Bennett Jr. of the New York *Herald*, had sent him halfway around the world to ascertain the truth. He was most pleased, the young man said, to be greeted by a healthy Livingstone who was very much alive. The world would be overjoyed with the good news, and so would Bennett.

Livingstone smilingly protested that he had not been lost at all, knew his whereabouts perfectly, and had been in touch with his wife and family. He was gratified that so many people had taken an interest in his whereabouts and welfare, and surprised that a leading American newspaper, particularly one with a reputation for sensationalism, would have mounted such an expedition and not some august organization like the Royal Geographic Society. He was too polite to ask the young man's name. Instead he suggested his unexpected visitor might be tired from the arduous trek and would like to rest.

Not until the next day over tea did the young man identify himself. He said he was an American named Henry Morton Stanley. But that was a name he had been given by another Henry Stanley, an American businessman who, he was to repeat many times, had informally adopted him in his teens. Nor was he an American citizen. He had been born in the small village of Denbigh, in northern Wales, on January 28, 1841. The Denbigh parish register noted the baptism of John Rowlands Jr., bastard, born on that date to Elizabeth Parry, unmarried, and John Rowlands. Even the name of the father may have been a fiction. Elizabeth, eighteen, was "no

**1871:**

**January 6** Arrives in Zanzibar to begin Livingstone expedition.

**November** After ten months and 1,000 miles through trackless territory, locates Livingstone in African village. Greets him with now-famous opening, "Doctor Livingstone, I presume?"

**1866:**

**June** Becomes freelance newspaper correspondent, covering Indian wars in West.

**1868:**

**January 20** Assigned by Bennett to cover wars in Africa.

**1895:**

Returns to Great Britain, restores his British citizenship, and serves i n Parliament.

**1865:**

**April 9** Confederate General Robert E. Lee surrenders to Union army, ending Civil War.

**1867:**

**February 16** Approaches James Gordon Bennett of *New York Herald* for job as overseas correspondent.

**1869:**

**October 27** Directed by Bennett to "find Livingstone," English missionary-explorer David Livingstone missing in Africa.

**1872:**

**March** After exploratory trips with Livingstone, returns to Europe and United States as famous and controversial celebrity.

Conducts explorations throughout Africa. Assists King Leopold of Belgium in establishing ruthless and exploitative regime in Congo.

**1904:**

**May 10** Dies in London.

better than she should be," in the local vernacular; John Rowlands was the town drunk. Denbigh gossip said the real father was a prominent local attorney, James Vaughan Horne, who had paid Rowlands to swear paternity for the price of a few drinks. A century later, a Stanley biographer conducted a lengthy investigation and concluded that the gossips were probably right.

## "WHERE ARE WE GOING, DICK?"

The teenage mother had little interest in either matrimony or motherhood. (She would eventually bear five more children, apparently by several fathers, all but the last out of wedlock.) Rather than be subjected to the taunts of the townspeople, she left her newborn in the care of her seventy-year-old father and fled to London. Moses Parry was a kindly retired butcher who had come upon hard times and was now living in a two-room cottage with two grown sons. Still, he welcomed the boy, played with him, dandled him on his knee, took him for walks and to church, and taught him to trace the letters of the alphabet on a slate.

Then, suddenly the old man died, almost literally in little John's arms, in 1846. Decades later he could describe tearfully how the old man had cried out, clutched both hands to his chest, collapsed, and died. Custody now fell to Moses's two unmarried sons. They shortly decided that raising a five-year-old was too much of a burden and farmed him out to a middle-aged couple, the Prices. After six months, they stopped paying the caregivers.

One day the Prices' twenty-seven-year-old son Richard scooped up the boy and, first carrying him on his shoulders and then prodding him along, hurried him through the town. "Where are we going, Dick?" the boy plaintively cried out in Welsh. "To see your Aunt Mary," Dick lied. Instead, the two stopped in front of a giant iron gate. When the gate opened, Dick shoved the five-year-old inside. Eager hands clutched him, and the gate closed as the boy screamed and wailed.

## STANLEY'S TEENAGE MOTHER HAD LITTLE INTEREST IN EITHER MATRIMONY OR MOTHERHOOD. (SHE WOULD EVENTUALLY BEAR FIVE MORE CHILDREN, APPARENTLY BY SEVERAL FATHERS, ALL BUT THE LAST OUT OF WEDLOCK.)

St. Asalph's workhouse was a dumping ground not only for unwanted children but also for the detritus of Welsh society—those too old to work, the feeble-minded, the very ill, the disabled. Males and females, even husbands and wives, were scrupulously separated. They subsisted on a diet of bread and gruel, and were dressed uniformly—men in coarse-woven, dun-colored suits and women in striped dresses, making them easily recognized if they managed to escape.

They slept two to a bed, and Stanley was to report later that he had been exposed to "all manner of depravity," as well as frequently beaten by the teacher, James Francis. In truth, however, flogging was routine at many English schools, even premier institutions like Eton. And St. Asalph's Francis gave him a solid education. He learned to read and love reading, and he had access to many books, many of them sappy morality tales but including classics such as *Robinson Crusoe*.

One dinner hour just before his tenth birthday, Francis called John aside and pointed to "a tall woman with an oval face, and a great coil of dark hair behind her head." Francis asked John whether he knew the woman.

"No, sir," I replied, Stanley wrote years later in his autobiography draft.

"What, do you not know your own mother?"

"I started with a burning face, [Stanley wrote] and directed a shy glance at her and perceived her regarding me with a look of cool, critical scrutiny. I had expected to feel a gush of tenderness toward her, but her expression was so chilling that the valves of my heart closed with a snap."

Elizabeth Parry was not there to see her son; she and two of her other illegitimate children had been consigned to the workhouse as destitute paupers.

Mother and son were not to meet again until he was twenty-two years old, but he obviously yearned for such a relationship. He made several trips to Wales to see her, but he was not accepted until later, when he was prosperous.

At age ten, John made an attempt to escape, according to Stanley's questionable autobiography, climbing over the workhouse wall and walking 8 miles (13 km) to his uncle Moses's home. He spent a day and a half laughing, chattering, and playing with his young cousins. Then Uncle Moses returned him to the workhouse. What would the neighbors think if he housed a workhouse refugee?

By the time John left the workhouse at age fifteen, he had high marks in arithmetic and geography, and Francis was pushing to have him admitted to a major public school. The teacher even called on John's uncle Moses to help, saying John was "an excellent scholar and endowed with extraordinary talents." Moses ignored the plea.

But in 1856, fifteen-year-old John got a chance to further his education, and another taste of freedom and family life. Moses Owen, twenty, was the second son of Elizabeth Parry's older sister, Mary. Just appointed headmaster of a school in Brynford, he volunteered to take in the obviously bright boy and tutor him. John remained in Moses's household for nine months, over the objections of Moses's wife.

When summer came, Moses sent the boy "temporarily" to a farm owned by Mary Owen. John enjoyed the fresh air and the farm work, even the plowing and weeding, after the confinement of St. Asalph's. And that taste of freedom was enough. When he was not invited back to Moses Owen's household, he tried another relative, his mother's oldest sister, Maria, in Liverpool. Maria and her husband brought him to Liverpool and found him a clerkship in an insurance office. When the insurance company failed, he followed the "boy wanted" signs and successively worked as errand boy for a haberdashery and a butcher.

One day, delivering meat to a vessel at the Liverpool docks, he was asked whether he would like to sign on as a ship's boy. He immediately accepted, only to learn on a seven-week voyage that the workhouse beatings and harassment were mild compared to those he endured on the ship. The day the *Windermere* docked in New Orleans, he jumped ship.

## JOHN BECOMES HENRY

From the moment the seventeen-year-old Welsh boy stepped onto the New Orleans dock in 1858, he fell in love with America. To begin with, there was the boom and buzz of a great city, humming with life, its polyglot mixture of faces and tongues from everywhere, lively music, spicy aromas, and beautiful, well-dressed women. Most of all was the sense of freedom and a new life. Here he was not the discarded waif of the workhouse or the lowly deckhand of the *Windermere*. No one bossed him or pushed him around; no one snubbed him or looked down on him for his supposedly disgraceful origins. No one knew anything about him, or his illegitimacy or workhouse days. For the first time in his life, he wrote later, he was treated as a reasonable and worthy human being. It was nothing like Wales, and certainly not like the workhouse.

The first night he slept on a cotton bale on the docks. When morning came he set out looking for "boy wanted" signs or other opportunities. He also began the metamorphosis from John Rowlands to Henry Morton Stanley.

How this was accomplished, if not the stuff of myth, is at least arguable. According to Stanley's initial stab at autobiography in 1890, he accosted a man sitting outside a wholesale grocery, reading a newspaper. "Do you want a boy?" he asked the man, whom he assumed was the store's owner. The man asked him to read a sentence in the newspaper to prove he was literate, then engaged him on the spot. The man was named Henry Stanley, said to be an itinerant cotton broker who had a desk inside the grocery, which was owned by one James Speake.

The enterprising youth was to spend the next two years with Stanley, traveling with him on business calls along the Mississippi and its tributaries as far as St. Louis. Stanley came to treat him as his own son and even conducted a mock baptism in which he rechristened the boy "Henry Morton Stanley," the "Morton" because that was the maiden name of Stanley's late and beloved wife. "Mister Stanley" made plans to formally adopt him. Then his benefactor/foster father went to Cuba to visit an ailing brother, while John was sent to Pine Bluff, Arkansas, to explore the possibility of opening a store there. Here he learned that "Mister Stanley" had died in a Cuban yellow-fever epidemic, Speake had also died, and his store had burned to the ground. Meanwhile, John, now using the name Henry Stanley, was clerking in a grocery in Cypress Bend, Arkansas, when the Civil War caught him in 1861.

Various authors and critics have cast doubt on aspects of Stanley's story, and in his masterful 2007 biography, author Tim Jeal, after some astute and painstaking investigation, concluded that much of the tale was fiction. The 1860 census showed only one Henry Stanley in New Orleans—Henry Hope Stanley. He was indeed a prosperous cotton broker with a posh office near the Customs House and scarcely in need of rented desk space in the rear of a wholesale grocery. This Henry Stanley did not die in Cuba but lived until 1868 as a prominent New Orleans business leader. There was no evidence that he had ever intended to adopt the youth; no adoption papers had ever been drafted. If anyone had been the boy's benefactor, it was Speake. Records showed John Rowlands worked for Speake for two years and was indeed treated as a family member.

When Abraham Lincoln was elected president in November 1860, Cypress Bend, like much of the South, was caught up by war fever. Seven Southern states seceded from the Union to form the Confederacy. Arkansas, a slave-holding state but a poor one, hung back until Confederates fired on Fort Sumter in Charleston Harbor in April 1861 and Lincoln called for troops to put down the insurrection. Then Arkansas joined three other earlier holdout states in declaring secession. The young men of Cypress Bend rushed to enlist in the glorious cause, cheered on by wives and girlfriends. Stanley held out. As a British citizen, he felt it was not his quarrel. ("I could never understand," he once said, "why white people were killing each other over the rights of black people.")

Then one day he received a package addressed by a feminine hand. The package contained a young woman's chemise and slip, clearly mocking his supposed cowardice. He believed the "gift" had come from one of the "beautiful" daughters of James L. Goree, a wealthy physician and plantation owner who was one of the store's best customers. Deeply stung by the sender's derision—it was "far from being a laughing matter to be called a coward," especially by a young woman—he promptly enlisted in a local militia unit, the Dixie Grays, using the name William H. Stanley.

## SERVING THE "BONNY BLUE FLAG"

On April 4, 1862, carrying an antique flintlock musket and wearing an ill-fitting Confederate uniform, he found himself one of ninety thousand Union and Confederate troops locked in the decisive Battle of Shiloh, or Pittsburg Landing, on the Tennessee River. It was the battle that brought the victorious

Major General Ulysses S. Grant to national attention. The battle also cost the Confederacy its commanding general, Albert Sidney Johnston.

For Private William H. Stanley, the Battle of Shiloh was also mercifully brief but grisly. As the Grays advanced against the Union lines, he saw his best friend killed, torn apart by a fusillade to his midsection, and others from Cypress Bend wounded or killed. Then the Union troops counterattacked, scattering the Confederates. Stanley was caught between the lines and captured.

He was taken first to a prisoners' holding pen and then to Camp Douglas near Chicago, a camp overflowing with cases of dysentery and typhoid. More than two hundred men died the first week he was there. The death toll and misery, the conviction that, in the old Southern adage, he "didn't have a dog in this fight," and the belief that the Confederacy was doomed to defeat persuaded him to switch sides and join a Union artillery regiment as a "writer," or clerk. He became ill again, then was sent home until his health improved (or simply deserted, as some authors have written). After a quick trip back to Wales in which he was inhospitably received by his mother, he returned to the United States and began to shape a career as a journalist.

First, though, Stanley enlisted in the Navy, again serving as a "writer," on the frigate *Minnesota*. One official duty was to write accounts of the vessel's actions. When the *Minnesota* participated in the bombardment and subsequent capture of Fort Fisher, which protected the port of Wilmington, North Carolina, the creative Stanley wrote a glowing account of the *Minnesota*'s role that he sold to several newspapers. After the war ended, these clippings convinced the *Missouri Democrat* in St. Louis to sign him as a freelance correspondent, covering the turbulent Colorado gold fields.

Stanley briefly left the United States in 1866 for another trip to Wales. This time his mother accepted him as a respectable member of the family; he was wearing an American naval officer's uniform (which he had "borrowed"). A foray into Turkey followed, where he and a companion were robbed, beaten, and briefly jailed in a hideous Turkish prison, all of which he wrote about for papers back home.

When he returned, he was hired by the *Missouri Democrat* as a full-time employee. His first assignment was to travel with and report on an expedition against Indian tribes led by the Civil War hero General Winfield Scott Hancock.

**Dandified James Gordon Bennett published America's most famous and sensationalist newspaper, the *New York Herald*. He commissioned Stanley to "Find Livingstone!"** Library of Congress

His blood-and-gore reporting caught the eye of other editors and he was soon selling his reporting on the Indian wars to several of them, including James Gordon Bennett, publisher of the nation's largest newspaper, the New York *Herald*. When Hancock's expedition ended, he went to New York and on December 16, 1867, approached Bennett for a job.

Bennett put him off until Stanley offered a counterproposition. Britain had just declared war on Abyssinia (Ethiopia), whose bizarre King Theodore had

kidnapped the British consul and ten English missionaries, imprisoned them, and subjected them to torture, supposedly because Queen Victoria had failed to answer his letter proposing a royal diplomatic meeting. Britain was poised to attack the African kingdom. Stanley proposed to accompany the British invaders, pay his own expenses, and accept whatever payment Bennett chose if his reports were timely and interesting. It was an arrangement few freelance journalists would offer or accept, but Bennett agreed and Stanley set out for Africa, arriving there on January 20, 1868.

The venture made Stanley a journalistic celebrity. The British overwhelmed Theodore's larger but primitive army. The king was hunted down and executed. Stanley wrote colorful accounts of the fighting and the king's death, and smuggled them out via the diplomatic pouch to Cairo, where he had bribed a telegrapher to give his messages priority. His articles drew attention not only in America but also in Britain. They were richer in detail than the British newspapers, and beat them into print by five days. Bennett was ecstatic. He directed Stanley to meet him at his hotel in Paris.

## "WHATEVER THE COST, FIND LIVINGSTONE!"

In his after-the-fact best seller, *How I Found Livingstone*, Stanley wrote a gripping but possibly embroidered account of that meeting. Going to the publisher's room in the Grand Hotel well after midnight, he woke a somewhat groggy Bennett, who admitted him and then abruptly asked, "Where do you think Livingstone is?" At that point, October 27, 1869, Livingstone had not been heard from for nearly two years, and international alarm had been growing about the missionary-explorer's possible fate.

Livingstone was not revered just for his missionary work and discoveries. He had been an early apostle of stamping out the slave trade, which he declared the greatest deterrent to the development of Africa and "the open sore of the world." It was a view that Bennett believed would resonate with his readers, whose country had just fought a war over the slavery issue. Livingstone was a great hero in the antislavery pantheon.

**Five years before he was "found" by Stanley, medical missionary and antislavery crusader Dr. David Livingstone sat for this formal portrait.**

"I really don't know, sir," was Stanley's reply to Bennett's question.

"Do you think he is alive?"

"He may be or he may not be."

"Well, I believe he is alive, and that he can be found, and I am going to send you to find him."

"What? You mean for me to go to Africa and search? Have you considered seriously the great expense you are likely to incur?"

"What will it cost?"

Stanley mentally calculated the costs he knew had been incurred by other explorations, and he estimated at least £2,500. Bennett responded: "Well, draw a thousand pounds now, and when you have gone through that, draw another thousand, and when that is spent draw another thousand, and when you have finished that, draw another thousand, and so on . . . But, find Livingstone!"

The two men then sat down and discussed other overseas topics and places to visit before beginning the search—the inauguration of the Suez Canal, a forthcoming British military expedition up the Nile, new archeological findings in Jerusalem, difficulties between the sultan and the khedive in Constantinople, the construction of the Euphrates Valley railway, a tour of the old Crimean War battlefields. They shook hands, and Stanley left by the eleven o'clock train that evening for Marseille on the first leg of this remarkable assignment. On January 6, 1871, fifteen months after the midnight interview, he had completed all of Bennett's wish list and reached Zanzibar, the island jumping-off place for trips into the interior, today part of Tanzania. The greenhorn explorer was now ready to track down Livingstone, who was still missing.

## INTO THE BUSH

Not only had Stanley never led nor organized such an ambitious expedition before, but he also had never commanded any expedition. He had not even been an employer building and directing a workforce. But he had given a lot of thought and planning as to how to conduct the venture.

**Explorations by Livingstone and Stanley opened large areas of "the dark continent" of Africa in the nineteenth century.** English School / Getty Images

# A MAP OF
# AFRICA
## TO ILLUSTRATE THE TRAVELS OF
# LIVINGSTONE, STANLEY AND CAMERON.

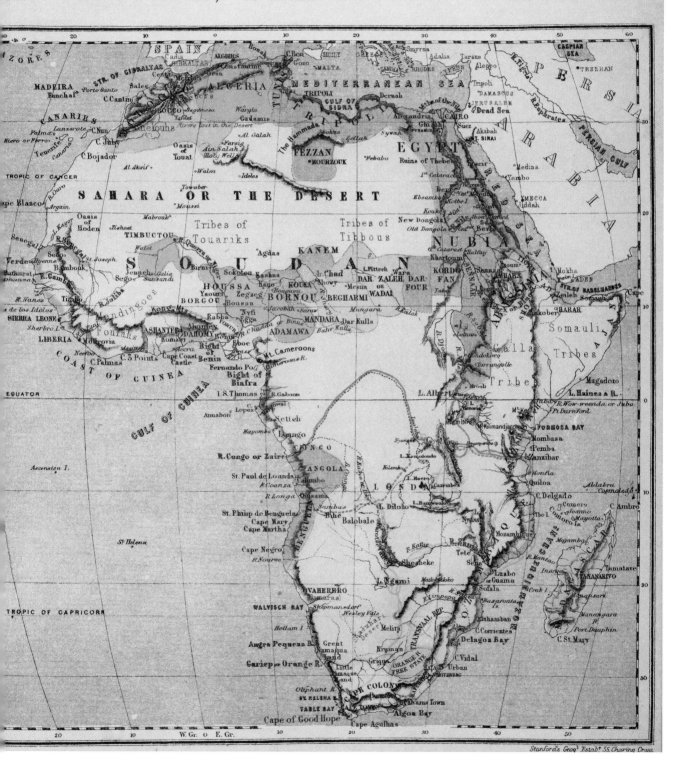

Stanford's Geog.l Estab.t 55, Charing Cross.

Stanley lined up a full complement of personnel, including two other adventurous white men who had been ship's officers, along with Selim, a young Syrian Christian from Palestine, who would serve as interpreter. He recruited six Africans experienced with previous explorations, nearly two hundred natives who were to serve as bearers, and another twenty-three *askari*, military-trained natives who would be warriors and guards. He commandeered huge supplies of special beads, wire, and cloth that he was told would serve as local currency. He also armed the party with rifles, pistols, muskets, swords, and daggers—just in case—and enough food to last two years. Thoughtfully, he brought a food supply for Livingstone in case he was starving. He also obtained two horses and twenty-four mules.

Then, informed that large caravans moved slowly and thus invited attack, he split the unwieldy group into six smaller caravans. It took nearly two months to get the whole procession underway. Its immediate destination was Ujiji, a settlement on Lake Tanganyika, 750 miles (1,207 km) away. Ujiji was the last place anyone had definitely seen Livingstone.

It soon developed that many of Stanley's preparations were misguided. Instead of dense jungle, the trail led across savannah, rough, rugged terrain covered with impenetrable waist-high brush. The weather was fiercely hot and sticky, temperatures reaching into the upper 120 degrees Fahrenheit (49°C). The party was afflicted by all manner of unfamiliar tropical diseases and insect-borne infections. Elephantiasis, a frightening disease causing enlargement of the lower limbs and scrotum, took the life of one of the white officers. Dysentery, smallpox, malaria, and miscellaneous fevers were recurrent. Stanley himself was repeatedly felled by fever and had to be carried in a litter.

Pack animals were attacked by *tryptopanosomiasis*, the dread "sleeping sickness" transmitted by the tsetse fly. Bearers deserted or stole goods, raiding the precious food supply. Stanley followed an old Arab caravan route; chiefs along the way had become accustomed to collecting exorbitant tributes for crossing their lands and insisted Stanley pay up. He spent hours haggling over terms while the caravan came to a standstill.

**Resplendent in glittering tunic, the onetime workhouse waif was ennobled by Britain and served in the House of Commons after finding Livingstone.**

## A MEMORABLE MEETING

The procession was an estimated eight days' march from Lake Tanganyika when Stanley received electrifying news from a caravan traveling in the opposite direction. The caravan had passed through Ujiji, and had seen a white man there. At first Stanley was alarmed: Had someone else reached his destination ahead of him? He questioned the informant further: Was the white man young? Older? Fat? Did he appear ill? No, the informant insisted, he was an old man with "white hair on his face." Some wrinkles. Dressed in white. Perhaps a doctor. Livingstone! There could be no doubt. Excited, Stanley offered an extra payment of valuable cloth to any man who would consent to push forward without taking a rest stop.

Early in November 1871, ten months after leaving Zanzibar and a trek of nearly a thousand miles, the party crested a hill and Stanley saw before him a village nestled by the shimmering blue waters of the lake. He ordered the American flag unfurled and carried at the head of the procession. At the edge of the village, he stopped in surprise. The open clearing was crowded with people. Suddenly Selim the interpreter cried out: "There he is! I see the doctor, sir! Oh, what an old man!" Stanley pushed through what he described as "avenues of natives'" until he confronted the pale, weary-looking white man. Then, doffing his helmet, which he had polished along with his boots in preparation for the meeting, he spoke the words that were to echo through history:

"Doctor Livingstone, I presume?"

The other man smiled faintly and lifted his cap. "Yes," he said.

The two shook hands and Stanley said, "I thank God, doctor, that I have been permitted to see you."

Livingstone answered, "I feel thankful that I am here to welcome you."

Stanley had been warned in Zanzibar that Livingstone could be a crotchety old man, imperious in his manner and difficult to deal with. Instead, the two got along famously. Stanley stayed four months and accompanied Livingstone on another exploration around Lake Tanganyika, where they determined that the Rusizi River flowed into the lake, not out of it, as had been believed. Soon, however, it was time for Stanley to return to the United States and report to Bennett. On March 14, 1872, Stanley and Livingstone, whose names would be forever linked, parted for the last time. Stanley tried to persuade Livingstone to leave with him, but the old man was determined to remain where he had spent so much of his life. He died in Africa in 1873.

After Livingstone's death, Stanley returned to "the dark continent" and became an explorer in his own right. He began a search for the source of the Nile, then stumbled onto the headwaters of the Congo and followed the great river across the continent to its mouth in the Atlantic. He circumnavigated Lake Victoria and showed it to be the second-largest freshwater lake in the world.

He advised King Leopold of Belgium on his ruthless one-man colonization of the Congo in what became known as "the rubber atrocities." Leopold's brutalization of native labor and Stanley's role as Leopold's advisor brought sharp worldwide criticism. The Belgian parliament overturned Leopold's personal rule. The episode severely blackened Stanley's reputation. In the United States, Stanley was befriended by Mark Twain, who organized lecture tours and a flurry of book contracts for him. In 1895 he restored his British citizenship, returned to Britain, sat in Parliament, and in 1899 received a knighthood. As Sir Henry, the boy who had been dumped at the workhouse as an unwanted bastard had reached the pinnacle of honor and fame.

# CHAPTER 11

# JACK LONDON

## REBELLIOUS MOTHER, REBELLIOUS SON
## 1876-1916

**JACK LONDON DIDN'T FIND OUT HE WAS ILLEGITIMATE UNTIL HE WAS TWENTY-ONE YEARS OLD. THE DISCOVERY LAUNCHED HIM ON A FRENZIED LIFE OF ADVENTURE AND A LITERARY CAREER THAT PRODUCED FIFTY-THREE BOOKS.**

THE YOUNG MAN WAS STARTLED AT FIRST. THEN HE BECAME ANGRY, THEN outraged. He balled up his fists and pounded the table where he sat.

Twenty-one-year-old Jack London had been slowly leafing through yellowing newspapers in the Oakland, California, public library that day in 1897 when a brief item brought him up short. The young aspiring writer often browsed the library's back issues, seeking some small news item that might contain the kernel of a potential short story, or even a novel. Sometimes that search paid off.

Today the few paragraphs that caught his eye were a twenty-one-year-old sensationalized police report. On June 4, 1875, a pregnant young woman named Flora Wellman of Oakland, California, had attempted suicide after her "husband," one William Chaney, had deserted her because of the pregnancy. Flora Wellman was the name of Jack London's mother. Jack had been born January 12, 1876, six months after the suicide attempt. But William Chaney was not his father. In fact, Jack London had never heard of anyone named William Chaney. As far as he knew, his father was the man whose house he shared, the disabled Civil War veteran he called "Dad." That man's name was John London.

Could it be that Jack had been born illegitimate? That he was, in fact, a bastard?

**Jack London poses for an outdoor portrait in 1912. London found out he was illegitimate at age twenty-one, while leafing through old newspaper clippings.** akg-images

## 1876:

**January 12** Born to Flora Wellman in San Francisco. Father is listed as William Chaney, an itinerant astrologist and preacher who abandoned her during pregnancy.

**October** Flora marries John London, a disabled Civil War veteran. Her ten-month-old boy is named John London, nicknamed Jack.

**Autumn** Ex-slave Virginia "Mammie Jennie" Prentiss joins household and becomes surrogate mother to Jack.

## 1893:

Signs on to schooner bound for Japan. Unable to find work on return, travels cross-country as freight-hopping hobo. Jailed for vagrancy for thirty days in Buffalo, New York—an experience he is to use in later writing.

## 1896:

Seeking ideas for short stories, stumbles across 1875 newspaper clipping identifying Flora Wellman as having attempted suicide when her "husband," named as William Chaney, leaves her on news of her pregnancy. He has never heard of Chaney.

## 1899:

**January** Publishes first writing, a short story entitled *To the Man on the Trail*, about hobo life. He is never paid.

Short story, *A Thousand Deaths*, is published in *Black Cat* magazine. Receives $40, his first payment for writing.

## 1889:

Aged 13, works 13–18 hours a day in fish cannery. With loan from Mammie Jennie buys sailing sloop and becomes "oyster pirate" in San Francisco Bay. Attacked by other pirates, he joins California Fish Patrol.

## 1894:

Becomes socialist and speaks on street corners as "The Boy Socialist." Runs unsuccessfully for California governor.

Completes high school. Enrolls in University of California but withdraws for lack of money. Begins writing for school publications.

## 1897:

Tracks Chaney to Chicago and writes him. Murky reply admits relationship but denies paternity.

**September** Joins Klondike gold rush. Remains in Alaska throughout winter, suffering from scurvy, kidney disorder, and beginning of alcoholism.

Jack slapped the newspaper shut, hurried out of the library, and rushed home. He accosted his mother fiercely, demanding to know the truth. Who was this man Chaney? Was he really Jack's father? If so, why had Jack never seen him? Why had Chaney never visited? Why, why, had Jack never been told?

After several tearful, explosive, hand-wringing sessions, Flora confided her story in dribs and drabs. Even though Chaney was listed as the child's father, and they lived together as husband and wife, she and Chaney had never been married. Just as the newspaper stated, he had left Flora when she was three months pregnant. She had not been in contact with him since. He had never contributed to the boy's support. She had no idea of his whereabouts. She supposed he might still be somewhere in the San Francisco Bay area. End of information.

**IN TIME, LONDON ACCEPTED THE FACT OF HIS ILLEGITIMACY, BUT HE NEVER SPOKE OPENLY OR WROTE ABOUT IT, THOUGH HE SOON BECAME RECONCILED WITH HIS MOTHER. HE NEVER COMPLETELY FORGAVE HER, HOWEVER, FOR KEEPING FROM HIM THE TRUE CIRCUMSTANCES OF HIS BIRTH.**

As skilled and indefatigable a researcher as a cub reporter himself, Jack set out to track down his putative father and in due time located him—in Chicago.

**1903:**
Submits long short story to *Saturday Evening Post*.
Turns it into a novel, *The Call of the Wild*, which is widely
praised and reprinted and brings him international fame.
Eventually becomes an American classic.

**July** Separates from Bessie and moves out of house.
They divorce, bitterly, two years later, with ongoing
battles over custody of children.

**1905:**
Buys land in Sonoma County, California, and builds
"Beauty Ranch," showplace near Glen Ellen.

Later, builds 15,000 square foot mansion at Beauty
Ranch. Two days before occupancy, house burns to the
ground and is never rebuilt.

**1900:**
Marries Bessie Maddorn, a business
associate. They have two daughters,
Joan and Bessie (Becky).

**1904:**
Meets Charmian Kittredge
and falls in love. They
marry in 1905, after his
divorce.

**1916:**
**November** Suffers attack of dysentery, complicated
by ongoing kidney disease and alcoholism. Takes
increasing doses of morphine to control pain. Dies
in his bed at Beauty Ranch on November 22. Death
is attributed to kidney failure, complicated by heavy
morphine. Suicide is suspected but never proven.
He leaves behind legacy as one of America's
greatest writers.

He wrote the man a letter and eventually received a weaselly worded, oily, ambiguous response. Chaney might possibly be his father, he admitted. But so, he wrote, might any number of others. Flora was promiscuous, he alleged. She had had several lovers. He left when he made that discovery. He also left because she "slandered" him. She said he had ordered her to have an abortion, which was not only illegal but also against his deeply held religious convictions as a self-ordained minister. Oh yes, Chaney wrote, he was a very sick man, and these false accusations about an event two decades ago had placed great strain on his weakened heart. He pleaded with "Mister London" not to pursue the matter further.

After a final confrontation with his mother, Jack stormed out of the house and set off on an adventurous life that was to bring him fame and recognition as one of America's greatest writers. In time, he accepted the fact of his illegitimacy, but he never spoke openly or wrote about it, though he soon became reconciled with his mother. He never completely forgave her, however, for keeping from him the true circumstances of his birth.

## JUST A LITTLE GIRL FROM OHIO

Flora Wellman, not unlike her son, seemed born with a rebellious streak. The fourth of five daughters of a wealthy Massillon, Ohio, contractor and canal builder, she was her father's favorite, the one chosen for piano lessons, private

PROF. W. H. CHANEY,

PRINCIPAL OF

## College of Astrology

AND KINDRED SCIENCES.

~~426 Park Avenue.~~

CHICAGO, ILL.

**2829 CALUMET AVE,**

Prices for Nativities:

Oral Delineation, $1     Written, $5, Upward.

Date of Birth should include Sex, Place of Birth, Day of
the Month and Hour as near as possible; as when
date of birth can be given correct a personal interview is not necessary.

tutors, riding instruction on her own pony, and specially tailored frocks from New York. When she contracted typhoid fever, which stunted her growth so that she never reached 5 feet (1.5 m) tall, she had round-the-clock private-duty nurses. Her mother died when Flora was four years old. When her father eventually remarried, the favorite child dug in her heels and refused to speak to her stepmother.

At age twelve, Flora ran away from home. Brought back by her frantic father, she ran away again. When she was seventeen, she left home for good; she only visited and corresponded with her family in Massillon episodically thereafter. When the Civil War broke out, she volunteered for the Sanitary Commission, which tended sick and wounded soldiers and was a kind of forerunner of the American Red Cross. Afterward, she wound up in Seattle, then a raw frontier town. There she met William Chaney. Chaney, an astrologer and sometime preacher, was moving to wide-open San Francisco and suggested she accompany him. That appealed to Flora's sense of adventure, and off they went.

In California, Chaney lectured on horoscopes and preached on the falsehood of organized religion, while Flora taught music and worked at a feminist publication. She embraced spiritualism, held séances, and convinced herself that she could communicate with the dead. And then she became pregnant.

The crumbling San Francisco *Chronicle* article that caught young Jack's attention was headlined "A Discarded Wife." A despondent Flora Wellman, the article melodramatically reported, had shot herself in the forehead, causing a superficial, grazing wound, after Chaney, described as her husband, had insisted she "destroy her unborn child." Chaney then stalked off and disappeared. Flora moved in with friends and gave birth to a son on January 12, 1876. She placed the child in care of a wet nurse, Virginia Prentiss, a former slave who had just given birth to a stillborn child. "Jennie" Prentiss was to become an influential figure in Jack's life. She was to remain at his side until his death, applauding, praising,

**Jack London's mother, the diminutive Flora Wellman, was short, moody, and an indifferent parent.** The Huntingdon Library

disciplining, insisting on his education, and supporting his dreams and ambitions. He referred to her as "Mammie Jennie."

Subsequent biographers (including London's second wife, Charmian) have disagreed about Flora's role in Jack's upbringing. In later memoirs, London pictured his childhood as troubled, abusive, and love-deprived, as well as poverty-stricken. Others say he exaggerated the hardships for dramatic effect. He was a fiction writer, after all, and would naturally want his story to read more grippingly.

Certainly his was a mixed-up childhood. Flora was an inattentive mother, to say the least. She left much of the actual mothering to Jennie Prentiss while she pursued her interest in spiritualism and the suffrage movement. Ten months after Jack's birth, she married John London, a carpenter and disabled Civil War veteran. War injuries limited London's employment, and Flora supported the family—barely—by giving piano lessons and taking part-time jobs. The family moved repeatedly, from San Francisco to Oakland to Berkeley and back again. The boy, who now called himself Jack, spent scarcely a few months in one school before he was transferred to another.

But Jack's education thrived. He was later to say that he taught himself to read, while giving credit for his voracious appetite for books to an Oakland librarian, Ina Coolbrith, who later became California's first poet laureate. He haunted libraries, reading and studying books to learn the techniques of writing and expressing himself. Although weak in arithmetic and other subjects, Jack completed elementary school, and it was recommended that he go on to Oakland's public high school, one of the first high schools established in California. But Flora insisted he seek a job to bring income to the hard-pressed family, which included London's two daughters by his first marriage.

## THE BOY SOCIALIST

At age thirteen—there were no effective child-labor laws in 1889—Jack was working in a cannery, putting in shifts of up to eighteen hours a day. The inde-

**Neat in striped shirt and bowtie, ten-year-old Jack London posed with his dog Rollo for this schoolboy photo in 1886. Two years later, he was working 12 hours a day in a fish cannery.** The Huntingdon Library

pendent youth soon had enough of slave conditions. He persuaded Jennie to lend him money and bought the sloop *Razzle-Dazzle*, the first of many vessels he would own and use as background for stories. He became an "oyster pirate," poaching on shellfish beds in the San Francisco Bay mudflats at night and selling his loot in the Oakland fish markets in the morning. Oystermen ganged up on him and rammed his vessel. Then he switched sides and joined the California Fish Patrol. Next he signed on to a sealing schooner, the *Sophie Sutherland*, bound for Japan. When he returned, jobs were scarce, and he took up the life of a hobo, hopping freights and traveling cross-country on the new transcontinental railroad.

London later wrote vividly—and horrifyingly—about that period. He was arrested for vagrancy in Buffalo, New York, and sentenced to thirty days in the Erie County Penitentiary. "Manhandling was only one of the minor unprintable horrors of the Erie County Pen," he wrote in *The Road*, his story of his hobo life. "I said 'unprintable,' but in justice I should say 'unthinkable.'" Returning home again, he worked long and arduous hours in a jute mill and then in an electric power station. Those experiences and what he saw as the exploitation of the working class turned him into a socialist. Soon he was making fiery speeches against the ownership class on Oakland street corners. He became known as "the boy socialist" and even ran for governor.

All this convinced London, as he later wrote, that he must earn a living by his brains, not his hands and muscles. He went back to Oakland High School at the age of nineteen—this time with his mother's (and Mammie Jennie's) encouragement—and earned a diploma. He also began writing, starting with two stories in the student magazine. It was this drive to find interesting stories and plots to write about that brought him to the old newspaper files in the Oakland Library in 1896.

When Jack received the response from his supposed father and confronted Flora with it, he was devastated. Not that he considered Chaney an admirable father figure; he viewed Chaney's charges of Flora's infidelity despicable, and his claim that he could not have fathered a child because he was impotent, ludi-

**In single file, an army of goldseekers left their makeshift tent city to cross a mountain pass in quest of the supposed riches of the Klondike.** The Granger Collection, New York

crous. (Chaney, it turned out, had been married three times before he met Flora, and he was to marry three more times after deserting her. By "impotent," he apparently meant "sterile.") Jack had no sympathy for the man who claimed he was the victim, the one wronged and slandered. But Jack had now, at age twenty-one, been brought face-to-face with the hidden truth about his birth: He was illegitimate. He had to get away and wrestle to comprehend that knowledge.

## IN CANADA, LONDON DEVELOPED SCURVY AND SUFFERED THE CLASSIC CONSEQUENCES—SWOLLEN GUMS, DETERIORATION OF THE JAWBONES, YELLOWING COMPLEXION, AND SUBCUTANEOUS BLEEDING AROUND THE FACE. IT WAS ALSO THE BEGINNING OF HIS HEAVY DRINKING AND CONSEQUENT ALCOHOLISM.

In July 1897, two ships arrived in Seattle carrying miners loaded with bags of gold taken from Dawson Creek in Canada's Yukon Territory. The news also coincided with a severe economic downturn and financial panic in the United States. Within days a stampede of eager gold seekers headed for the Yukon and the adjoining Klondike area of Alaska. Eleven days after the first cries of "Gold!" Jack joined the stampede, seeking relief from the emotional pressures of the previous few months, but also adventure and the prospect of perhaps getting rich in the process. As winter 1897 set in, Jack, his brother-in-law James Shepard, and others were frantically finishing up a jerrybuilt cabin in the Skagway area of Alaska.

It was a hideous winter. Canada had set strict rules that immigrants to the area must carry a half year's supply of food. But when more than 100,000 would-be prospectors descended on the frozen territory, famine quickly set in. Many of the miners faced starvation and took to eating anything at hand, like Charlie Chaplin boiling his shoes in *The Gold Rush*. Jack developed scurvy, an affliction caused by vitamin C deficiency because of a lack of fresh vegetables and fruits in the diet. He suffered the classic consequences—swollen gums, deterioration of the jawbones, yellowing complexion, and subcutaneous bleeding around the face. He lost his four front teeth, and his complexion was blotched with pockmarks that he carried the rest of his life. It was also the beginning of lifelong kidney disorders and of his heavy drinking and consequent alcoholism.

However, he emerged with a treasure trove of experiences that he drew on for his most famous literary works, including *Call of the Wild, White Fang, To Build a Fire*, and *Burning Daylight*.

## A WRITER'S PRODUCTIVE LIFE

Jack had always regarded writing as a ticket out of poverty, a way of making a comfortable living without hard physical labor, and he struggled to prove it, a struggle he described in his semi-autobiographical novel of a young writer, *Martin Eden*. His first short story, since widely reprinted and anthologized, was "To the Man on the Trail," published in January 1899. It was a story of hobo life, for which he was offered—and was never able to collect—five dollars. He first vowed to give up the whole business, but then, prompted by his mother, tried again. This time, a magazine called *The Black Cat* accepted his short story "A Thousand Deaths." He received forty dollars, his first payment ever for writing. His career as a writer was off and running.

Thanks partly to improved printing presses run by electric power, popular magazines were thriving and formed an insatiable maw for short-story writers. Book publishing was booming, too. Not only London but also other writers benefited. He became part of a prominent turn-of-the-century writers' group, much of it based on the West Coast, that included many whose names were to become familiar and whose works were to become classics—Frank Norris, Stephen Crane, Richard Harding Davis, Theodore Dreiser, and Lincoln Steffens. It was also the heyday of the muckraker. London began turning out stories at a torrid pace. Most were immediately gobbled up.

In 1903, London sent unsolicited to *The Saturday Evening Post* the completed manuscript of a very long short story. It depicted the life of a domesticated mixed-breed dog that had been snatched from a family farm in Northern California, then sold in Alaska for use as a sled dog. There the dog is brutalized, breaks free, and joins a wolf pack. He eventually becomes its leader.

The *Post* editor replied that he would purchase *The Call of the Wild* if the author would cut five thousand words from it and name a price. London agreed and set the figure at three cents a word. Published first by the *Post* and then as a book by Macmillan, it immediately became a huge seller, and it grew into a classic. The book London once described as "just another dog story," has been republished many times, has been translated into more than twenty languages, and occupies a prominent niche in the pantheon of American literature. London was to say ruefully later that perhaps he should have named a somewhat higher price.

But if *Call of the Wild* didn't bring London riches, it did bring him fame. Now he was not only a best-selling author but also a national—even international—celebrity. After *Call of the Wild*, in 1903, London turned himself into a virtual writing machine. In rapid succession came *The Sea Wolf* (1904), *The Game* (1905), *Before Adam* (1907), *The Iron Heel* (1908), *Martin Eden* (1909), *Burning Daylight* (1910), and *Adventure* (1911). And that was only the novels. In between came short-story collections, autobiographical memoirs such as *The Road*, and *The People of the Abyss*, a polemical report of the plight of the slum dwellers in the East End of London.

London set out to write one thousand words each day and largely reached his goal. And they were well-crafted words, too. Near the end of his career, needing money badly, he was turning out potboilers that admittedly had little literary merit. But his earlier works were almost universally well received and admired. All told, he wrote fifty-three books, and by 1913 he was earning the 2009 equivalent of $2 million a year.

London's personal life was frenzied—and tumultuous—too. In 1900 he married Bessie Maddern, as his career was taking off. They had been friends

## IN 1916 JACK LONDON TURNED FORTY, AND IT WAS AN UNHEALTHY FORTY. THE LONG YEARS OF HEAVY DRINKING TOOK THEIR TOLL.

for several years and agreed that they had married out of friendship and convenience, not love, and because they both wanted children. They had two daughters, Joan and Bessie, later called Becky. Joan was to become herself a writer, depicting, sometimes harshly, the family relationship in her memoir, *Jack London and His Times*.

At first, "Mother Girl" and "Daddy Boy," as they called each other, seemed a compatible married couple. They both doted on the children, as family photos show. But Jack's drinking increased, and he would frequently stay out all night. Bessie came to believe that he was visiting prostitutes. Fearing he might contract a venereal disease and thus infect her, she "refused to let him in the

room with her at night," wrote biographer Clarice Stasz. The marriage became increasingly strained.

On July 24, 1903, Jack notified Bessie that he was leaving her and moving out of the house. Several bitter years followed while a divorce settlement was negotiated. The family split. Jack's mother Flora complained, apparently with justification, that Bessie was manipulating the daughters and turning them against Jack, allegedly in the hope of obtaining a juicier property settlement. She took her son's side uncompromisingly and refused to see Bessie again. Bessie struck back by denying Flora's efforts to visit her granddaughters.

In 1904, Jack's publisher, George Platt Brett Sr., hired a new secretary and introduced her to Jack. Charmian Kittredge was livelier, bubblier, and defi-

**Jack and Charmian London visited Hawaii during a year-long Pacific cruise. The result was a bestselling book, *The Voyage of the Snark*, which is credited with promoting Hawaii as a tourist destination.** akg-images

nitely prettier than Bessie. She was also openly sexier. "Finding that this prim and genteel lady was lustful and sexually vigorous was like discovering a hidden treasure," Stasz wrote in *American Dreamers: Charmian and Jack London*. Jack quickly found a pet name for her, too. He called her "Mate Woman."

They married in 1905. They were a perfect couple, friends said. They went everywhere together and shared the same interests; she read and critiqued his writing, and he helped her with her own writing. She was eventually to write three books. In 1907, London bought a yacht, the *Snark*, and they spent two years cruising the Pacific; London turned the voyage into another best seller, *The Cruise of the Snark*. They also spent six weeks in Hawaii, which had just become an American territory. The Hawaii-based stories London wrote afterward are credited with Hawaii overcoming the stigma as a leper colony and turning it into a tourist destination.

London needed best sellers by then. In 1905, he bought one thousand acres in Sonoma County, California, in the remote Valley of the Moon near the village of Glen Ellen (now comprising Jack London State Historic Park). He called it Beauty Ranch and endeavored to make the property a model ranch and showplace for his ideas of progressive land use and agriculture, which are now recognized as well ahead of their time. He purchased more land and confessed that he now wrote "for no other purpose than to add to the beauty that belongs to me." He was chronically in debt.

London began constructing a 15,000-square-foot mansion built of local redwood and stone and brought in architects from Japan and Europe as well as the United States to design it. Two weeks before he and Charmian were to move in, "Wolf House" burned to the ground. Arson was suspected, but no one was ever arrested. (The Wolf House ruins, left undisturbed, are an attraction at Jack London State Historic Park.) The ranch itself was a financial failure, a steady drain on his income that he struggled to staunch. Neighbors said the city boy was a poor manager and absentee owner who neglected the property for months at a time.

In 1916, Jack London turned forty, and it was an unhealthy forty. The kidney disorder that had plagued him for years steadily worsened, causing great pain that he could only assuage with increasingly stronger injections of morphine. The long years of heavy drinking took their toll, too. By November his kidneys were failing, and he was slipping in and out of consciousness. Still he insisted on writing, and he began making notes for an autobiography.

On November 22, he had an acute attack of dysentery, compounded by the kidney failure. Clearly sinking, he gave himself a morphine injection and then propped himself up in bed to read. When Charmian looked in later, his eyes were closed, his head on his chest. She assumed he was asleep and tiptoed away. Next morning the man who had risen from illegitimate birth and hardship to become one of America's literary lions was found dead, the open book still in his hand.

Because London had written so often and so graphically about suicide, the rumor spread (and still persists) that he took his own life, perhaps with a deliberate overdose of morphine. The death certificate gave the official cause of death as uremic poisoning, complicated by morphine.

His "Mate Woman" outlived him by many years, dying in 1955. The mother who had once wept of her "badge of shame" outlived him, too. Flora Wellman London, long crippled by arthritis, died on January 4, 1922, aged seventy-nine. Jennie Prentiss, the bastard child's loyal "other mother," was with her.

# CHAPTER 12

# LAWRENCE OF ARABIA

## LEGENDARY, BUT NOT LEGITIMATE
## 1888-1935

**THE "ARAB REVOLT" OPENED A NEW CHAPTER IN
THE WORLD WAR I STRUGGLE FOR THE MIDDLE EAST.
THE MAN WHO ENGINEERED IT WAS THE BASTARD SON OF
A BRITISH NOBLEMAN WHO WOULD GO DOWN IN HISTORY.**

IT WAS ALL SO UNEXPECTED. MINUTES BEFORE, WORLD WAR I TURKISH infantrymen were mobilizing in trenches cut into a desolate desert hillside above the Gulf of Aqaba, at the tip of the Sinai Peninsula, in 1917 part of the Ottoman Empire, now Jordan. The July morning sun already glared down mercilessly, blurring their vision and conjuring up mirages that danced across the barren landscape. The Turks looked longingly yet nervously toward the cooling Gulf waters and the Red Sea beyond. Their commanders were wary of a possible assault on their position from the sea, so the trenches had been constructed to repel attacks from that direction. Behind them, to the east, lay the Great Nefudh Desert, one of the most desolate, water-less, and forbidding deserts on Earth. No attack could possibly come from that direction. The Nefudh was an impassable barrier.

Suddenly the stillness of the desert morning was broken by the crackle of rifle fire, then the thunder of pounding hooves. As still-sleepy soldiers turned toward the noise, a wave of horse-men, firing their guns and shouting in a mysterious language, roared down on their unprotected rear. Then startlingly and frighteningly, the horsemen were joined, even outpaced, by a pha-lanx of desert tribesmen on camels, hundreds of camels, their desert costumes flapping, their steeds' necks stretched out until they were almost parallel to the ground. Standing as they rode, the riders picked off Turks before they had an opportunity to raise their weapons.

**Sun-bronzed and dressed in flowing robes and headdress, "Lawrence of Arabia" passed for an Arab although he was only five feet, six inches and spoke Arabic with an Oxford accent.**

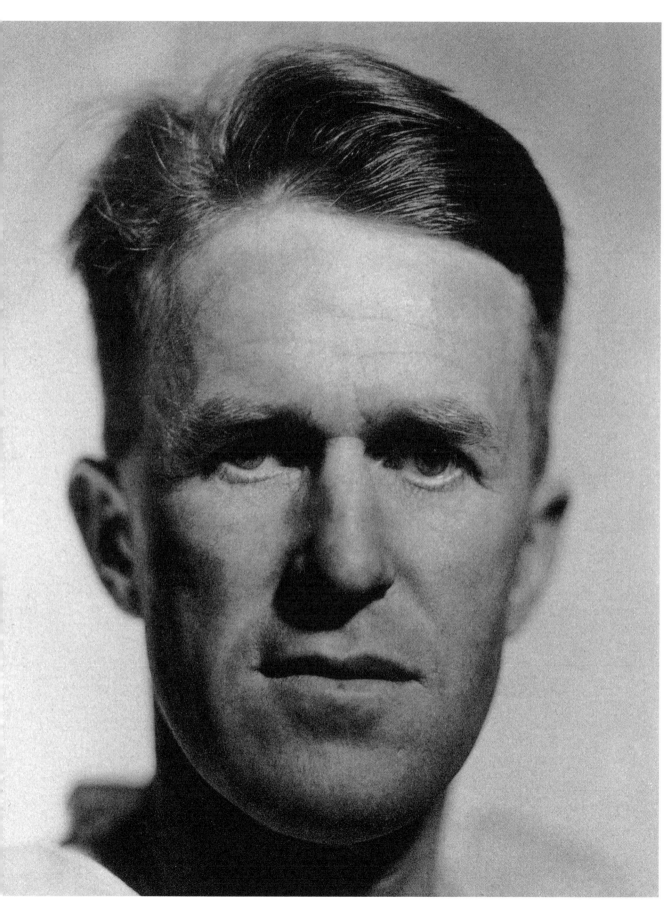

## 1888:
**August 16** Born in Wales, to Sarah Junner and Sir Thomas Robert Tighe Chapman, Anglo-Irish nobleman. Second of five illegitimate sons born to the couple. Sarah is former nanny to Sir Thomas's daughters by first marriage. She uses name "Lawrence," from family with whom she once lived and sons are given that name.

## 1889:
**September** Family moves to Brittany in France.

## 1895:
**Summer** Family returns to England, living on estate near Southampton and then in Oxford, where Ned enters school.

## 1899:
**Summer** Sets off alone on three-month bicycle trip through northern France, visiting old Crusader castles and fortifications. Lifetime interest in archeology begins.

## 1907:
**October** Enters Jesus College, Oxford.

## 1909:
**Summer** Undertakes solitary walking tour of Middle East, exploring old ruins. Stays in Arab homes, adopts Arab dress, and becomes fluent in language.

## 1911:
**Summer** Joins Oxford-based archeological expedition to explore old Hittite civilization in Middle East, serving as interpreter and liaison to Arab workmen.

## 1913:
**Summer** Joins new expedition ostensibly looking for old Israelite sites in Sinai. Expedition is actually cover for intelligence gathering for British.

---

The frightened infantry were no match for the attackers. The Arabs' leader, in a voluminous white robe with pristine Arab headdress and on a racing camel, overtook the others and positioned his camel at the head of the attack. He was only yards from the foremost Turkish troops when his mount suddenly stumbled and plunged forward. The rider was catapulted headfirst over the camel's neck. His head struck the ground with an emphatic thud. While the Turks scattered, fled, or held up their hands in abject surrender, the attacking force hurried to the side of their fallen leader. Woozily he waved them away and spoke first in the language of the desert Bedouins, then in the crisp English of an Oxford-educated gentleman.

"Aurens! Aurens!" the relieved riders called to him, for they never had been able to master the pronunciation of his surname. "Lawrence of Arabia," technically a major in the British army but actually an adviser to the Arab irregulars, that day vaulted from illegitimacy to legendary hero, a leader and architect of the "Arab Revolt" that helped bring Allied triumph and redrew the map of the Middle East.

## THE FIVE BROTHERS

Thomas Edward Lawrence—known as "Ned" as a child—was the second of five sons, all illegitimate by puritanical Victorian standards. His Anglo-Irish father, Sir Thomas Robert Tighe Chapman, was a nobleman who drew an inheritance

## 1914:

**August** World War I begins in Europe. Britain joins Allies in war against Germany and Austria-Hungary.

**November** Joins British Imperial General Staff as civilian geographer.

## 1916:

**June** Arab tribes rise up against ruling Ottoman Turks, a German ally.

**Autumn** Now a captain, travels with three-man high-level mission to tribal leaders in Arabia as interpreter and liaison. Remains as permanent liaison to Arabs. As top adviser to Arab leader Faiṣal, develops hit-and-run guerrilla strategy against Turkish installations and railways in Arabian desert.

## 1918:

**September** Arabs and British take Damascus, last Turkish bastion in Middle East.

**November 11** World War I ends with Allied victory.

## 1922:

Seeking anonymity, enlists in British Royal Air Force under name "John Hume Ross." Serves ten months before true identity is discovered.

Publishes highly-acclaimed account of Middle East career, *Seven Pillars of Wisdom.*

## 1915:

**January** A commissioned lieutenant in British army, is assigned to Arab Bureau in Cairo.

## 1917:

**July** Surprise assault by Lawrence-led camel corps and cavalry captures Aqaba, last Red Sea port in Turkish hands and ensuring successful British-Arab offensive against Turkish-held Palestine and Syria.

**Christmas** Leading Arab force, accompanies British commander Sir Edmund Allenby on triumphant entry into Jerusalem.

## 1919:

Special adviser to Arab delegation at Versailles Treaty negotiations. Feels personally betrayed by final document, denying independence to Arabs, and establishing French and British colonial "mandates."

## 1935:

**May 13** Suffers severe head injuries when thrown from motorcycle trying to avoid two boys on bicycles.

**May 19** Dies in Oxford after six days in coma. Accorded state funeral led by Winston Churchill.

---

from estates across Ireland acquired with the help of Sir Walter Raleigh in Elizabethan times, and who would become 8th Baronet of Westmeath in 1914.

Sir Thomas married Edith Hamilton, daughter of another wealthy land-owner, and had four daughters. Edith is described by historians as a bitter, vindictive woman who became increasingly obsessed with religion and insisted that the family and household staff hold prayer sessions several times a day. She lectured the family incessantly about sin, a category in which, it is said, she eventually came to include marital relations.

In the late 1870s, a young Scottish woman, Sarah Junner, joined the household as the girls' nanny. Sarah herself was illegitimate, had been brought up by a Scottish Episcopal clergyman uncle, and later lived in the household of one John Lawrence before moving to Ireland. A troubled Sir Thomas fell in love with Sarah, who was fifteen years younger. When Sarah became pregnant in 1885, she moved from the Chapman estate to Dublin, using the name "Miss Lawrence." Three months after Sarah's child was born, Sir Thomas moved in with her. The newborn was given the name Montagu Robert Lawrence, although he was known as Robert, and the four brothers who followed also carried the name Lawrence. The couple never married.

It was a peripatetic family. From Ireland, the Lawrences moved to Tremadoc, in Caernarvonshire in north Wales, where Thomas Edward was born

August 16, 1888. When Ned was thirteen months old, the family moved across the English Channel to Dinard, a summer resort in Brittany. They remained in France until Ned was almost seven, then moved back to Britain to an estate near Southampton, and then finally to Oxford, for the boys' education, where Ned attended the Oxford High School for Boys.

Ned was sixteen before he had any whisper of the circumstances of his birth. Even then it was only suspicion from a few chance remarks or fragments of letters, not incontrovertible evidence. At one point it was rumored around Westmeath that Sir Robert was not the boys' father. Ned half-believed it at first, then discarded the rumor as impossible. He was close to his mother, although in his teens, like many adolescents, he complained she was too controlling. Sarah was an educated, thoughtful woman with strong ambitions for her sons. His father, a large, strong man and heavy drinker, was distant. He left management of the family estates to the two cousins who preceded him as baronet,

## LAWRENCE WAS SIXTEEN BEFORE HE HEARD ANY WHISPERS OF THE CIRCUMSTANCES OF HIS BIRTH.

occupying himself with what he called his "pastimes." He was a camera enthusiast, purchasing always the latest and most advanced models, and an ardent bicyclist, with a new up-to-date model every year.

But although father and son were not close, Sir Robert's example apparently was a significant influence on young Ned's life. Like his father before him, the boy became an ardent cyclist and hobbyist photographer, given to long, solitary bike trips with a camera slung around his neck. After returning to England, the family continued to maintain their house in Brittany; at age eleven, Ned set out from there on his bicycle, carrying only a blanket and backpack, to pedal around northern France alone. He spoke fluent French from his early school days; his early childhood playmates had been French, as had been his governess. He intended to blend into the landscape as inconspicuously as possible. He didn't want to be seen as an English visitor observing the natives. His goal was to be part of the environment, to be absorbed in it—to be, as he said later in following the same policy in Arabia, "like a fish in the water, like a bird in the sky."

## ON THE TRAIL OF THE CRUSADERS

Ned's bicycle took him past the castles of northern France, and they fascinated him. He climbed over fortifications, turrets, towers, walls, and moats, photographing them all with his trusty camera, usually rolling out his blanket and sleeping under the stars. He became particularly interested in the role of the Crusaders in building and occupying the massive structures. He made several follow-up trips, and when he entered Jesus College at Oxford, in October 1907, he wrote a thesis, *The Influence of the Crusades on the Medieval Military Architecture of Europe.* The paper brought him to the attention of D. C. Hogarth, newly appointed keeper of the Ashmolean Museum of Antiquities at Oxford. With Hogarth's guidance, given reluctantly at first, because of the older man's fear of the potential dangers of such a solitary trip in unknown territory, and after a crash course in Arabic languages, Ned set off on a walking tour, alone, of the Holy Land to inspect the Crusaders' castles there.

It was a long trek, starting from Sidon, in what is now Lebanon, continuing to the fabled city of Damascus, then and now the capital of Syria, and on to places whose names still resound in the troubled Middle East—Beirut, Aleppo, Antioch. The second stage of Ned's journey took him through northern Syria almost into Turkey itself and as far as the headwaters of the Euphrates River.

Hogarth had warned Ned of the intense heat and blinding sun reflected on the sands—"almost more than an Englishman can bear"—but within a few days of being "a fish in the water, a bird in the sky" he recognized the protective advantages of the Arabs' flowing robes and headdress, and chose them as his standard garb. He wanted to be seen as just another Arab, and accepted that way—even though he was an unlikely Arab with his short stature (he was only five feet six [168 cm]), blue eyes, and fair if sunburned complexion. He adopted other Arab habits, such as eating with his fingers and limiting food and water intake. He often stayed overnight in Arab homes, to better polish his command of the colloquial language.

After nearly four months of walking 20 to 25 miles (32 to 40 km) a day, and having been beaten and robbed of his precious camera plus some artifacts he was bringing for Hogarth's museum, Ned returned to Oxford for his final examination. He was just twenty-one. Hogarth immediately recruited him to return to Carchemish in the area he had just covered, for an archeological dig near the

Euphrates, the site of an ancient Hittite civilization. Hogarth—
"Every job I ever had, except the RAF, I owe to him," Lawrence
was to say later—also arranged for a four-year Oxford demyship,
a kind of junior fellowship, which would cover his expenses and
travel. Lawrence became an assistant to Leonard Woolley, head
of the expedition. Lawrence's major duty was as liaison to the two
hundred Arab workmen. He ate, chatted, joked, and spent eve-
nings with them.

The work went on for three years, and Lawrence was
accepted as one of them. Then, as it was winding down, the two
men received a cable from London, asking them to undertake an
archeological expedition in the Sinai Peninsula, under the aus-
pices of the Palestine Exploration Fund (PEF). They were to trace
the route of the Israelites in the Wilderness of Zin described in the
Old Testament, and particularly to look for the spot where Moses
supposedly smote a rock and brought forth a rushing spring.

Arriving in the Sinai, however, they were met by Captain
Francis Newcombe, a British intelligence officer. Newcombe
discreetly explained that the archeological expedition, for
which PEF had received approval from Turkish authorities, was
merely a cover story. The true purpose of the expedition was
intelligence-gathering. Newcombe, himself an archeologist,
would accompany them, mapping the territory and pin-
pointing sites of possible military importance in the event of
war—roads, trails, and particularly water sources. The fiction
that they were seeking Moses's spring and the Israelites' route
was pure camouflage.

## THE GUNS OF AUGUST BARK

By 1913, political and economic rivalry between Britain and a rising Germany
was approaching a crescendo. Much of it centered on the Middle East. "The
jewel in the crown" of the British empire was India; its possession was key to the
empire's wealth. The route to India lay across Ottoman lands, bisected by the
British-controlled Suez Canal, and British-administered Egypt. Thus Suez and

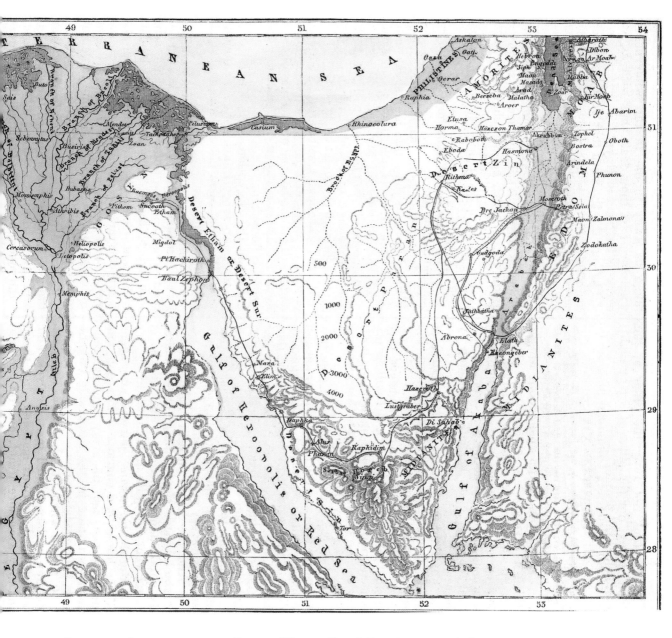

Egypt were of prime importance. In 1909, Winston Churchill, as First Lord of the Admiralty, had switched Britain's battle fleet from coal to oil. The Ottoman Middle Eastern lands had a chokehold on the world's oil supply. The Middle East was the fleet's lifeline.

Imperial Germany saw no reason why it should be shut out of the region and its potential wealth. Courting impoverished Turkey, known as the "sick man of Europe" for its backward government and medieval economy, Germany financed and built railways and communications facilities linking the disparate parts of the Ottoman empire. Its prime project was a Berlin-to-Baghdad railway,

**The Arabia of Lawrence: The long tongue of the Sinai Peninsula, shown in an early map, was fought over by Ottoman Turks and Lawrence's Arab irregulars in 1916-1918. The Gulf of Aqaba at right was the site of Lawrence' most famous battle.** Time & Life Pictures/ Getty Images

which would bring German locomotives within a few hundred miles of India. Encouraged by the Sultan, Germany began construction of the Hejaz Railway, stretching across the Arabian Desert to Mecca and Medina. Faithful Muslims were supposed to visit the holy cities at least once in a lifetime; thanks to German engineers and financing, that trip would be easier. Of course, the railway, when completed, would also allow Germany access to the vast oil supply of the peninsula. Moreover, after the "Young Turks" revolt by the Turkish military took over the government, their strongman Enver Pasha had signed a secret treaty with Germany requiring the two countries to come to each other's aid in the event of war. He brought in German officers to modernize the Turkish army. None of this went down well in London.

## LAWRENCE WANTED TO BE SEEN AS JUST ANOTHER ARAB, AND ACCEPTED THAT WAY—EVEN THOUGH HE WAS AN UNLIKELY ARAB WITH HIS SHORT STATURE (HE WAS ONLY FIVE FEET SIX [168 CM]), BLUE EYES, AND FAIR IF SUNBURNED COMPLEXION.

Britain and Turkey had had mixed relations for nearly a century. The two had stood together against Napoleon and in the Crimean War from 1864–1856, split when Britain supported Greek rebels against Ottoman rule, then divided again in the Balkan wars that ousted Turkey from southeastern Europe. Turkey's pact with Germany and Britain's lining up with Russia drove in the final wedge.

In the hot summer of 1914, while Lawrence was back in Oxford compiling a final report on Carchemish, the guns of August sounded. German troops hurtled into France, Britain and Russia joined France, and the world plunged into the Great War of 1914–1918. In November, Turkey joined the Central Powers of Germany and Austria-Hungary, and war came to the Middle East.

Like many young Britons, Lawrence's brothers immediately volunteered. (Both were lost in the early fighting in Flanders; Will, who had joined the Royal Flying Corps, died in a crash, and Frank was listed as missing after a heavy bombardment of his unit. His body was never found.) T. E., as he now styled himself, waited until November, when the Carchemish report was finished. Then he joined the geographical section of the Imperial General Staff as a civilian. Within a few weeks, he was put into an army uniform as a Special Lists officer,

not attached to any unit. By January 1, 1915, Lieutenant Lawrence was in Cairo, where the British were assembling officers with Middle Eastern experience as a specialized intelligence unit, later named the Arab Bureau.

Lawrence spent nearly two years in a desk job, eventually wearing the bars of a captain, and he chafed at it. He considered the Middle East a vital theater of war, but the higher-ups did not. The main event for them was the bloody, brutal trench warfare of the Western Front, and anything else was merely a sideshow. Lawrence protested that the Arabian tribes were ready to revolt, which should be encouraged; an Arab uprising would force the Turks to send troops to Arabia, relieving pressure on the Russians or causing Germany to send troops from the Western Front in their support. That kind of misguided thinking, he was firmly told, had led to the disaster at Gallipoli.

**Youthful archeologist Lawrence and expedition leader Leonard Woodley unearthed a massive Hittite bas-relief in diggings near the Euphrates River, 1913.**
Rue des Archives / The Granger Collection, New York

## THE ARAB REVOLT

Then, in June 1916, the Arabs took matters into their own hands. Confident that British support would be forthcoming, Grand Sherif Hussein, emir of Mecca, called on all Arabs in Hejaz, the vast desert east of the Red Sea, to rise up against their fellow Muslims, the Turks. His four sons, Ali, Abdullah, Faişal, and Zeid, each had a small private army. They would lead the way and rally other sheiks to join in a generalized Arab Revolt.

The rebels enjoyed some success at first, overwhelming small Turkish garrisons. But they were untrained and under-equipped, without cannon or machine guns, and with only ten thousand rifles, many of them antiques, for a potential force of fifty thousand. And there was no unified command or central strategy, even for such mundane matters as feeding or paying the troops. It was a case of every tribe for itself. After three months, the revolt was falling apart.

The British sent a three-man mission down the Red Sea to Hussein at Jiddah hoping to shake things up. The mission was headed by Sir Ronald Storrs, a senior official in the Egyptian administration, and Colonel C. E. Wilson. Lawrence accompanied them as a combination note taker and linguist. Hussein was courteous but vague. The trio called on Ali, Hussein's eldest son, and his second son, Abdullah. The meetings were full of bombast but with little result. Then they traveled 100 miles (161 km) deep into the desert where the third son, Faişal, was already fighting. Lawrence, whose words were being more and more listened to by Storrs and Wilson, immediately sized up Faişal as the most capable leader. Lawrence returned briefly to Cairo, then back to Faişal's camp as Britain's designated adviser to the revolt. One of his first moves was to shed his uniform and again adopt Arab dress; Faişal said he did not want a uniformed British officer seen at his camp, and Lawrence was only too willing to oblige. Thereafter the two men were full partners, with Lawrence developing strategy and Faişal directing the fighting on the ground, usually through subordinates.

Lawrence had neither military training nor experience, but he recognized that the tribesmen could not hope to stand up in a set-piece battle against the superior firepower and organization of the German-trained and disciplined Turks. Instead,

**Sir Ronald Storrs headed a special British mission to Arab tribal leaders, with Lawrence as an aide.** Library of Congress

**Sheik Faişal teamed up with Lawrence to lead successful Arab revolt of 1916–1918. Faisal later became king of newly-established Iraq.**
Library of Congress

he preached hit-and-run raiding against Turkish supplies and installations, the kind of fast-moving in-and-out guerrilla warfare the tribesmen had long practiced. Defeating the Turkish army on the battlefield was not the objective. The body count was unimportant.

"The death of a Turkish bridge or rail, or machine or gun or charge of high explosive is more profitable to us than the death of a single Turk," he declared. Moreover, attacks on the railway or supply depots would compel the Turks to transfer combat troops to guard duty and thus reduce their battle effectiveness. He made the Hejaz Railway, the Turkish main supply route, the primary target. Almost every day, a stretch of track was booby-trapped and wrecked. Lawrence himself planted some of the pressure-sensitive explosives and watched delightedly as locomotives smashed into the torn-up rails and careened into the desert, sabotaging a load of supplies for the large Turkish stronghold at Medina.

But the Turks in Hejaz could still be supplied by sea, so he led Faişal's force in an attack on the small Red Sea port of Wejh, and after three days of fighting the garrison capitulated. That left only one key port in Turkish hands: Aqaba. Aqaba must be neutralized if the British were to push north to Gaza, Jerusalem, and Damascus in Syria. It could not be left behind as a potential dagger in the British back. And Aqaba was protected from land attack by the intolerable heat and emptiness of the Nefudh Desert.

## LEARNING FROM THE MASTERS

But Rome had felt secure from land invasion, too, behind the bulwark of the Alps, before Hannibal and his elephants disabused them of the idea. At Oxford Lawrence had studied military thinkers such as Clausewitz, Saxe, and Hannibal. Lying in his tent one night slowly recovering from an attack of dysentery, he tried to apply their lessons to a strategy for Aqaba. The revolt had recently been joined by a tenacious warrior from the north named Auda Abu Tayi of the Howeitat tribe. Auda had come to Faiṣal to complain that fighting had been going on, and he hadn't been invited to the party. After all, in his desert-fighting career, he had personally killed twenty-eight men and captured countless others. Lawrence bonded with him immediately, seeing in the large, bearlike Auda a figure out of medieval romance.

"His mind is packed (and generally overflowing) with stories of old raids and epic poems," Lawrence described him later. And he knew the desert, having fought over virtually every square meter. He could identify every oasis and water source. With Faiṣal, the two developed a strategy. They would make a giant loop around Aqaba, feigning a northward assault toward Damascus, and then swoop down the narrow Wadi Sirhan toward the sea, approaching Aqaba from behind.

Nearly two months passed before the fighters were in place on the arid terrain above the port, the time spent in rallying other tribes to the revolt. They were joined by another legendary warrior, Sherif Nasir of Medina, who now shared command with Lawrence and Auda. After repeated stops for feasting designed to enlist other tribes, Lawrence grew edgy over the seemingly slow pace. One day in early July 1917, he and Nasir were resting near a muddy pool when Auda rode up. The big man smiled, scanned the position, and asked Lawrence, who had criticized his tribe earlier, "What do you think of the Howeitat now?" Annoyed, Lawrence shot back, "By God, indeed they shoot a lot and hit a little." Auda was enraged at the insult. He tore off his headdress, threw it to the ground, and raced off toward his men. "Get your camel if you want to see an old man's work," he flung back over his shoulder. Lawrence reached the hilltop just in time to see Auda's fifty Howeitat horsemen pounding down the valley toward the Turkish position. Minutes later, the four hundred men of the camelry followed, racing (according to Lawrence's estimate) at 30 miles (48 km) an hour.

In the David Lean Academy Award–winning film *Lawrence of Arabia*, the majestic charge is mistakenly shown to have been directed at Aqaba itself. In fact, the assault targeted Abu el Lissal, halfway down the slope, where the Turks had built a blockhouse and entrenchments against attack from the sea. Abu el Lissal was actually stronger than usual, a Turkish relief column having come that day to replace the garrison. Nonetheless, the combination of fifty horsemen in front and four hundred camels on their flank overwhelmed the Turks, especially

Helmeted Turkish infantry move across the desert to confront British and Arab allies. Well-equipped and German-trained, Turks were frequently outflanked by Arab hit-and-run tactics. Getty Images

since their entrenchments protected them only from the front, not the flank or rear. Opposition crumpled in a few minutes. It was a complete slaughter by the vengeance-seeking Arabs. Three hundred Turks were killed and another 150 taken prisoner, most of them wounded. The next day the Aqaba garrison troops emerged, hands upraised in surrender.

The capture of Aqaba was the turning point of the Arab Revolt—and the beginning of the Lawrence legend.

## BETRAYAL

In September 1917, a new British commander, Edmund Allenby, arrived in the Middle East from the Western Front, where he had been nicknamed "the Bull" for his formidable presence and forceful offensive tactics. Unlike his predecessor, he quickly accepted Lawrence and his Arab irregulars. They formed the right flank of Allenby's army as the British moved northward toward Damascus. By Christmas 1917 they had taken Jerusalem, and in September 1918 Lawrence and the Arabs triumphantly rode into Damascus at Allenby's side to accept the Turkish surrender. Although the war officially continued until November, it effectively ended in the Middle East with the fall of Damascus.

Lawrence felt betrayed by the ending. He had convinced Faişal and the other Arab leaders that they were fighting for their own freedom, not on behalf of imperial powers. Instead, at the Versailles peace conference, where Lawrence sat at Faişal's side as his adviser, the Middle East was carved up between Britain and France, under the guise of League of Nations mandates. Despite its Arab population, Palestine was set aside as a homeland for the Jews.

Lawrence was maddened by the results. He went back to Oxford to write a memoir, *Seven Pillars of Wisdom*. He collaborated with the American journalist Lowell Thomas on Thomas's book, *With Lawrence in Arabia*. The book sold five million copies and made him an international celebrity. To avoid the spotlight he signed up for the Royal Air Force under the name "John Hume Ross." Aircraftman Ross served nearly a year before his true identity was revealed.

Instead of the bicycles of his boyhood, he took up motorcycling, roaring around the narrow roads in the Oxfordshire hills. On May 13, 1935, returning from a post office errand, he came over a rise to see two young delivery boys on bicycles ahead. He swerved, clipped one, and spilled to the ground, his head heavily hitting the pavement. He lay in a coma for six days and died on May 19, aged forty-six. His father had died of pneumonia while "T. E." was attending the Versailles peace conference, but his mother outlived all five sons, dying in 1951 at the age of ninety-eight. He was buried two days after his death, amid elaborate mourning. Winston Churchill read the eulogy for the illegitimate youth who had made a name for himself half a world away, declaring:

"We shall never see his like again . . . His name will live in history. It will live in the annals of war. It will live in the legends of Arabia."

# CHAPTER 13

# BILLIE HOLIDAY

## HOW A PARENTLESS AND POVERTY-STRICKEN CHILD BECAME A JAZZ LEGEND
## 1915-1959

BILLIE HOLIDAY'S CHILDHOOD WAS MARKED BY PARENTAL
REJECTION, HARDSHIP, A SUCCESSION OF CARETAKERS,
AND PROSTITUTION. YET, HOLIDAY EVENTUALLY CHANNELED
HER PAIN AND SORROW INTO SONG TO EMERGE AS ONE OF THE
GREATEST JAZZ SINGERS OF THE TWENTIETH CENTURY.

ALICE DEAN COUNTED OUT A HANDFUL OF COINS FOR HER YOUNGEST
employee, twelve-year-old Billie Holiday. The madam of a Baltimore brothel, Dean had hired
the girl to help keep her "sporting house" clean. She also sent Billie out to pick up groceries and
various sundries for the women who worked in the brothel.

Billie's work was done, but the girl refused to accept her pay, gently dropping the coins back
into Dean's hand. The madam was confused. Dean had a collection of jazz records in the parlor,
along with a wind-up Victrola. In lieu of her pay, Billie asked if she could stay for a while in the
parlor, playing Louis Armstrong and Bessie Smith records. Amused by the girl's request, and
happy to save on a salary, Dean agreed. Billie retired to the parlor, where she sat, wide-eyed, on
the floor, listening raptly to Armstrong's freewheeling skat and Smith's honeyed voice. Billie fell
in love with the music, and with the way it made her feel.

Years later, she recalled, "Sometimes the record would make me so sad I'd cry up a storm.
Other times the damn record would make me so happy I'd forget about how much hard-earned
money the session in the parlor was costing me."

While still a child, Billie Holiday experienced more hardships than many do in a lifetime. She was
raped, sent to reform school, turned tricks in a brothel, and served time in New York workhouse.
Holiday channeled her pain into her music.

**1915:**

**April 7** Is born Eleanora Harris in Philadelphia. Mother is Sara "Sadie" Harris, who worked as a maid, and father is Charles Fagan, a grocery boy training as a musician, who abandons her as an infant.

**1926:**

Is raped by neighbor Wilbert Rich, who is sentenced to three months in jail. Eleven year-old Holiday is returned to Catholic-run school until 1927.

**1930:**

Arrested for prostitution at age fourteen and sentenced to four months at New York's Welfare Island.

**1933:**

Records her first record, "Your mother's Son-in-Law" with Benny Goodman Orchestra.

**1925:**

Is sent to reform school for truancy for nine months. Lacking parental supervision, she drops out of school permanently.

**1929:**

Moves to New York with her mother, where she starts working as a prostitute.

**1931:**

Begins singing at a variety of Harlem jazz clubs.

**1937:**

Is nicknamed "Lady Day" by saxophonist and lifelong friend Lester Young.

From the time she was an infant, Holiday was shuttled between households, raised by a revolving cast of relatives. Her mother worked frequently and took jobs out of state; her father spent much of the year touring with a band and showed little interest in her. Holiday channeled the pain of a life filled with rejection, loneliness, despair, and yearning into her music. Her voice could touch—and break—the hearts of those who heard her sing. Filled with sorrow and longing, it was a voice born from a hardscrabble life and the trauma of illegitimacy.

## FROM THE TIME SHE WAS AN INFANT, HOLIDAY WAS SHUTTLED BETWEEN HOUSEHOLDS, RAISED BY A REVOLVING CAST OF RELATIVES.

She moved frequently; she made friends, but had to leave them behind when her mother uprooted her to another neighborhood. Billie became a loner, playing in the street by herself, or working to help support her mother. She babysat for neighbors, scrubbed steps, and ran errands for money. "Always working at some job or another, I never had a chance to play with dolls like other kids," she recalled as an adult.

All her life, she searched for love, and for a father figure to protect and shelter her from a cold, hard world. Her pain is palpable in all her songs, especially the last one she wrote. In "Left Alone," Holiday notes:

**1938:**
Tours with the Artie Shaw orchestra, becoming one of the first black singers to perform with an all-white band.

**1941:**
Marries trombonist Jimmie Monroe.

**1956:**
Publishes her autobiography *Lady Sings the Blues*, which is later made into a movie starring Diana Ross.

**1959:**
Gives her last performance in New York City.

**July 17** Dies of heart failure.

**1939:**
Records two of her best-known songs, "God Bless the Child," and "Strange Fruit," the latter about the lynching of African-Americans.

**1947:**
Is found guilty of drug possession, and sentenced to a year and a day in prison.

**1957:**
Marries Louis McKay, a man with alleged ties to organized crime.

**2000:**
Is inducted into the Rock and Roll Hall of Fame.

Maybe fate has let him pass me by

Or perhaps we'll meet before I die.

Hearts will open, but until then,

I'm left alone, all alone.

## A LEGACY OF ILLEGITIMACY

In 1915 Sara "Sadie" Harris was nineteen years old and single when she gave birth to the child who would go on to become one of the most celebrated singers in history. Harris herself had been an illegitimate child. Her father, Charles Fagan, abandoned her when she was an infant. He spurned her mother, Sussie Harris, and married another woman when Harris was a toddler. His new wife did her best to keep the child out of Fagan's life. His parents and siblings were equally cold to Sadie and Sussie, whom they considered low class.

The rejection by her father and his family was extremely painful for Sadie. She yearned for his acceptance and support. When her father converted to Catholicism, Harris followed suit, in an effort to draw closer to him. Fagan worked a variety of jobs, including operating an elevator. His diligence allowed him and his wife to enjoy a comfortable lifestyle. Harris and her mother, however, struggled to eke out a living. It was a pattern Harris would repeat with her own daughter.

Harris was working as a maid in Baltimore when she met Clarence Holiday, a sixteen-year-old grocery delivery boy who was training to become a musician. Harris was short and pretty; Holiday was young and handsome and had no intention of settling down. Years later, he would brag about "stealing" Harris's virginity. The relationship resulted in pregnancy.

Shortly afterward, Harris secured transportation employment that took her to Philadelphia. At the time, it was common for wealthy white Northern families to pay Southern black women transportation fees and a salary to work in their homes as domestic servants. It wasn't long before Harris's pregnancy began to show. Her employers promptly fired her and ordered her to vacate the premises. Homeless, unwed, and pregnant, Harris brokered a deal with Philadelphia General Hospital. In exchange for cleaning the floors and washing the windows, she was given a bed and obstetric care.

On April 7, 1915, Harris gave birth to a daughter. She named her Eleanora—a name the child would trade for Billie. Weeks later, Harris shipped the baby off to live with her half-sister Eva and her new husband, Robert Miller, back in Baltimore. They in turn handed Billie off to Miller's mother, Martha. It was Martha Miller who raised the future jazz singer for the first years of her life. Clarence Holiday stopped by a few times to visit his daughter, but the young man, still in his teens, was more interested in pursuing a musical career than being a father. When World War I broke out, he was drafted and sent oversees for two years.

Holiday returned to the United States in 1919 and resumed his musical training. He got booked by a touring band and left Baltimore. The following year, Harris, now back in Baltimore, married Philip Gough. Billie went to live with the couple. She thrived in the family atmosphere. "I was happy for a little bit," Billie later recalled. The happiness came to an end three years later. "He was a good stepdaddy to me as long as he lived, which was only for a little while," Billie said. In fact, Gough did not die, but deserted Sadie and her child. It is unclear whether Billie knew the truth. In any case, she was left without a father figure once again.

## REFORM SCHOOL AND RECORDS

Harris, as she would do throughout Billie's childhood, left town and left the girl in the care of Martha Miller. Billie was fond Miller, whom she called "grandmother," but she missed her parents terribly, and feeling unwanted, she began to act out. The child skipped school, used foul language, and shoplifted socks and trinkets from a local five-and-dime store. Billie "was neglected by her mother," her cousin Evelyn recalled. "She left her all the time and that was the problem. The child had an attitude, I guess from being neglected."

Clarence Holiday saw the child a few times a year, on those occasions when his band played in Baltimore. Billie adored him, but Clarence, an up and coming jazz guitarist, seemed indifferent to his daughter. Billie began skipping school on a regular basis when she was eight years old.

Truant officer Anna Dawson pleaded with the girl to attend school, explaining that she was headed for trouble. Her attempts to reform Billie failed. Despite her intervention on Billie's behalf, the child was ordered to juvenile court, where a judge, noting her absentee parents, declared her "a minor without proper care and guardianship." She was sent to the House of the Good Shepherd for Colored Girls, an institution run by the Catholic Church. The constant supervision and regular routine had a good effect on the young girl. Billie grew close to one of the nuns working at the institution. Sister Margaret Touhe was a caring woman who encouraged Billie to complete her studies, and more significantly, to sing for her classmates. It was while at Good Shepherd that Billie was baptized. "She was so happy, poor child," recalled a Good Shepherd staff member. "She was in there with the rest of the girls, all of them in white dresses and veils; she was grinning from ear to ear . . . the Sisters gave her Mary rosary beads. She was so tickled."

Nine months later, in October 1925, Billie was released into Harris's care. Forced to support herself and her daughter, the single mother resumed her pattern of leaving Billie with relatives and friends of the family. Lacking real supervision, the child dropped out of the fifth grade; it was the highest level of education she would complete. "School never appealed to me," she said years later.

In the winter of 1926, Harris was back in town. She and Billie lived together in an apartment in a rundown section of Baltimore. On Christmas Eve, 1926, Harris returned home, after a night on the town with a boyfriend, to find her neighbor Wilbert Rich sexually assaulting eleven-year-old Billie. She called the police. Rich was arrested and sentenced to a mere three months in jail. Billie, however, was sent back to the House of the Good Shepherd for Colored Girls, where she was ordered to remain until she was twenty-one. Although it was obviously unfair for the court to punish the victim, Billie would most likely have received better care under the guardianship of the Sisters of the Good Shepherd. Harris visited her father Charles Fagan and managed to enlist his help (and

financial support) in obtaining a lawyer for Billie. The child was released back into her care in February 1927.

Harris ran a restaurant out of their apartment, where she served home-cooked beans, collard greens, and pigs' feet to some of the city's more colorful residents. Her customers, who arrived at all hours, included hustlers, musicians, entertainers, and various ne'er-do-wells. It was here that Billie met up with Alice Dean, the madam of a local brothel. Dean hired Billie to scrub the steps of the brothel and run errands. Billie was big for her age; she was a pretty girl, and already well developed. She looked several years older than she was.

Biographers speculate that Billie may have done more than run errands for Dean. Some contend that the twelve-year-old worked as a "pretty baby," a very young prostitute who appealed to customers with a predilection for pre-teen girls. Holiday was busted for prostitution several times in her life, the first arrest occurring when she was fourteen.

## HARLEM NIGHTS

Around 1929, Billie relocated to New York, where Harris was then living. Domestic work was one of the few areas of employment open to African American women at the time. Harris found work as maids for both of them. Billie wasn't interested, declaring, "I ain't gonna be no maid." Instead, she went to work for legendary Harlem madam Florence Williams. This time Billie was certainly turning tricks. "In a matter of days, I had my chance to become a strictly twenty-dollar call girl. And I took it," she recalled in her autobiography.

She was just fourteen when she was arrested during a raid on the brothel. Harris lied in court about Billie's age, telling the judge her daughter was twenty one to save her from being sent to a reformatory school. Billie was sentenced to 100 days in a workhouse on Blackwell's Island (today known as Roosevelt Island), located in the East River of New York City.

Upon her release, Billie began to search for work as a performer in one of the many nightclubs and speakeasies that populated Harlem. She was deter-

**Billie Holiday's poise and penchant for feathers, flowers, and finery inspired her close friend, musician Lester Young, to nickname her "Lady Day."** Redferns / Getty Images

mined to make a living as a singer. She was also fortunate to be living in Harlem, home to a burgeoning and exciting music scene. Billie found work as a singer in a variety of nightclubs. In one of these, a club called Monette's, Billie caught the eye—and ear—of record producer John Hammond.

"She had an uncanny ear, an excellent memory for lyrics, and she sang with an exquisite sense of phrasing," Hammond said. "I had found a star." The country was in the midst of the Great Depression, and financially strapped record companies were unwilling, and unable, to take a chance on recording a new, unknown artist. Hammond was frustrated but convinced that Billie, "the best jazz singer" he had ever heard, was destined for musical success.

## THE BIRTH OF BILLIE HOLIDAY

By then, Billie had taken on her now-famous first name. "My name, Eleanora, was too damn long for anyone to say," she said. "Besides, I never liked it." The screen actress Billie Dove inspired her new moniker. "I was crazy for her," Holiday said. "I tried to do my hair like her and eventually I borrowed her name." She also took her father's surname, a bold move that earned his ire.

As a featured guitarist and banjo player in the Fletcher Henderson band, Clarence Holiday frequently played clubs in Harlem. Billie sought him out, sometimes going to his shows. When money was tight, she would ask him for a handout. Financially, Holiday had been a deadbeat dad, leaving Harris to support their child on her own. He wasn't inclined to part with his money now that Billie was a teenager, but only did so to get rid of her. He felt Billie was bad for his image and didn't want her hanging around him. "Please, whatever you do, don't call me Daddy in front of these people," he told her. "I'm going to call you Daddy all night unless you give me some damn money for rent," retorted Billie.

John Hammond knew Clarence Holiday and was delighted to learn that the amazing new singer on the scene was his daughter. Holiday was less enthused, telling Hammond, "For Christ's sake, don't talk about Billie in front of all the guys," he told him. "They'll think I was old. She was something I stole when I

**Establishments like the Cotton Club were immensely popular with wealthy white patrons who flocked to Harlem on weekends to listen to live music, usually performed by black artists.**

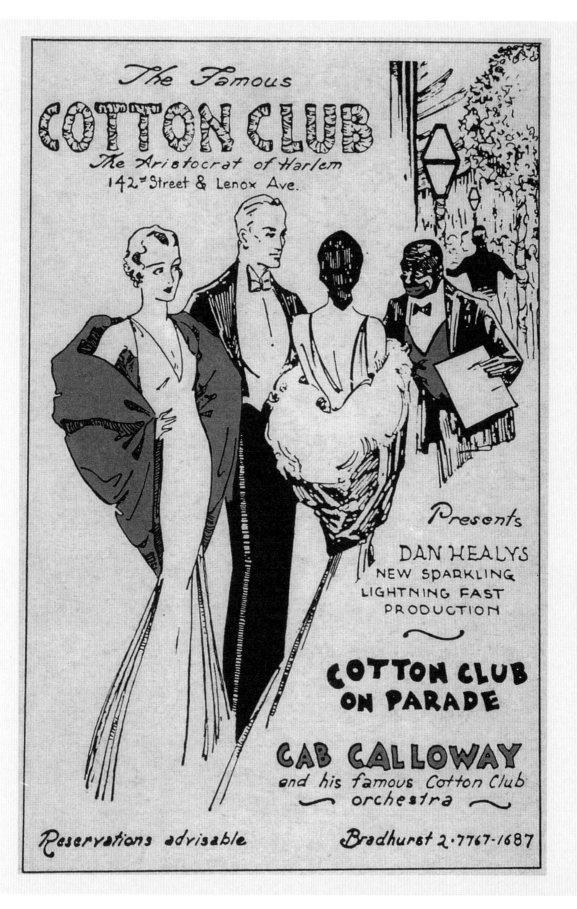

was fourteen," Holiday said. Years later, Hammond wrote, "I didn't know what 'stole' meant. I had never heard a parent referring to a child with so much contempt and horror. So I knew there was no relationship between them."

With Hammond's help, Billie recorded her first song, "Your Mother's Son-in-Law," with the famed Benny Goodman orchestra. Goodman was impressed by Billie and hired her as a vocalist for his band. One of the first black singers to work with a white band, Billie broke racial barriers, and as a result gained many white fans, including actors Paul Muni and Charles Laughton. She went on to record with Count Basie, Artie Shaw, and Lester Young, a gifted sax player who christened her "Lady Day." Billie nicknamed him the "Pres." The two remained lifelong friends.

In 1939, Billie Holiday recorded two of her best-known songs. "God Bless the Child," which she also wrote, was inspired by her own childhood. The song, a paean to self-reliance, includes the lyrics "God bless the child that's got his own/He just worry 'bout nothin' cause he's got his own."

Based on a poem written by a white Jewish schoolteacher, "Strange Fruit" told the story of the lynching of an African American man. "Strange fruit" was a metaphor for the swinging bodies of black lynching victims. It was a powerful, haunting, provocative song; it also broke new ground musically. Holiday referred to it as a "personal protest" against the evils of racism. Alarmed by the subject matter, and worried about a potential backlash from Southern retailers, Columbia Records refused to record "Strange Fruit." But Billie was determined. Eventually, Commodore Records agreed to record it. The song became one of Billie's hallmarks. Decades after it was recorded, *Time* magazine dubbed "Strange Fruit" the "song of the century."

"The first time I sang it, I thought it was a mistake," Holiday said. "There wasn't even a patter of applause when I finished. Then a lone person began to clap nervously. Then suddenly everyone was clapping and cheering." According to scholar and political activist Angela Davis, the song "almost single-handedly changed the politics of American popular culture and put the elements of protest and resistance back at the center of contemporary black musical tradition."

**Saxophonist Lester Young and Billie Holiday were kindred spirits who remained lifelong friends. Holiday referred to Young as the "President of the Tenor Saxophonists."** Getty Images

## HEARTBREAK, ABUSE, AND ADDICTION

After being rejected by her father one too many times, Billie finally gave up on Clarence Holiday. Of course, once her fame eclipsed his, Holiday began boasting that she inherited her talent from him. His crowing was too little, too late. During her career, Billie hired hundreds of musicians—and nearly every guitarist in Harlem—except her father. He was bitter about this slight, conveniently forgetting how he had abandoned Billie as a child. For Billie it was a form of payback.

Professionally, Billie's star was on the rise. Her personal life, however, was rife with heartbreak and disappointment. She seemed desperate for someone to love and accept her. She was drinking heavily, and she developed an addiction to heroin. Billie carried on a string of love affairs, each one more disastrous than the last. Her lovers, several of whom were female, preyed on her insecurities. They also drained her growing bank account. She married trombonist Jimmie Monroe in 1941 but left him for another musician, trumpet player Joe Guy.

In 1947, Billie Holiday was tried and found guilty of drug possession. She was sentenced to a year and a day in West Virginia's Federal Reformatory for Women. The drug treatment the judge promised Billie would receive was not forthcoming. Billie quit heroin cold turkey, sweating and writhing in agony on a thin mattress in her cell for nearly three weeks. When she recovered, she was assigned prison cleaning duties. The facility was made up of a half dozen buildings, each housing fifty women. Holiday washed the floors and windows and kept the prison tidy.

She refused to sing, even when the warden asked her to participate in the prison talent show. "The whole basis of my singing is feeling. In the whole time I was there, I didn't feel a thing," Holiday said. A model prisoner, Holiday was granted early release after eight months. Her manager arranged for her to sing at Carnegie Hall two weeks later. According to a music critic for *Down Beat* magazine, she received "one of the most thunderous ovations ever given a performer in this or any other hall."

In 1957, Billie married Louis McKay, a man with alleged ties to organized crime. McKay tried his best to help his new wife stay off drugs. He wasn't suc-

**Billie Holiday began abusing drugs and alcohol in the early 1940s; she developed a heroin addiction that would plague for the rest of her life. In 1947, Holiday was sentenced to a year and a day in a West Virginia jail for drug possession.**

cessful. Billie continued in a sad downward spiral. Her dreams of having a loving, supportive family died with her parents. She was depressed and unable to kick her heroin addiction.

Billie Holiday gave her last concert in Manhattan in May 1959. Two months later, on July 17, she died in Metropolitan Hospital while under arrest for drug possession. She was forty-four years old. Doctors attributed her death to lung congestion and heart failure.

All her life she longed to be loved, never realizing that she was beloved by everyone who heard her sing. Fifty years after her untimely demise, her voice continues to captivate and deeply move listeners. In his autobiography, President Barack Obama described the first time he heard her sing: "Beneath the layers of hurt, beneath the ragged laughter, I heard a willingness to endure . . . and make music that wasn't there before."

In 1972, Diana Ross portrayed Billie in the film version of her life story, *Lady Sings the Blues*. Holiday influenced countless singers, from Ella Fitzgerald to Frank Sinatra, Peggy Lee, Nina Simone, and Janis Joplin. In 2000, Billie Holiday was inducted into the Rock and Roll Hall of Fame. She remains a seminal figure in jazz music.

**One of the first African American singers to perform with an all-white band, Billie Holiday broke down racial barriers in the music industry. Offstage and on the road however, she experienced discrimination because of her color.** Redferns / Getty Images

# CHAPTER 14

# EVA PERÓN

## A STRUGGLING ACTRESS REMAKES HERSELF INTO A CULTURAL ICON
## 1919-1952

**SHE BEGAN LIFE POOR, PLAIN, AND ILLEGITIMATE. AN IRON WILL, RELENTLESS AMBITION, AND HER OWN SEXUALITY TRANSFORMED HERSELF INTO THE WEALTHY, GLAMOROUS, AND CONTROVERSIAL FIRST LADY OF ARGENTINA.**

THEY WAITED OUTSIDE FOR HOURS, FILLING THE STREETS IN THE CENTER of Buenos Aires. It was spring 1944, and the weather in the capital of Argentina was perfect. The women stood shoulder to shoulder, clasping the hands of their small children. The men gathered on the sidelines, smoking cigarettes and feigning disinterest. The soft rumble of a pair of automobiles filled the air.

An excited murmur spread through the crowd as two sleek, freshly polished black sedans approached. Four military officers exited the first car and approached the second, out of which emerged Juan Perón, the handsome secretary of labor. At forty-eight, he cut a dashing figure in his crisp uniform. He carried himself with an air of relaxed authority. His power was evident in the way he walked and in the deferential way the officers treated him.

"You are very popular, sir," one of the officers said. "The people love Perón." It was true: Juan Perón's popularity was growing, a fact that pleased the man who aspired to be president of this southern South American country. However, he was fully aware that the crowd was not there for him. No, they were there to see Evita. Their intense affection for his lover was unprecedented. Evita's brilliant success with the poor and the working class pleased him. A vain man, Perón thought of Evita as his creation, and as creator, he basked in her reflected glory. Without

**Born in a rural town and raised in poverty by a single, unmarried mother, Eva Perón carved out her own destiny—and a place in history when she became Argentina's First Lady.** The Granger Collection, New York

him, the twenty-four-year-old would still be a struggling actress. Of course, Evita viewed her success much differently.

The crowd surged forward, pushing, craning their necks for a closer look. And then suddenly, she emerged, slipping from the darkness of the car into the night air. Her golden hair, pinned up to resemble a conch shell, glistened under the street lamps. Perón moved aside, allowing the crowd an unobstructed view of Evita. Women cried out, children sung out her name. Perón grinned broadly, clearly enjoying the effect his lover had on the Argentine people.

As they called out her name and reached forward to touch her hands, it was clear that she belonged not to this proud, powerful man, but to them, the people. The officers gently pushed the crowd back. But Evita was not afraid. She waved, and then bowed deferentially to the crowd.

Evita's clothes were a stark contrast to the threadbare rags worn by many of the people who called out to her. Her gown, custom designed and created, rivaled that of any Hollywood movie star. A string of precious gems embraced her neck. The shoes that adorned her feet, and raised her height several inches above her five-and-a-half feet, were handmade from the finest Italian leather. Those shoes cost more than some Argentines made in a year.

Yet, rather than begrudge Evita these excesses, the crowd cheered its approval. She hailed from humble origins, just like they did. When she draped herself in furs and jewels and donned the latest European fashions, she did it

**1948:**
Creates the Maria Eva Duarte de Perón Foundation, an Argentine charity.

**1951:**
Helps secure women the right to vote in a national election.

Accepts the nomination for the office of vice president, but withdraws due to military opposition.

**1955:**
Perón is overthrown. Anti-Perónists steal Eva Perón's remains and hide them in Italy.

**1947:**
Lobbies for suffrage for Argentine women.

**1949:**
Forms the Perónista Feminist Party.

**1952:**
Is given the title "Spiritual Leader of the Nation" by Argentine Congress.

**July 26** Dies from ovarian cancer. Mourning lasts two weeks in Argentina.

**1974:**
Perón, back in office, dies. His third wife repatriates Eva Perón's remains and has them buried next to her husband's in a crypt in the presidential palace.

as much for them as for herself. She represented them—having been born poor and raised in the most unpretentious circumstances. Her success was their success, and they wanted her to look every bit as glamorous as she did. No one understood this better than Eva herself.

Despite her dazzling appearance and the adoration of the common people, Evita was persona non grata with many Argentines. In hopes that her beauty and haute couture would gain her acceptance by the oligarchy—the elite group of Argentines that ran country—Juan Perón had spared no expense on Evita's wardrobe that night. But they openly snubbed her. They saw her as common, an illegitimate girl from the rural Pampas—worse still, as a social-climbing actress who used sex to gain entrance into the most vaunted circles.

Evita was not ashamed that she had escaped a life of insignificance and obscurity. She held her head high and continued to appear at Perón's side, as if she had every right to be there. If the oligarchy thought she would simply go away, they were terribly wrong. If Evita could not make the upper classes love her, then she would do without their love. And she would make them pay.

## HARDSHIP AND HUMBLE BEGINNINGS

Evita came into the world on May 7, 1919. Named María Eva Duarte, she was the youngest of five illegitimate children born to Juana Ibarguren and Juan Duarte, a wealthy, married man who maintained another, legitimate family in another

town. The Ibarguren-Duarte family lived in a small house on the ranch that Juan Duarte operated on the Pampas, the vast fertile Argentine plains near the rural village of Los Toldos. They lived like any other family, if not a little better, as the income Duarte earned from the ranch enabled him to buy his children good, leather shoes. Most children in the area wore espadrilles. Straw-soled, fabric shoes with fabric ankle ties, espadrilles were the shoes of the lower classes.

Eva was a small child who often accompanied Duarte as he made his rounds on the ranch. He hoisted her high on his shoulders, providing her with an unobstructed view of the vast Pampas. Juana was a heavy-set, voluptuous woman who viewed herself as a wife, not a mistress. The children had the run of the ranch and considered their family to be like any other. Their contentment was shattered with the arrival of the real Mrs. Duarte. While she visited her husband, Juana was relegated to the role of a cook, and the children were ordered to remain out of sight.

Not long after that visit, Juan Duarte returned to his legal family, leaving Juana and the children destitute. Forced to vacate the ranch, they moved into a one-room apartment in a rundown part of a nearby town, Junín. Juana did her best to support her large brood, working as a maid during the day and making alterations on her sewing machine at night for money. Sometimes she would hint that Duarte would be back. In fact, the family would never see him alive again.

Although they were poor, Juana kept her children well dressed and well scrubbed. She was vigilant about their appearances and made all their clothes herself. They outgrew the leather shoes Duarte bought them and now wore espadrilles instead.

In Junín, people stared whenever the Ibarguren-Duarte family passed by. Many of the townspeople shunned them. Some children were forbidden from playing with Eva and her siblings. A classmate told Eva it was because of Juana. A rumor spread through town that Eva's grandmother had sold Juana to Duarte, like one sells a horse to a rancher, or a cow to a farmer. In school one day, two classmates teased Eva and her sister Erminda about their last name. "You're not

**Eva never forgot her roots. As First Lady, she expressed a deep affection and understanding for the poor and underprivileged classes known as los descamisados—who in turn, adored her. She helped enact social welfare programs to support the indigent and her suffrage campaign was instrumental in winning women the right to vote.** AFP/Getty Images

really Duartes," the girls said. Eva didn't understand. Later, her brother Juancito explained their illegitimacy to her. Seven-year-old Eva had trouble sleeping that night. She curled up on her side listening to the hum of her mother's sewing machine and wondering whether what Juancito had told her was true.

Eva was quiet and well behaved, though she resented her humble home, her espadrilles, and the way the townspeople whispered about her family. She spent hours poring over glossy star magazines. She loved the Hollywood style and fantasized about becoming a movie star. Canadian-born Norma Shearer was her favorite actress. Eva knew she was special—but no one else seemed to notice this. She knew that one day the world would see how special she was. She would wear the latest fashions and the best leather shoes, and walk with her head held high.

She was seven when Juan Duarte died. Juana felt it was their duty—and their right—to attend his funeral. Juana dressed in black, like a widow, and shepherded her children to Duarte's house in time for the funeral. Eva and her siblings stared at the palatial home in awe. Juana knocked on the door. A woman answered and began yelling. Frightened, Eva hid behind her mother. A man with a hard face gently ushered the woman back inside. He told Juana she alone could come inside to view the body. He seemed to look through the children as if they were glass. Absently brushing Eva's hand from her leg, Juana followed the man, leaving her children outside waiting on the doorstep.

Eva heard raised voices inside the house and then wailing. Juana left the house a few minutes later, her posture erect and proud, her eyes red and swollen. Eva knew she had been crying. The Ibarguren-Duarte family waited outside, like beggars, for what seemed like hours. Finally, the people inside the house emerged. A few of them stared at Eva's family with angry eyes. There were children, too; Eva would later learn that these were her half-siblings. The man who had closed the door on them spoke to Juana in hurried, hushed tones. Juana nodded silently.

Several men carried out a coffin. Juancito told Eva that their father was inside the coffin. Eva was silent. She had little memory of her father. But seeing her mother and sisters cry made her cry, too. She and her sister Erminda huddled together, wishing they were elsewhere.

Eva was not sure which was worse—being stared at by angry eyes or being invisible. She had trouble understanding the business of adults, but she did know that these rich people hated her mother, Eva, and her siblings. The strangers scared her, but they also made her angry. Eva's clothes were homemade, but she was just as good as these people in the fancy house.

Even at that age, she had a keen awareness of the injustice of their situation.

Decades later, she recounted the ordeal in her autobiography. "I remember very well that I was sad for many days when it occurred to me that in the world there were poor and there were rich; and the strange thing is that it was not so much the existence of the poor that made me sorry as the knowledge that there were rich at the same time."

**DETERMINED TO REMAKE HERSELF AND TRANSCEND HER CLASS, EVA NEVER FORGOT HER BEGINNINGS AND MADE IT HER PRIORITY TO HELP THE LOWER CLASSES WHEN SHE BECAME FIRST LADY OF ARGENTINA.**

Eva was unsettled that some people could have so much while others had so little. The inequality rankled her. Determined to remake herself and transcend her class, she never forgot her beginnings and made it her priority to help the lower classes when she became first lady of Argentina.

## A TINY GIRL WITH BIG DREAMS

With Eva's older siblings working and pitching in financially, the family was able to move into a small house in a better section of town. Money was still tight, and to make ends meet, Juana began taking single male borders in. Eva tried to ignore the whispers of peers and townspeople, who said her mother did more than cook for these men. It hurt Eva to hear such talk, and she felt deeply ashamed—of her mother and of herself, for being Juana's daughter. These feelings aroused a sense of guilt in the young girl. Juana worked so hard to support the family; Eva knew she should be thankful to have a roof over her head. She was conflicted: She loved her mother, and she was embarrassed of her.

In the rural towns and villages, most girls stayed at home, married local boys, and repeated the pattern their parents had established. Eva was not like these girls; a mundane life in a small town was not good enough for her. She was afraid of spending her life in obscurity. The images in the Hollywood maga-

zines she pored over filled her head. Eva dreamed of wearing glittering designer gowns, hobnobbing with movie stars, and leading a life of pure glamour. She longed to emulate the beautiful screen goddesses she read about.

When Eva was fifteen, she left Junín for Buenos Aires. Like much of her life, the manner in which she arrived in the Argentine capital is uncertain. Several biographers contend that the teenager hooked up with a much older, married singer named Agustín Magaldi, and that it was Magaldi who brought Eva to the big city. However, an equal number of historians argue that Eva never met Magaldi, and that she moved to Buenos Aires on her own.

Whatever the truth, within a year Eva was living on her own, eking out a meager living as a theater actress. Her roles were small, and most were nonspeaking. A mere slip of a girl, the brunette Eva purposely starved herself, perhaps afraid of looking, and thus becoming, like her fleshy, morally ambiguous, stout mother. Eva looked nothing like Juana, but as a young adult she followed her mother's lead and used her sexuality as a means to survive and get ahead in a strictly patriarchal society. One lover cast her in a play, another helped her land work as a print model, and yet another gave Eva her big break in radio. Every new role, every new lover, and every new connection brought her closer to her dreams.

## A MERE SLIP OF A GIRL, EVA PURPOSELY STARVED HERSELF, PERHAPS AFRAID OF LOOKING, AND THUS BECOMING, LIKE HER FLESHY, MORALLY AMBIGUOUS, STOUT MOTHER.

Eva's fortunes gradually improved. Movie stardom eluded her, but she did find success as a minor radio personality in Buenos Aires. The upper classes ridiculed her rural dialect and habit of mispronouncing words. However, her plain way of speaking endeared her to the poor and working class. Her fans loved that she spoke just like them. In 1944, Eva met Juan Perón, the newly appointed secretary of labor. The meeting—and a change in hair color—forever altered her life.

**Evita was a mediocre actress who found success as a radio host. Her slightly nasal intonation and plain way of speaking appealed to the masses; the upper classes, however, found her voice and on-air delivery distasteful and "common."**

## A MEETING OF THE MINDS

Juan Perón called her Evita, a diminutive meaning "little Eva." Evita played an increasingly prominent role in Perón's private and professional life. Within weeks of their meeting, she dispatched with his teenage mistress and moved him into an apartment next to hers.

Evita accompanied Perón everywhere, much to the chagrin of the military officers who reported to him. Argentine women were relegated to a subservient role. They could not vote and had no say in public policy. The officers objected to Evita's presence during their meetings with Juan Perón. Their objections were noted, and promptly ignored.

Besides sharing his bed, Evita also shared Perón's desire for power. Theirs was not a passionate love affair, however, but more of a meeting of the minds. She became his closest confidante and biggest supporter. Much of her radio show was now dedicated to promoting Perón and his political ideals. Evita flattered, built up, and advised Perón. He appeared to have complete trust in her. Together, they would change the face of Argentina—and, before they were done, nearly bankrupt the country.

## POWER AND PERÓNISM

Argentina in the 1940s was a political powder keg, with various factions vying for power. The population increased each year, as immigrants flocked to the South American country; fifteen million people called Argentina home in 1945. In October of that year, Juan Perón was arrested and imprisoned by rival officers who disapproved of his support of the labor unions.

Evita organized a massive pro-Perón demonstration outside the prison. She rallied the country's workers—the people whom the press and oligarchy disparagingly called *los descamisados*, "the shirtless ones." Evita recast the derogatory term in a positive light. The shirtless ones, she declared, were the real heart and soul of Argentina. Thousands strong, *los descamisados* descended on the prison, shouting, "Perón! Perón! Perón!" Their numbers and cries struck fear in Perón's captors, who released him for their own safety. From the balcony of the presidential palace, Perón greeted the demonstrators. He thanked them and pledged his undying support to the labor movement. Perón and Evita married several days later.

As a child, Evita wore simple pinafores and smocks hand-sewn by her mother. Later in life, she draped herself in dresses and gowns custom created for her by the most exclusive designers in the world, including Christian Dior.

In October of that year, Juan Perón was elected president, with strong support from the country's labor unions. He promoted his own political movement, dubbed *justicialismo*, which mixed elements of both capitalism and Communism. His style of government would become known as Peronism. Critics have likened Perónism to fascism.

Evita, the poor, illegitimate girl from the Pampas became the first lady of Argentina. She relished the role and her popularity, which surpassed that of her husband. It was ironic: The stardom that had dodged her as an actress enveloped her now that she had given up acting. In fact, she would give her greatest performances as Evita Perón. She also made those who doubted her, those who had looked down upon her in judgment, pay for their sins. Snubbed by the British during a world tour, Evita promptly cut off British imports to Argentina and ejected all British citizens from her country.

As she rose to power, Evita never forgave the oligarchy for rejecting her. Those who had turned up their noses at her found themselves on the wrong end of the law. Their businesses were confiscated, their profits distributed to the poor. In one case, several landlords had their property seized and given to the tenants whom Evita believed they had exploited. Club owners who refused her admission to their establishments found themselves investigated for political sedition. Those who dared complain faced prison, or worse. It was not uncommon for vocal critics of the Peróns to mysteriously go missing.

Evita occupied many roles in her seven years as first lady. She was a politically savvy counselor to her husband, a glamorous international star, a seductress, a mother to the people, a champion of the poor, and a living saint who worked tirelessly to protect the lower classes and promote women's rights. Through her efforts, women were given the vote, and hospitals, shelters, and charities flourished. Under Perónism laborers received better wages and more rights. But the good deeds and social reforms were eclipsed by nepotism, caprice, excess, revenge, and fascism. It was customary for the first lady to be appointed president of Sociedad de Beneficencia, a respected Argentine charity. However, the women who ran the charity disapproved of Evita and refused to offer her the position. Stung, Evita withdrew all government funding for the organization and formed her own charity instead.

Today, Evita remains the subject of much debate. Her life inspired numerous books and a hit Broadway play. Argentine writer Tomás Eloy Martínez described her as "the Cinderella of the tango and the Sleeping Beauty of Latin America."

Evita Perón died from cancer on July 26, 1952. She was thirty-two years old. An official day of mourning was declared. Buenos Aires closed down as thousands of people from all over the country flooded the streets to openly mourn the loss of the first lady. The lines to visit her body snaked for miles though the city. The mourning lasted for two weeks.

In 1955, Juan Perón was overthrown. The new government whisked Evita's corpse away in the middle of the night. Those in power worried (perhaps rightly so) that her grave would incite conflicting political passions in the people. Her body was kept in a hidden location in another country. Twenty-six years after her death, Evita was returned to Argentina. Her body lies inside a glass casket, 20 feet (6 km) under ground in a specially designed vault in Reloceta cemetery in Buenos Aires.

In her short life, Eva Duarte Perón battled poverty and the shameful stigma of illegitimacy. She emerged victorious to claim her place as one of history's most glamorous and enduring icons.

# CHAPTER 15

# FIDEL CASTRO

## AN ILLEGITIMATE CHILD SPARKS
## A REVOLUTION—AND REINVENTS A NATION
## 1926-

THE BOY WHO GREW UP TO BECOME A SWORN ENEMY OF CAPITALISM
AND A SELF-ANOINTED VOICE OF THE CUBAN PEOPLE WAS BORN
INTO WEALTH BUT OUT OF WEDLOCK. THE INCONGRUITY OF HIS
SITUATION SHAPED HIS CONTROVERSIAL VIEW OF POLITICS,
AND OF THE WORLD.

THERE WAS A STIR OF ACTIVITY IN THE LOBBY OF THE COLEGIO DOLORES in Santiago, Cuba. A cluster of boys had gathered around the bulletin board. The excitement was palpable as Fidel Castro approached the group. He was the last to arrive at school that day, a not uncommon occurrence. His classmates ran to him, all talking at once, their voices colliding as they ushered him over to the bulletin board. There, pinned proudly by a teacher for all to see, was a letter from the American President Franklin D. Roosevelt—a letter addressed to Fidel Castro! Fourteen-year-old Castro beamed and puffed up his chest.

Plucky and seemingly often overconfident, Castro secretly sought acceptance and craved attention. He carried a burden that he never discussed—a burden that his classmates whispered about behind his back. The bolder ones dared to talk about it within his earshot: Castro was illegitimate. It was a scandalous matter in a Catholic school, and in a predominantly Christian country. The scandal of his birth was temporarily upstaged by the arrival of Roosevelt's letter in the winter of 1940. That the president of the one of the most powerful countries in the world had written to Castro was a major social coup for the teenager. The prized missive was in actuality a

Fidel and Raul Castro talk politics and revolution in Havana, 1959. Nearly a half century later, Raúl Castro, known as the "softer" brother, was elected president of Cuba, after Fidel's ailing health forced him to retire.

## 1926:
**August 13** Fidel Castro is born in Birán, Cuba. His father is Angel Castro y Argiz, a Spanish immigrant, and his mother is Lina Ruz González, his father's cook. Castro grows up in relative wealth on his father's sugar plantation.

## 1941:
Is legitimized when his parents marry.

## 1948:
Marries fellow student Mirta Diaz Balart.

## 1952:
Runs for parliament, opposing Fulgencio Batista.

## 1955:
**May** Is released from prison on general amnesty, and exiled to Mexico, where he meets revolutionary Ernesto "Ché" Guevara.

Divorces Mirta Diaz Balart.

## 1940:
Receives a reply to a letter he wrote to President Franklin D. Roosevelt.

## 1945:
Enters law school at the University of Havana.

## 1950:
Receives his law degree.

## 1953:
Leads an unsuccessful armed attack on the headquarters of Batista. He is arrested, tried, found guilty, and sentenced to prison.

---

generic form letter sent by someone on Roosevelt's public relations staff. But its impact on the school was as deep as if FDR had written it himself.

Printed on official White House stationery, Roosevelt's letter thanked Castro for writing to him. Castro's schoolmates were awed by the reply from the American president. More impressive, and amusing, however, was the moxie young Castro expressed in writing to Roosevelt, and the bold request he made.

"My good friend Roosevelt," Castro wrote. "I don't know very [good] English, but I know as much as write to you. I like to hear the radio, and I am very happy, because I heard in it, that you will be president of a new period . . . I am a boy but I think very much . . . If you like, give me a ten dollars bill green American, in the letter, because never, I have not seen a ten dollars bill . . . and I would like to have one of them."

Castro told a classmate he was inspired to write to Roosevelt after reading about the American's election in the newspaper. The exchange made Castro a star at school. Castro was less enthused by the reply: Roosevelt had not sent him the ten-dollar bill he requested. Years later, when he became a thorn in the side of Roosevelt's successor, Castro joked, "[T]here are people who've told me that if Roosevelt had only sent me $10 I wouldn't have given the United States so many headaches!"

## TRUTHS AND FICTIONS

The beard, the burly stature, the military cap and fatigues, the cigars—for half a century, Fidel Castro has been the face and voice of Cuba. No political leader is

**1961:**
**April** The U.S. government secretly arms thousands of Cuban exiles to overthrow Castro's government. Castro's forces crush their landing at the Bay of Pigs.

**1965:**
Becomes first secretary of the Communist Party of Cuba, transforms Cuba into a single party socialist republic.

**1976:**
Adopts the title of President of the Council of State.

**2008:**
**February 19** Resigns as president due to ailing health. His brother Raúl takes over the presidency.

**1959:**
**January** Leads a guerilla army into Cuba and overthrows the Batista government.

**February** Becomes prime minister of Cuba.

**1962:**
The Soviet Union secretly places ballistic missiles in Cuba that could fire nuclear weapons on American cities. The world comes close to a nuclear war in the ensuing confrontation between the United States and Soviet Union. The Cuban Missile Crisis ends when the Soviet Union withdraws its nuclear weapons from Cuba in exchange for the United States removing its nuclear-armed missiles it had stationed in Turkey and no longer seeking to overthrow Castro.

**1970** (approximate):
Marries his second wife, Dalia Soto del Valle.

**1999:**
Celebrates four decades in power.

so inextricably linked to a country as Fidel Castro. His image and outsized personality are familiar to people around the world. But like many political icons, he has kept his private life far from the public eye. As a result he has been able to maintain fame—or infamy—without revealing much.

Castro is known for giving four-hour interviews and marathon speeches, including one that ran for seventeen hours. Yet for all that talking, he's never mentioned or alluded to his illegitimacy, a factor that clearly must have had a tremendous impact on him, having grown up in such a Christian country. An intelligent, curious boy, Fidel was not oblivious to the knowing glances and clucking tongues of neighbors who watched as the family continued to grow, fully aware that the lady of the house shared Angel Castro's bed but not his name. Most Cubans know very little about the man who figures so largely in their lives. His father, Angel Castro, was fond of saying, "A man is owner of his silence and prisoner of his words."

Castro has played fast and loose with the details of his life, coloring, softening, and revising events to recast himself in a more favorable light. Nowhere is Castro's revisionist history more evident than in Herbert L. Matthews's biography of him. Matthews, long deceased, was a star reporter at the *New York Times* when he was thoroughly charmed, and duped, by the Cuban leader. What Matthews believed was the truth about Castro was actually Castro's truth—reconfigured to advance his own agenda.

The biography, spoon-fed to Matthews by Castro, and Matthews's misguided admiration, effectively ruined the reporter's reputation, leaving a permanent stain on a once-stellar career. Matthews was just one of the myriad foreigners seduced by the charismatic, cunning former guerrilla leader with a knack for recasting his defeats into victories, and turning a blind eye to his personal failures. Television hosts Ed Sullivan and Jack Paar had also been taken in by Castro's charms. President Harry S. Truman would come to regret his initial description of the revolutionary leader as a "good young man trying to do what's best for Cuba."

"One thing is certain: wherever he may be, however and with whomever, Fidel Castro is there to win," said Nobel Prize–winning Colombian author Gabriel García Márquez. "I do not think anyone in this world could be a worse loser. His attitude in the face of defeat, even in the slightest events of daily life, seems to obey a private logic: he will not even admit it, and he does not have a moment's peace until he manages to invert the terms and turn it into a victory."

## CUBA'S FAMOUS SON IS BORN

Fidel Castro was born on the family sugar plantation in Birán, Cuba, in the early hours of August 13, 1926. "It was a conspiracy," he declared in his autobiography. "I was born a guerrilla, because I was born at night." He was the third child of Lina Ruz and Angel Castro; three more children were to follow. Neighbors noted the new addition to the Castro clan and gossiped about the fact that Angel Castro was still married to another woman. That woman, Maria Luisa, had borne him two children and left the house in humiliation after discovering her husband was carrying on an affair with Ruz, their teenaged maid. With Maria Luisa gone, Ruz promptly assumed her place as the female head of the household. This changing of the guard scandalized neighbors, in part because Angel Castro was not only already married but also a good twenty-five years older than his new paramour.

A Spaniard, Angel Castro had grown up poor in the impoverished, threadbare town of Galicia, in the northwestern part of Spain. In the nineteenth century, wealthy families often paid poor young men to serve in the military in

Angel Castro, a poor Spanish immigrant, found success and wealth running a sugar plantation in Birán Cuba. He employed most of the local residents.

place of their sons. According to Angel, he was paid to fight for Spain in Cuba's second War of Independence. He returned to Galicia after the war, but was unable to find work in the failing town. His ambition and will to survive took him back to the Caribbean island, where he eventually found great success running a sugar plantation. By the time Fidel was born, his father's plantation spanned nearly 2,000 acres, a sizable plot of land in an area where most people were too poor to afford shoes. Angel Castro made enough money to lease another 25,000 acres.

Although wealthy, the Spanish immigrant was seen as an interloper because of his heritage, and the fact that he had fought for Spain, *against* Cuba, in the island's struggle for independence. His flouting of marital conventions further underscored his status as an outsider. Angel Castro, however, was one of the richest men in the area, and the sole source of income, loans, and handouts for dozens of families.

Like his father, Fidel Castro was an outsider, envied for his wealth, and not considered a real member of the community. His childhood, much as his later life, was marked by contradictions. Fidel attended prestigious Catholic schools, and lived in a big house on stilts, and even had a radio and a phonograph—luxuries most of the neighbors could only dream about. The stilt house, though rustic and built by Angel Castro, was grand compared to the shacks and huts that dotted the nearby landscape and housed Fidel's early playmates.

Yet Castro did not fit in, and despite his bluster, he longed to be accepted by his peers. His did not take rejection well, although he was reticent about the alienation he felt. He used the surname Castro, like his siblings, but in reality he had not legally been given his father's name. In a rare moment, he confided in a friend who hailed from an aristocratic family, "Rafael, you have a name. I don't have a name. I have a negative name." His younger brother,

**Lina Ruz was a teenager when she was hired to work for the Castro family as a maid. Her affair with Angel Castro produced six children, including Fidel. The couple married when Fidel was a teenager.**

**Fidel Castro, right, is pictured here with his siblings Ramon and Angelita. The Castro family lived in a large house propped up on stilts; they were the wealthiest people in Birán.**

**As a child, Fidel Castro was competitive, clever, and occasionally short-tempered. He also loved being the center of attention. He's seen here (second from right, facing the camera) with classmates in 1940.**

and future political successor, Raúl, was sensitive and cried easily as a child. Fidel, however, presented a tough exterior even in his youth. He was brash and strong and had an explosive temper, lashing out with fists, feet, and teeth when challenged.

There were no schools near the Castro plantation. Many residents were illiterate; few received any formal education. Recounting his childhood, Castro stated that he demanded to be sent to school, and that his parents acquiesced, allowing him to attend several distant Jesuit-run institutions. However, some biographers contend that the Ruz-Castro children were sent away to boarding schools because Angel Castro was wary of keeping his illegitimate offspring on the plantation, in full and constant view of the neighbors. According to this theory, the patriarch wanted to lessen the appearance of impropriety, because he was still legally married to Maria Luisa, who could technically return to claim her place as his rightful wife.

## FROM THE PLANTATION TO THE SCHOOLROOM

"An excellent student and member of the congregation, he was an outstanding athlete . . . [who] won the admiration and affection of all," Castro's high school evaluation read. "He will study law, and we have no doubt that he will make a brilliant name for himself. Fidel has what it takes and will make something of himself." The praise implied that Castro was an exemplary student; in fact, he neglected his studies year-round, was distracted in class, and often got into trouble. He was more interested in sports than books, and he was highly competitive.

**CASTRO WAS DISINTERESTED IN THE HISTORY OF THE AMERICAS, LEADING HIS PROFESSOR TO REMARK, "HE TRIED TO MAKE IT, NOT STUDY IT."**

Castro was also high-strung, and occasionally eccentric. He dove off cliffs into unknown waters, bragged constantly, and was hospitalized after injuring himself by riding his bicycle into a wall on a bet. His behavior led classmates and teachers to dub him *loco Fidel*. It was a designation he did not appreciate. While attending the exclusive Jesuit-run high school Belén, Castro attacked classmate Ramón Mestre for calling him crazy. Mestre was a better fighter; Castro resorted to biting his opponent. Enraged by his defeat, Castro got a gun and threatened to kill Mestre. A priest wrangled the weapon away from Fidel and diffused the situation. Many years later, when Castro came into political power, he imprisoned the boy who had bested him.

His need to win—and gain recognition—bordered on obsession. Intent on mastering basketball, he practiced throughout the night in the darkened court. "Fidel drove me crazy," his athletic coach said, "always asking me what he had to do to be a leader, what he had to do to make himself known." Castro appeared to be looking for alternative ways to legitimize himself in society. His parents finally married in 1941, after Angel Castro obtained a divorce from his first wife. The elder Castro formally recognized Fidel as his son, legally entitling him to the surname he had used all his life.

As the end of the school semester approached, Castro was often on the verge of failing. But each time, he managed to ace his final exams by cramming an entire term's worth of work into a few days of marathon studying. It was an approach that confounded his teachers, and carried over to his collegiate years, where, ironically, the future leader of Cuba failed a class in Latin American studies. He was disinterested in the history of the Americas, leading his professor to remark, "He tried to make it, not study it."

## BIRTH OF A GUERRILLA

It was while attending law school at the University of Havana that Fidel Castro became interested in politics and social justice. The university was a breeding ground for political and revolutionary theories. Students actively criticized the government and called out for social reform. They were especially disillusioned with former president Fulgencio Batista, a revolutionary hero who led the military coup that unseated dictator Gerardo Machado in 1933. After leaving office in 1944, Batista installed a number of puppet presidents.

The strongest grievance against Batista was that he had not punished the corrupt officials and assassins who had worked for the Machado regime. Now these students formed violent gangs and exacted their own bloody revenge against Machado's deposed tyrants. A handful of gangs jockeyed for control over the student federation elections on campus. They fought each other with guns, out in the open. Numerous students were killed during this time. "Many of them who died as gangsters, victims of illusion, today would be considered as heroes," Castro said later.

In 1948, Castro married Mirta Diaz Balart, a fellow student from a well-to-do Cuban family. They had one child together. The marriage was an unhappy one, eventually ending in divorce. Castro graduated from law school and went to work as an attorney in a small law firm. Politically ambitious, he set his sights on a parliament position. Castro ran on the Orthodox Party ticket. The Orthodox

Party was a radical, nationalistic, anti-American group that sought to eradicate government corruption and cronyism. Castro's ambitions were thwarted when General Batista emerged out of retirement to lead a successful coup d'etat against President Carlos Prío Socarrás. Batista canceled the elections and declared himself provisional president. Castro attempted to bring legal charges against Batista for violating the constitution, but he was denied a hearing in court.

Furious, Castro abandoned his law practice and organized an army with the aim of deposing Batista. On July 26, 1953, Castro and his makeshift army attacked Moncada Barracks, Batista's largest military post. More than half of Castro's 160 soldiers were killed in the failed coup. Castro was arrested and tried for the audacious attack. At his trial he defended his actions in the now-famous speech "History Shall Absolve Me."

"I warn you, I am just beginning!" he told the court. "If there is in your hearts a vestige of love for your country, love for humanity, love for justice, listen carefully . . . I know that the regime will try to suppress the truth by all possible means; I know that there will be a conspiracy to bury me in oblivion. But my voice will not be stifled—it will rise from my breast even when I feel most alone, and my heart will give it all the fire that callous cowards deny it . . . Condemn me. It does not matter. History will absolve me."

He was sentenced to fifteen years in prison; he served two years before being released on general amnesty in May 1955. Castro left Cuba to live in exile in Mexico.

## THE REVOLUTIONARY RETURNS HOME

While in Mexico, Castro met Argentine revolutionary Ernesto "Ché" Guevera. Together, the two formed a guerrilla army and plotted to overthrow Batista. They called their planned action "The 26th of July Movement" after the first failed attack against Batista. Castro sailed into Cuba with eighty-two soldiers. Despite being grossly outmanned, the guerrilla army was successful—due in no small part to the support and assistance of Cuban citizens who joined the fight against Batista. Batista resigned and fled the island in January 1959. Over the next few years, Fidel Castro consolidated his power, installing his supporters in office, executing hundreds of real and imagined enemies, expropriating foreign-owned land, nationalizing all businesses, and declaring himself the voice

of the Cuban people. He also declared himself maximum leader, an omnipotent title affirming his leadership. Civil liberties were curtailed; dissenters were imprisoned, exiled, or worse.

Ironically, the wealthy boy despised capitalism and the oligarchy, identifying instead with the poor and the disenfranchised classes. "No doubt what has had the greatest influence is that where I was born, I lived with people of the most humble origins," he stated. "I remember the illiterate unemployed men who would stand in line near the cane fields, with nobody to bring them a drop of water, or breakfast, or lunch, or give them shelter, or transport. And I can't forget those children going barefoot. All the children whom I played with in Birán, all those I grew up with, ran around with, all over the place, were very, very poor."

Adamant about decreasing illiteracy, Castro implemented the state-sponsored "Great Campaign for Literacy." As a result, Cuban literacy rates increased more than 95 percent. A universal health care system was also implemented. Castro recreated the country; he molded and shaped it much the way a father shapes a son. Divorced, he sired several children by several different women, including five with his second wife, Dalia Soto del Valle, but his most beloved offspring was clearly Cuba. The illegitimate boy had fathered a nation, and in the process recast himself as the epitome of legitimacy. He heralded the transformation of the tiny island into the first Communist country in the Americas, and he formed a political alliance with the former Soviet Union. His Communist politics alarmed and alienated the United States. After an American embargo against Cuba, the island relied heavily on the Soviet Union for assistance.

In 1961, 1,400 insurgents, nearly all exiled Cubans trained by the American CIA, invaded the island's Bay of Pigs in an attempt to assassinate Castro. Castro's army captured 1,200 of them. Authorized by President John F. Kennedy, the covert mission was a colossal failure—and a huge embarrassment to the United States. One year later, the United States learned that Castro was allowing the Soviet Union to construct a missile base in Cuba. Both Castro and Soviet premier Nikita S. Khrushchev feared an American invasion of Cuba. And Kennedy

**Former Cuban president Fulgencio Batista fled the island in 1959, after being ousted from office during a coup led by Castro.**

feared the Soviets would deploy the missiles, launching them at the United States from a base less than 100 miles (161 km) from Florida. He called for the base to be dismantled. The United States began to block Soviet ships carrying armaments from reaching Cuba. The Soviets were on high alert, ready to deploy the nuclear missiles if attacked. For seven days, Kennedy and Khrushchev were deadlocked. Finally, the Soviet prime minister agreed to dismantle the base in exchange for a promise that the United States would not invade Cuba, and that the country would remove its own nuclear missiles in Turkey. Kennedy agreed

## IRONICALLY, THE WEALTHY BOY DESPISED CAPITALISM AND THE OLIGARCHY, IDENTIFYING INSTEAD WITH THE POOR AND THE DISENFRANCHISED CLASSES.

to the terms, and a nuclear war was narrowly averted.

The dismantling of the Soviet Union in 1991 left Cuba in dire financial straits, and without its strongest ally. Today, most Cubans teeter on the border of poverty. Eleven and a half million people reside on the island, which at 42,427 square miles (110,860 square kilometers) is roughly the size of Pennsylvania. Although the government pays medical and educational expenses, the average annual income is estimated to be a mere $240. Food shortages are common. Less than 10 percent of Cubans have a telephone. More than 1.5 million Cubans have been exiled from the country, and thousands have died trying to flee the island by boat. The suicide rate is among the highest in Latin America.

"This revolution is in ruins. There is no food, there's no freedom. People say it's all because of the *Yanqui* aggression, but that's a myth, as real as dragons and witches, a children's tale," Ché Guevara's grandson, Canek Sánchez Guevara, told Pulitzer Prize–winning reporter Andres Oppenheimer. "And if you graduate, there is no work in your field. They'll ask you to go to the countryside and work in agriculture. This place is hopeless."

Revolutionary, dictator, liberator, tyrant, megalomaniac—Fidel Castro has occupied a number of roles in his staggeringly long political career. His has been the longest political reign in Latin American history. In 2006, illness forced him to curtail his activities and appoint his brother Raúl acting president. In 2008, Castro resigned the presidency. The following year, newly elected American President Barack Obama expressed his desire to open a dialogue with Cuba. With the legendary dictator in declining health, his "softer" brother in charge, and the possibility of a truce with the United States, Cuba's future seems to be on the verge of being freed from Castro's iron grip—a grip that has lasted for half a century.

# BIBLIOGRAPHY

## INTRODUCTION

Hartley, Shirley Foster. *Illegitimacy*. Berkeley: University of California Press, 1975.

Laslett, Peter, Karla Oosterveen, and Richard Michael Smith. *Bastardy and Its Comparative History: Studies in the History of Illegitimacy and Marital Nonconformism in Britain, France, Germany, Sweden, North America, Jamaica, and Japan*. Cambridge: Harvard University Press, 1980.

Mangold, George Benjamin. *Children Born Out of Wedlock*. Columbia, MO: University of Missouri Press, 1921.

Mangold, George Benjamin. *Problems of Child Welfare*. Norwood, MA: The MacMillan Company, 1914.

Teichman, Jenny. *Illegitimacy: An Examination of Bastardy*. Ithaca, NY: Cornell University Press, 1982.

Zunshine, Lisa. *Bastards and Foundlings: Illegitimacy in Eighteenth-Century England*. Columbus: Ohio State UniversityPress, 2005.

## CHAPTER 1: WILLIAM THE CONQUEROR

Bradbury, Jim. *The Battle of Hastings*. Phoenix Mill, Gloucestershire, UK: Sutton Publishing, 1998.

Heyer, Georgette. *The Conqueror* (novel). Napierville, IL: Sourcebooks Inc., 1974.

Howarth, David. *1066: The Year of the Conquest*. New York: Viking Press, 1978.

Morillo, Stephen. *The Battle of Hastings*. Woodbridge Suffolk, UK: Boydell Press, 1995.

Musset, Lucien. *The Bayeux Tapestry*. Woodbridge, Suffolk, UK: Boydell Press, 2005.

Thomas, Hugh M. *The English and the Normans*. New York: Oxford University Press, 2003.

Thomas, Hugh M. *The Norman Conquest*. New York: Rowman and Littlefield, 2008.

## CHAPTER 2: LEONARDO DA VINCI

Freud, Sigmund. *Leonardo da Vinci and a Memory of His Childhood*. New York: W. W. Norton, 1964.

Kemp, Martin. *Leonardo*. Norman, OK: University of Oklahoma Press, 2004.

Nicholl, Charles. *Leonardo da Vinci: The Flights of the Mind*. New York: Viking, 2004.

Vallentin, Antonina. *Leonardo da Vinci: The Tragic Pursuit of Perfection*. New York: Viking, 1938.

## CHAPTER 3: FRANCISCO PIZARRO

Gabai, Rafael Varón, and Javier Flores Espinoza (trans.). *Francisco Pizarro and His Brothers: The Illusion of Power in Sixteenth-Century Peru.* Norman, OK: University of Oklahoma Press, 1997.

Goodman, Edward Julius. *The Explorers of South America.* Norman, OK: University of Oklahoma Press, 1992.

Kirkpatrick, F. A. *The Spanish Conquistadors.* London: A&C Black, 1934.

MacCormack, Sabine. *On the Wings of Time: Rome, the Incas, Spain, and Peru.* Princeton, NJ: Princeton University Press, 2007.

Wood, Michael. *Conquistadors.* Berkeley, CA: University of California Press, 2000.

## CHAPTER 4: ELIZABETH I

Axelrod, Alan. *Elizabeth I, CEO: Strategic Lessons from the Leader Who Built an Empire.* Paramus, NJ: Prentice-Hall Press, 2000.

Hibbert, Christopher. *The Virgin Queen: Elizabeth I, Genius of the Golden Age.* Reading, MA: Perseus Books, 1991.

Levin, Carole. *The Heart and Stomach of a King: Elizabeth I and the Politics of Sex and Power.* Philadelphia: University of Pennsylvania Press, 1994.

Ridley, Jasper. *Elizabeth I: The Shrewdness of Virtue.* New York: Fromm International, 1989.

Somerset, Anne. *Elizabeth I.* New York: St. Martin's Griffin, 1991.

Weir, Alison. *The Life of Elizabeth I.* New York: Ballantine, 1999.

## CHAPTER 5: JAMES SCOTT, 1ST DUKE OF MONMOUTH

Fraser, Antonia. *Royal Charles: Charles II and the Restoration.* New York: Dell, 1979.

James II, An Act to Attaint James Duke of Monmouth of High-Treason (Chapter II. Rot. Parl. nu. 2.), Statutes of the Realm: vol. 6: 1685–94 (1819), p. 2.

Johnson, David. *Monmouth's Rebellion.* New York: Viking Penguin, 1968.

Wigfield, W. MacDonald. *Monmouth Rebellion: A Social History.* Bradford-on-Avon, UK: Moonraker Press, and Totowa, NJ: Barnes & Noble Books, 1980.

Wigfield, W. MacDonald, comp. *The Monmouth Rebels, 1685.* New York: St. Martin's Press, 1985.

Wyndham, Violet. *The Protestant Duke: A Life of Monmouth.* London: Weidenfeld and Nicolson, 1976.

## CHAPTER 6: ALEXANDER HAMILTON

Brookhiser, Richard. *Alexander Hamilton: American*. New York: Simon & Schuster, 1999.

Chernow, Ron. *Alexander Hamilton*. New York: Penguin Press, 2004.

Flexner, James Thomas. *The Young Hamilton: A Biography*. Boston: Little, Brown & Company, 1978.

Hecht, Marie B. *Odd Destiny: The Life of Alexander Hamilton*. New York: MacMillian Publishing, 1982.

Lodge, Henry Cabot. *Alexander Hamilton*. Cambridge, MA: Houghton Mifflin Co., 1898.

## CHAPTER 7: JAMES SMITHSON

Bolton, Knowles Sarah. *Famous Givers and Their Gifts*. Manchester, NH: Ayer Company Publishers, 1896, reprinted 1971.

Burleigh, Nina. *The Stranger and the Statesman*. New York: Harper Perennial, 2004.

Ewing, Heather. *The Lost World of James Smithson: Science, Revolution, and the Birth of the Smithsonian*. New York: Bloomsbury, 2007.

Goode, George Brown. *The Smithsonian Institution, 1846–1896: The History of Its First Half Century*. Washington, DC: Smithsonian Institution, 1897.

Grimm, Robert T. *Notable American Philanthropists*. Santa Barbara, CA: Greenwood Publishing Group, 2002.

Oehser, Paul H. *Sons of Science: The Story of the Smithsonian Institution and Its Leaders*. New York: H. Schuman, 1949.

Rhees, William Jones. *James Smithson and His Bequest*. Washington, DC: Smithsonian Institution, 1881.

True, Webster P. *The First Hundred Years of the Smithsonian Institution, 1846–1946*. Washington, DC: Smithsonian Institution, 1946.

## CHAPTER 8: BERNARDO O'HIGGINS

Chasteen, John Charles. *Americanos: Latin America's Struggle for Independence*. New York: Oxford University Press, 2008.

Chissold, Stephen. *Bernardo O'Higgins and the Independence of Chile*. New York: Frederick Praeger, 1969.

Harvey, Robert. *Liberators: Latin America's Struggle for Independence 1810–1830*. Woodstock, NY: Overlook Press, 2000.

Herring, Hubert, *A History of Latin America*. New York: Alfred A. Knopf, 1968.

Prago, Albert. *The Revolutions in Spanish America*. New York: Macmillan, 1970.

Rodriguez, O., and Jaime E. Rodriguez. *The Independence of Spanish America*. Cambridge, UK: Cambridge University Press, 1998.

## CHAPTER 9: ALEXANDRE DUMAS FILS

Chandler, Frank Wadleigh. *The Contemporary Drama of France.* Boston: Little, Brown, and Company, 1921.

Gribble, Francis Henry. *Dumas, Father and Son.* Boston: E. P. Dutton & Co., 1930.

Maurois, André. *Three Musketeers: A Study of the Dumas Family.* London: Cape Publishing, 1957.

Maurois, André. *The Titans: A Three-Generation Biography of the Dumas.* Translated by Gerard Hopkins. New York: Harpers & Brothers Publishers, 1957.

Mellé, Rosine. *The Contemporary French Writers.* Boston: Ginn & Co., 1895.

Schwarz , Stanley H. *Alexandre Dumas, Fils: Dramatist.* Whitefish, MT: Kessinger Publishing, LLC, 2007.


## CHAPTER 10: HENRY STANLEY

Anstruther, Ian. *Dr. Livingstone, I Presume? A Biography of Henry Morton Stanley.* New York: E. P. Dutton, 1957.

Bierman, John. *Dark Safari: Behind the Legend of Henry Morton Stanley.* New York: Alfred A. Knopf, 1990.

Dugard, Martin. *Into Africa: The Epic Adventures of Stanley and Livingstone.* New York: Doubleday, 2003.

Farwell, Byron. *The Man Who Presumed.* New York: Henry Holt & Co., 1957.

Jeal, Tim. *Stanley: The Impossible Life of Africa's Greatest Explorer.* New Haven, CT: Yale University Press, 2007.

Pettit, Clare. *Dr. Livingstone, I Presume?* Cambridge, MA: Harvard University Press, 2007.

Smith, Frederika Shumway. *Stanley, African Explorer.* New York: Rand McNally, 1968.

Stanley, Henry M. *Autobiography of Henry Morton Stanley*, edited by his wife, Dorothy Stanley. Boston: Houghton-Mifflin, 1909.

Stanley, Henry M. *My Early Travels in America and Asia.* London: Duckworth, 2001.

Stanley, Henry M. *Through the Dark Continent. Vols. 1 & 2.* New York: Dover Press, 1988.

Wassermann, Jacob. *Bula Matari: Stanley, Conqueror of a Continent.* New York: Liveright, 1939.


## CHAPTER 11: JACK LONDON

Kershaw, Alex. *Jack London: A Life.* New York: St. Martin's Press, 1997.

Kingman, Russ. *A Pictorial Life of Jack London.* Foreword by Irving Stone. New York: Crown Publishers, 1979.

London, Jack. *John Barleycorn: An Alcoholic Memoir.* New York: Oxford University Press, 1978.

London, Jack. *Novels and Social Writings.* New York: Library Classics of the United States, 1982.

London, Jack. *Novels and Stories.* New York: Library Classics of the United States, 1982.

London, Joan. *Jack London and His Times: An Unconventional Biography.* New York: Book League of America, 1939.

Sinclair, Andrew. *Jack: A Biography of Jack London.* New York: Harper and Row, 1977.

Stasz, Clarice. *American Dreamers: Charmian and Jack London.* New York: St. Martin's Press, 1988.

## CHAPTER 12: LAWRENCE OF ARABIA

Aldington, Richard. *Lawrence of Arabia, a Biographical Enquiry.* Chicago: Henry Regnery, 1955.

Barr, James. *Setting the Desert on Fire: T. E. Lawrence and Britain's Secret War in Arabia, 1916–1918.* New York: W. W. Norton, 2008.

Brown, Michael. *Lawrence of Arabia: The Life, the Legend.* New York: Thames & Hudson, 2005.

Graves, Robert. *Lawrence and the Arabs.* New York: Paragon House, 1991.

James, Lawrence. *The Golden Warrior: The Life and Legend of Lawrence of Arabia.* New York: Paragon House, 1993.

Knightley, Phillip. *Lawrence of Arabia.* New York: Thomas Nelson & Co. 1977.

Lawrence, T. E. *Seven Pillars of Wisdom, A Triumph.* Garden City, NY: Doubleday, Doran & Co., 1936.

Liddell Hart, Sir Basil Henry. *Colonel Lawrence, the Man behind the Legend.* New York: Dodd, Mead, 1934.

Thomas, Lowell. *With Lawrence in Arabia.* Garden City, NY: Doubleday & Co., 1967.

Wilson, Jeremy. *Lawrence: The Authorized Biography of T. E. Lawrence.* New York: Atheneum, 1990.

## CHAPTER 13: BILLIE HOLIDAY

Chilton, John. *Billie's Blues.* New York: Stein and Day, 1975.

Clarke, Donald. *Wishing on the Moon.* New York: Viking, 1994.

Davis, Angela Y. *Blues Legacies and Black Feminism: Gertrude "Ma" Rainey, Bessie Smith, and Billie Holiday.* New York: Vintage, 1998.

Greene, Meg. *Billie Holiday.* Westport, CT: Greenwood Publishing Group, 2007.

Griffin, Farah Jasmine. *If You Can't Be Free, Be a Mystery: In Search of Billie Holiday.* New York: Ballantine Publishing Group, 2001.

Holiday, Billie, and William Dufty. *Lady Sings the Blues.* Garden City, NY: Doubleday, 1956.

Nicholson, Stuart. *Billie Holiday.* Boston: Northeastern University Press, 1995.

O'Meally, Robert G. *Lady Day: The Many Faces of Billie Holiday.* New York: Arcade Publishers, 1991.

## CHAPTER 14: EVA PERÓN

Barnes, John. *Evita: First Lady.* New York: Grove Press, 1978.

Bourne, Richard. *Political Leaders of Latin America.* New York: Knopf, 1970.

Evita Perón *Historical Research Foundation* website. http://evitaperon.org.

Martinez, Tomas Eloy. *Santa Evita.* Translated by Helen Lane. New York: Random House Inc, 1997.

Ortiz, Alicia Dujovne. *Eva Perón.* New York: St. Martin's Press, 1996.

Perón, Eva. *La razon de mi vida.* Buenos Aires: Editorial Peuser, 1951.

## CHAPTER 15: FIDEL CASTRO

Bourne, Peter G. *Fidel: A Biography of Fidel Castro.* New York: Dodd, Mead & Company, 1986.

Castro, Fidel, Ignacio Ramonet, and Andrew Hurley. *Fidel Castro: My Life.* New York: Scribner, 2008.

Castro, Fidel, with Deborah Shnookal and Pedro Álvarez Tabío. *Fidel: My Early Years.* New York: Ocean Press, 2005.

Castro, Fidel, David Deutschmann, and Deborah Shnookal. *Fidel Castro Reader.* New York: Ocean Press, 2007.

Coltman, Leycester, and Julia Sweig. *The Real Fidel.* New Haven, CT: Yale University Press, 2003.

Geyer, Georgie Anne. *Guerrilla Prince: The Untold Story of Fidel Castro.* Boston: Little, Brown & Company, 1991.

Leonard, Thomas M. *Fidel Castro.* Westport, CT: Greenwood Press, 2004.

Matthews, Herbert L. *Fidel Castro.* New York: Simon & Schuster, 1969.

Oppenheimer, Andres. "After 50 Years, Cuba Has Little to Show." *The Miami Herald,* December 12, 2008.

Skierka, Volker, and Patrick Camiller. *Fidel Castro.* Malden, MA: Polity Press, 2004.

## ACKNOWLEDGMENTS

I would like to thank my coauthors Edwin Kiester Jr., Ed Wright, and Alan Axelrod for their help writing this book. Many thanks also to my gifted, patient editor, Cara Connors, who kept me focused and on track. Lastly, thanks to Tom Donnarumma for all his support and encouragement.

## ABOUT THE AUTHOR

Juré Fiorillo is a freelance writer specializing in history and criminology. She was a contributor to *History's Greatest Lies* and *Before They Changed the World.* The coauthor of *True Stories of Law & Order* and *True Stories of Law & Order: Special Victims Unit,* she has a master's degree in criminal justice.

# INDEX

*Note: Page numbers in italics indicate figures.*